W9-ADW-173

January 1961

The Message of the Fourth Gospel

John

Christian Board 3.95

ERIC LANE TITUS

THE
Message
OF THE
Fourth Gospel

NEW YORK   ABINGDON PRESS   NASHVILLE

SET UP, PRINTED, AND BOUND BY THE
PARTHENON PRESS, AT NASHVILLE,
TENNESSEE, UNITED STATES OF AMERICA

TO

DR. WALTER R. GREENWOOD

who taught me the meaning of eternal life

this book is affectionately dedicated

Preface

COMMENTARIES ON THE FOURTH GOSPEL ARE LEGION. THE ADDI-
tion of another to the list requires adequate justification. If
the present volume deserves to exist, it is largely because of a
fundamental approach which has been followed throughout.
This approach may be stated as follows:

1. The commentary assumes that the Fourth Gospel is a
thoroughgoing interpretation of Jesus; at no point is this assumption weakened by the tendency to mix history and interpretation.

2. An understanding of the evangelist's method is held to be
basic to an adequate interpretation; exegesis is therefore made
at every point in the light of the contextual evidence of literary
techniques involved.

3. The assumption is that the fourth evangelist was a popular
religionist, not a philosopher.

4. The commentary proceeds on the assumption that John
was dependent mainly on Paul and the Synoptics, and that
Hellenistic writers (such as Philo) contributed to the evangelist's
thought only in the sense that Hellenism was his native "atmosphere." Little effort is therefore made to relate Johannine
thought and symbol to *specific* Hellenistic thinkers or movements.

5. A radical difference between this commentary and the vast
majority is that it deals with the Gospel material section by
section, not verse by verse. An attempt is made to identify natural
units of material and to isolate their meaning.

6. It is further assumed that current New Testament *intro-
ductions* contain all information at present available on introductory problems. Except for general suggestions as to authorship
and date of writing, no attempt has been made to recanvass
the area.

Translation of passages is my own. The reader will do well to use a critical Greek text or a good English translation in conjunction with his study of the commentary.

The book is divided into two parts. Part I discusses three areas which seem especially relevant to the approach presented in the commentary. These areas are: literary method; the Logos doctrine; and the concept of the Spirit. Part II consists of the commentary. The reader will find it helpful first of all to acquaint himself with the points of view set forth in Part I, since they are reflected in the interpretation of individual pericopes of the Gospel.

Footnote references indicate, in part, the authors to whom I am indebted.

ERIC L. TITUS

Contents

9

PART I

INTRODUCTION

CHAPTER I

The Evangelist's Literary Method

No SATISFACTORY APPRECIATION OF THE FOURTH GOSPEL CAN BE
gained apart from a thorough grasp of its author's literary
method. Couched in the form of a life of Jesus, it is natural
for the modern mind, unaccustomed to ways of antiquity, to
view the material as history. This view has vitiated even the best
of modern commentaries, which, while recognizing the Gospel's
symbolic and interpretative character, nevertheless feel called
upon to find data there for a reconstruction of the historical
career. To be sure, the older notion that the Synoptics are history while the Fourth Gospel is interpretation must be dis- •
pensed with; the difference between the two has increasingly
diminished in our thinking. But it is not that the Fourth Gospel
is recognized as standing closer to the Synoptics viewed as history, but that the Synoptics are now seen to be nearer to John
viewed as interpretation.

Still, it must be maintained that a real difference exists between John and the Synoptics. For all their interpretative interest, in one aspect of their function the Synoptists were compilers
of earlier tradition. The result of this would be the preservation
of early tradition, no matter how incrusted with interpretative
elements. The isolation of this primitive tradition is the task
of the historian of the life of Jesus, and it is still assumed by
many that this may be accomplished with some degree of success. On the other hand, the fourth evangelist was in no sense
a compiler of earlier tradition, but a composer in the true sense •
of the word. The term "creative" best describes his religious
and literary genius. Under his pen a source becomes transformed
into something quite new and different. It is evident that the

13

historical events per se had little importance for him. If, at any point, his narrative conveys information on the subject, it is more by accident than by intent.

It is of interest that in spite of all that has been said in recent years about the essentially unhistorical character of the Fourth Gospel, we are now seeing the resurgence of an attempt to give it historical value. This development is due in part to the work of Maurice Goguel, who, in his Life of Jesus,[1] finds considerable biographical data in the Fourth Gospel. An illustration of Goguel's influence is seen in the recent work of Vincent Taylor, The Life and Ministry of Jesus, in which he uses the framework Goguel had reconstructed largely from the Fourth Gospel. Regarding this framework, Taylor writes:

This hypothesis concerning the course of events depends on our acceptance of the historical statements in the Fourth Gospel, and it is increasingly recognized that we have good reason to accept these statements, in spite of the interpretative element which undoubtedly is to be found in that Gospel.[2]

Yet Goguel himself recognizes that the historical aspects (which he gleans from reconstructed "sources") are not at all due to an attempt to satisfy "historical curiosity," since the evangelist's purpose was edificatory and religious.[3]

Goguel's success in finding historical material in John is not convincing even when due allowance is made for his great discernment in the field of source identification. In the main, his arguments for such sources and for their historical accuracy are altogether too subjective, and fail to take into account the literary character of the book. Goguel predicates too much logical thought to a writer whose mind was essentially mystical and contemplative.

It is possible that the current interest in historical elements in the Fourth Gospel is related to the development of his-

[1] Tr. Olive Wyon (New York: The Macmillan Co., 1944).
[2] (New York and Nashville: Abingdon Press, 1955), p. 16.
[3] Op. cit., p. 157.

torical skepticism. If the critic, who is also a churchman, feels that the quest for the historical Jesus is futile, it is easy for him, quite unconsciously, to create a Jesus congenial to his theological point of view, or to conclude that the Christ of the early church differed little from the Jesus of history.

One may, of course, make too deep a cleavage between history and interpretation. All descriptions of events constitute interpretation. Nevertheless, there is a difference between the relatively objective presentation of historical events and artistic representation. This difference may be seen when one compares the two statements that follow:

Jesus was a Galilean Jew who gathered together a group of disciples and went about the country teaching about the coming kingdom of God. During a visit to Jerusalem he was seized by the Roman authorities, convicted of treason, and put to death by crucifixion.

Jesus was the Son of God who came down from heaven, chose disciples from the lower world to become members of the higher realm of eternal life, and taught the things which he had learned from God. At the time appointed by God he went to Jerusalem to be glorified and to give his Spirit to the church.

The first statement is probably more accurate as a record of facts; the second is theological, and is clothed in the language of religious faith.

Yet it is wrong to assume that the unadorned statement of the facts is thereby more "true" than the other. Indeed, the truth about the career of Jesus would be essentially unknown if a thoroughgoing "life" were written in "factual" terms. Events need interpretation; and interpretation does not consist merely in the cataloguing of dates, geographical movements of the subject, and the like. If all this were known we would still be called upon to express in religious language the meaning of that vital spiritual impulse that men had experienced in Jesus of Nazareth. This is but to say that something like a Gospel was bound to be written. The Synoptics represent one phase of the process of interpretation, a phase which used as part of its method words and incidents which attached to the historical person. The Fourth Gospel presents us with a more advanced chronological stage in the development, uses tradition with more freedom, and is concerned primarily with the problem of meaning. It is therefore highly selective in its use of the earlier tradition, using only those elements which relate to the problem of meaning, and, even then, reconstructing them to conform more adequately to its purpose.

This means that important items such as the ethical teachings of Jesus are omitted. This does not necessarily mean that the evangelist had no interest in the ethical side of religion; it means, rather, that the ethical element was not his immediate concern. It is possible that he would conceive of the believer, participant in the higher order of eternal life, as embodying those virtues which we call ethical. But he does not discuss this in his Gospel.

This absorption in the meaning of Jesus caused the evangelist to range far and wide for concepts and symbols which would support his purpose. In terms of literary antecedents we may be confident that he used Mark and Luke. It is probable that he used Matthew. It is almost certain that he used a number of Paul's letters also. In addition, there seem to be definite reflections of the book of Acts. There is proof, of course, that he used the Old Testament. It is highly probable that he made use of a Gnostic (or possibly Stoic) hymn to the Logos. It is impossible to go beyond this assessment of sources with any degree of assurance. But the rich world of Hellenistic symbolism and idea was open to him and the indications are that he exploited it to good advantage.

These materials are combined and arranged in the Gospel in such a manner as to suggest to the contemplative mind the character and quality of God's revelation in Jesus. The Gospel is not so much a narration of events as it is a complex combination of meaningful artistic and religious symbols designed to capture the imagination and elevate the thoughts to the level

16

of mystic contemplation which, we must suppose, the evangelist himself enjoyed.

With regard to history, the evangelist's interest was in the *event*, not in the events. It was important for him that the Incarnation had occurred in history. But for him to embark on a quest for the historical Jesus would be to make the same error as that committed by the Jews of his Gospel—to place emphasis on the externals of the event. Historical concern must yield to discernment. This principle is so central in the Gospel that, on its own grounds, we are led away from the historical problem to the theological one of revelation.

If a modicum of "history" is to be found in the Gospel it must be due to two factors: (a) the generally known facts regarding the career of Jesus; e.g., that he was a Galilean (Nazareth) Jew; that he was a teacher; that he had disciples; that he performed mighty works; that he was accused of treason; that he died by crucifixion; (b) the concern of "the Jews" with Jesus as a man making presumptuous claims; e.g., that they know his father and mother; his Nazareth origin is known to them; he is a Sabbath-breaker. But history on either of these levels is likely to be either traditional or artificial, i.e., constructed for purposes of structural literary development. This kind of history serves only as the base for interpretation which elevates Jesus above it.

We may take the most obvious historical item, the Crucifixion, as an example. The historian would say that Jesus was put to death by the Romans on grounds of treason. In the light of our knowledge regarding the problem, i.e., what we can learn from a critical study of the Synoptics in the light of Jewish and Roman legal procedures, we are led to make this kind of decision. But such a "historical" statement would be foreign to the thought of the evangelist. For him, the enemies of the light are the Jews, and it is they who put Jesus to death. But in doing so they are instruments of the divine purpose. Crucifixion itself, historically conceived as an instrument of Roman justice, is transformed into a device whereby the Son of

17

man is lifted up, i.e., exalted and glorified. That which was in history turns out to be above history and something entirely different from what the historian conceives it to be.

We find the same motivation in operation in relation to the Nazareth origin of Jesus. From the historical viewpoint we would have to say that Jesus' home was Nazareth of Galilee. As a historical statement it is true enough, but for the evangelist it is untrue since it identifies Jesus with "this world"; hence the assertion that Jesus has come from God and that his home is heaven. If we take the evangelist's position on this problem as normative, we are left with no historical information at all. If, on the other hand, we conclude that Jesus was, in fact, a Nazareth product we place ourselves within the circle of the disbelieving Jews. (In this regard critical scholars and the disbelieving Jews have much in common!) But all this is but to say that the evangelist's concern is with the meaning of Jesus for religious faith. "Historical" data whether real or fictitious are but foils for his message about Jesus, the Son of God.

The literary techniques employed by the fourth evangelist may be classified under eleven headings:

1. Apocalyptic technique, which permits Jesus to "predict" future events.

2. Appropriation of materials: stories, symbols, and ideas from certain literature current and from Hellenistic life generally.

3. Construction of Gospel units so as to move progressively toward a climax; the movement is from the materialistic to the spiritual. This climactic movement is also evident in the Gospel as a whole.

4. Literary opportunism.

5. Use of the "sign."

6. Individuals used as representations or symbols.

7. The use of individuals whose stupidity creates an opportunity for teaching.

8. Individuals who unconsciously testify on behalf of Jesus.

9. Use of dramatic technique.

10. Use of the rabbinical method.

11. Use of words with double meaning.

Apocalyptic technique. One of the convenient by-products of the evangelist's use of the gospel literary form was the readiness with which it lent itself to the predictive element. In that regard it provided him with essentially the same technique used by the apocalyptists. The apocalyptist takes his stand in the past and then "predicts" the future. In fact, of course, he is but reviewing history. In much the same way the evangelist is able to survey certain important religious developments which have occurred in the church. He differs from the apocalyptist, however, in that he has Jesus do what the apocalyptist would claim for his pseudonymous author; he places predictive words on the lips of Jesus, thereby giving an authority for his writing far superior to that gained by associating it with some worthy of the faith.

This predictive element is dominant in the Discourses, but is reflected throughout the Gospel. When analyzed it breaks down into the following categories: (a) predictions of the betrayal (6:70-71; 13:10b, 11, 18-19, 21, 27; 17:12); (b) predictions of Peter's future (13:7, 36-38); (c) predictions regarding Jesus' death (3:14; 8:28; 10:17-18; 12:7, 23-24, 27, 31); (d) predictions as to the safety of the disciples (10:28; 17:12, cf. 18:9); (e) predictions concerning the reactions of the disciples to Jesus' death (16:6, 20-22; 6:62; 10:17-18; 16:20b); (f) predictions of the disciples' enlightenment attendant on the resurrection faith (13:7; 16:13-15, 20-24; cf. 2:22; 12:16); (g) predictions of the Jewish rejection (8:24; 9:40-41; 10:26; 12:48; 15:24-25; cf. 2:23-25; 12:37-40); (h) predictions of his return—the giving of the Spirit (7:37-38; cf. vs. 39; 14:3, 16-17, 18-21, 23, 26; 15:26; 16:7-10, 13-15, 16-23); (i) predictions regarding the Gentile ingathering (10:16; cf. 12:20-22; 17:20); (j) predictions of persecutions (15:18-20; 16:1-4).[4]

This list represents a breakdown of the specifically predictive elements. But it would be wrong to assume that they ex-

---

[4] The categories tend to shade into one another; this is particularly true of those dealing with the death and resurrection, since the evangelist seems to consider them as one event.

haust the predictive aspect of the Gospel; in a real sense the Gospel as a whole represents a gigantic thrust of the life and thought of the developing church back into the career of Jesus. Antagonism toward the Jews, as represented, for example, in ch. 8, the coming of the Greeks, the definition of worship as spiritual requiring no need of temples at Jerusalem or Gerizim, reflect developments well known to the historian of the early period of Christian history.

Appropriation of materials. The assumption that John used the Synoptics as a literary source, dominant for many years, has more recently been challenged. Dodd, in his important book *The Interpretation of the Fourth Gospel*, questions the validity of the assumption. He holds that the main factor involved in the perpetuation of the faith and the story was oral tradition, and to assert that John used the Synoptics as a literary source assumes that "the writings of early Christianity must have formed a documentary series, in literary dependence on one another." [5] But this position too readily overlooks the careful work of men like B. H. Streeter[6] and Hans Windisch,[7] who concluded that the Fourth Gospel was dependent on Mark and probably on Matthew and Luke as well.

Part of the problem is due to the fact that the Johannine stories, even those most closely resembling their Synoptic counterparts, display a high degree of individuality. But there is no guarantee that the evangelist would take less liberty with independent tradition than with the pericopes of Mark, Matthew, and Luke. Here we find the crux of the matter: Was the evangelist at all interested in faithfully reproducing a source? Dodd thinks we may assume "he intended to record that which happened, however free he may have felt to modify the factual record in order to bring out the meaning." [8] But we can too

---

[5] (Cambridge: The University Press, 1953), p. 449. Used by permission.
[6] *The Four Gospels* (New York: The Macmillan Company, 1925).
[7] *Johannes und die Synoptiker* (Leipzig: J. C. Hinrichs'sche Buchhandlung, 1926).
[8] *Op. cit.,* p. 447.

easily assume this. The assumption seems unwarranted in view of the fact that he feels free to transfer the cleansing of the temple incident from its position at the end of Jesus' ministry to the very beginning and to construct the story of the raising of Lazarus from elements appearing in Mark and Luke. The impression gained is that he viewed tradition as a vehicle for the communication of inner, spiritual truth, and that the question of the historical accuracy of the medium of communication is quite beside the point. If this is so, then what is demanded of the interpreter is an approach imaginative enough to match that of the evangelist himself.

Is there any real reason why we may not allow this kind of creativity to the fourth evangelist? Certainly his creative genius was sufficient to produce the Discourses and the great prayer of ch. 17. What we often fail to see is that the same mind that produced this material is at work in the narrative sections also. In other words, the narrative sections differ little from the Discourses; they, too, show the creative mind of the author—the thought, mood, and spirit of the Discourses are transferred to the narrative. This is but to say that the same creative mind is at work throughout. John cannot use tradition without transforming it!

Long ago Streeter saw the need for approaching the problem of sources through recognition that the fourth evangelist was a mystic:

> The starting-point for any profitable study of the Fourth Gospel is the recognition of the author as a mystic—perhaps the greatest of all mystics. To him the temporal is the veil of the eternal, and he is ever, to use von Hügel's phrase, "striving to contemplate history sub specie aeternitatis and to englobe the successiveness of man in the simultaneity of God." But, if this is so, it follows that any inquiry into the sources of the Fourth Gospel will be futile which does not approach the subject from the standpoint of the psychology of the mystic temper.[9]

[9] Op. cit., p. 366. Used by permission of The Macmillan Company.

21

While we would not rule out the possibility of other lines of tradition reaching the evangelist, the method is doubtful which "finds" it in the Gospel apart from control material. The various Logia and the apocryphal gospels (Hebrews and Egyptians are most relevant here) may perhaps be brought in as evidence, but the independence of these traditions from the canonical Gospels cannot be assumed.[10] The writings which reflect the brand of Christianity which survived, namely, the apostolic fathers and the apologists, certainly rely largely on the canonical Gospels in their appeal to tradition. This is true of Ignatius; it is true of Justin Martyr also. It may be that the isolated remark of Papias regarding his preference for "the living and abiding voice" has been overworked.

The question of the date of composition of the Gospel properly belongs here, since the argument for dependence of John on the Synoptics is to some degree based on the extent to which the latter had become established in usage. The time reference "about A.D. 110" has become a new dogma maintained largely out of custom. It is possible to place the writing of the Gospel anywhere in the time span, A.D. 95 to A.D. 140. A date no later than roughly A.D. 110 has been chosen largely on the grounds that Ignatius used the Fourth Gospel. But this is by no means certain.[11] It is of interest that Marcion, who would have found the anti-Jewishness of John much to his liking, neglects the Fourth Gospel. Furthermore, the faint reflections of John in Justin Martyr, if such they are, suggest that in his time the Gospel is at most in the early stages of becoming established. It is a possibility that the Gospel should be dated toward the end of the time span suggested above.[12] If so, the Synoptics

[10] See Leon Wright, *Alterations of the Words of Jesus* (Cambridge: Harvard University Press, 1952), pp. 103-7, for a good discussion on the Oxyrhynchus sayings in this connection.

[11] Sanday, *The Gospels in the Second Century* (London: Macmillan and Company, 1876), pp. 274-76. Sanday attempts to make a case for dependence but, in our opinion, does not succeed.

[12] In the interest of an earlier dating, scholars have tended to stress the importance of Rylands Papyrus 457 and Egerton Papyrus 2. The uncertainty of the relationship between the Egerton papyrus and the Fourth Gospel is well known;

22

were already well established in the churches when the Gospel was written, a fact which helps account for its dependence on this particular line of tradition.

A further point may be noted in connection with John's use of sources. There is no reason to think that the early transmitters of the tradition felt called upon to preserve it with a great degree of accuracy. Even the fact that it eventually came to be scripture did not prevent change. This is particularly true of the fluid pre-Origenic period, though change did not stop with Origen as any textual critic knows. And not all these changes were of the accidental variety. The present writer made a study of changes made in the New Testament text by Justin Martyr and Clement of Alexandria in terms of motivating factors involved. The study showed that several motivating forces were at work; they were classified as follows: historical, dogmatic, harmonistic, stylistic, ethical and practical, and explanatory. By far the most important category was the dogmatic.[13]

There is no reason to think that a difference existed between the use of particular readings by the Fathers and of tradition by John. As in the case of the Fathers, the fourth evangelist's religious interests must be viewed as a controlling factor in the selection, contextual adaptation, and internal modification of Synoptic materials. The sharp distinction often made between canonical and noncanonical books tends to blur the features of this aspect of the process. But the phenomena of contextual adaptation and internal modification may be discerned at the

---

consequently, no conclusions as to date can be based upon it. The problem is different with respect to the Rylands fragment. Paleographers date it at approximately the middle of the second century. Even then allowance must be made for a degree of error. Taking the fragment into account, Barrett argues for limits of A.D 90-140 for the writing of the Gospel: C. K. Barrett, *The Gospel According to St. John* (New York: The Macmillan Company, 1955), p. 108.

[13] E. L. Titus, "The Motivation of Changes Made in the New Testament Text by Justin Martyr and Clement of Alexandria" (unpublished Ph.D. dissertation, University of Chicago, 1942). A more recent study has been made by Leon E. Wright, who canvasses the literature of the second century, and, indeed, goes beyond it to include Origen, who, in spite of his interest in an accurate text, displays "the moulding dynamics of motivating interests of a religious and practical character," Wright, *op. cit.*, p. 9. Used by permission.

genesis of the process, i.e., in the manner in which Matthew and Luke used Marcan tradition. A good illustration of this is Luke's adaptation of Mark's story of Jesus' rejection (Mark 6: 1-6). Luke 4:16-30 changes the order of Mark, and makes it "a dramatic frontispiece to Jesus' public ministry." [14] But it is a great deal more than a "frontispiece": whereas in Mark the story is merely one of a *local* rejection by Galilean Jews who know Jesus and his family too well for them to view him as an exceptional person, in Luke it becomes a prelude to the subject of the Jewish rejection and the Gentile acceptance to which Luke's two-volume work is largely dedicated. This new function is made possible by the appending to the story of the rejection proper, allusions to Elijah and Elisha in their traditional, favorable relations with Gentiles (Luke 4:25-27).

One further point may be observed. Streeter has pointed out that, with regard to the reporting of the discourses of historical personages, two different traditions existed in antiquity—the Jewish and the Greek.

In the Jewish tradition care was exercised to preserve the maxims of the "wise men," such sayings being preserved in books like Proverbs, Ecclesiastes, and the Wisdom of ben Sira. The attachment of the name "Jesus, son of Sirach," to the last named about 130 B.C. begins a period in which the author's name is attached to epigrammatic sayings. Before this the collections had been anonymous. Streeter holds that

it is to the continuance, in the preponderantly Jewish communities in the Early Church, of this Jewish practice of preserving as far as possible the exact words of the teacher that we owe the different collections of sayings of Christ which are preserved to us in the Synoptic Gospels.[15]

The Greek tradition, on the other hand, felt free to compose speeches for characters involved. Thucydides expressly states that

[14] S. MacLean Gilmour, in *The Interpreter's Bible* (New York and Nashville: Abingdon Press, 1952), VIII, 89.
[15] *Op. cit.*, p. 369.

he did so. The same method undoubtedly holds true for the Dialogues of Plato. Since the fourth evangelist was writing in a Greek city, his readers, both Greek and Jewish-Christian, would be acquainted with this method. They would know that the ideas set forth in the Discourses were not intended to be a verbally exact record of what Jesus actually said but that the doctrine propounded was "organically related to what Christ . . . would have taught had he been explicitly dealing with the problems confronting the Church at the time the Gospel was written." [16]

These considerations, added to the comparative work of scholars like Streeter and Windisch, make the fundamental dependence of John on the Synoptics a probability not quickly to be put aside.

It is generally held that the Fourth Gospel reveals a large degree of dependence on the thought of Paul. The concept of the Spirit, the emphasis on the unseen world as the real world, and the idea of the new creation illustrate areas of dependence. But the evangelist's willingness to modify the apostle's thought is still more striking. In this he shows the same creative genius that we have seen in his use of the Synoptics. The Spirit becomes the dominant concept without the limitations of an imminent eschatology; the idea of the new creation is brought into relation with the Spirit's operation apart from sacramental mediation; resurrection is conceived in terms of a present depth-dimension experience, unrelated to eschatology. "In general, it can be said that the Gospel writer's mind is attracted to those areas of Paul's thought which are embraced by the rather elusive term 'mystical.' " [17]

Certain areas of Paul's thought, on the other hand, apparently held no attraction for the evangelist. Paul's view of the cross when conceived in terms of propitiatory sacrificial practice, juridical procedure, or vicarious sacrifice seems to be completely foreign to the less rationalistic mind of John. Yet in Paul himself

---

[16] *Ibid.*, p. 371.
[17] Ernest C. Colwell and Eric L. Titus, *The Gospel of the Spirit* (New York: Harper & Brothers, 1953), p. 48. Used by permission.

the death is explained in ways that transcend the Jewish sacrificial and juristic systems. Death and resurrection combined (death-resurrection) in "the unity of one salvation-occurrence: 'He who died' is also 'he who was raised up' (Rom. 8:34; II Cor. 5:15; 13:4)." [18] It is obvious that John can reject the one and accept the other.

A similar pattern is apparent with respect to eschatology. Of course the evangelist was not dependent solely on Paul for this feature, but, being so truly a Paulinist, one may imagine that he contemplated this massive aspect of Paul's thought with no small degree of concern. Nevertheless, he rejects it, and puts a radical substitute in its place: the doctrine of eternal life through the indwelling Spirit.

Finally, while Paul holds to the importance of sacramentalism,[19] the Fourth Gospel shows a disparagement of all ritualistic religion. The minimizing of water baptism, stress on the believer's mystical participation in the spiritual nature of Jesus, the absence of an account of the Lord's Supper, and the description of the Spirit's visitation as unpredictable, all testify to the author's viewpoint on this matter.

For him the Spirit is functionally and dynamically present in the church's experience leading its members into ever-enlarging experiences of awareness of meaning and value. The sacramental view of religion is consequently too mechanical for him to embrace it. We would go so far as to say that the Fourth Gospel represents a reaction to an increasing suppression of spontaneous religious experience through the substitution of an ex opere operato sacramental ritual.[20]

It is difficult to determine with any real degree of certainty the extent to which John made use of sources beyond the Synop-

---

[18] Rudolf Bultmann, *Theology of the New Testament*, tr. Kendrick Grobel (New York: Charles Scribner's Sons, 1951), I, 293. Used by permission.
[19] *Ibid.*, pp. 311-14.
[20] Colwell and Titus, *op. cit.*, pp. 51-52.

tics and Paul's letters. There is reason to believe, however, that he drew some ideas and at least one phrase from the book of Acts.

Acts, it must be remembered, represents an artistic interpretation of the westward march of Christianity. Literarily speaking, it has much in common with the Fourth Gospel itself. At the outset it presents the theme of the book on the lips of the risen Jesus: "But you will receive power when the holy Spirit has come upon you and you will be my witnesses in Jerusalem, in Judea, in Samaria, and to the end of the earth" (Acts 1:8). John has the same general pattern: the Jews, the Samaritans, and the Greeks. The similarity is, of course, too general to be taken as proof that John used Acts, but, taken in combination with other factors, it becomes a reasonable possibility. John is a Gospel of the Hellenists, but it recognizes both that "salvation is out of Judaism," and that a mission to the Samaritans preceded the coming of the Greeks.

A second possible base in Acts for Johannine material is found in the story of Pentecost (Acts 2:1-36). It is entirely possible that the miracle at Cana owes important elements to that story: the "good wine" (John 2:10) compares with the "new wine" (Acts 2:13), which is intoxicating (John 2:10; cf. Acts 2:15), and is symbolic of the Spirit which is to be given when Jesus' hour has come (John 2:4; cf. Acts 2:17).[21] In other words, the Cana miracle symbolically anticipates the Johannine "Pentecost" (20:22-23), which is itself a reconstruction of the Pentecost story of Acts.

The story of Jesus and the Samaritan woman in the fourth chapter of John may be in some respects related to the story of the Samaritan mission in Acts (8:5-25). The Simon legend enlarges in the second century, and it may well be that John, like Justin Martyr, reflects it. The possibility is strengthened by some verbal similarities.[22]

[21] Infra, pp. 87-88.
[22] Infra, p. 105.

Finally, and perhaps most significantly, the fourth evangelist, when commenting on the story of Jesus healing the official's son (4:46-54), says, "And he and his whole household believed" (4:53). There is no Synoptic precedent for this saying, but it is fairly common in the Acts narrative (Acts 16:15, 31, 34; 18:8).

The cumulative force of these instances is in the direction of probability that John used Acts. The Acts narrative, with its stress on the triumphant westward spread of Christianity under the leadership of the Spirit beginning with Pentecost and its demonstration in particular events of the power of the Spirit working through the disciples, is a good example of the "greater works" which the disciples will perform when the Spirit is liberated into the community; in the Discourses of the Fourth Gospel there is an implicit "Acts of the Apostles."

A further source for the Fourth Gospel writer was the rich symbolism of Hellenistic religion generally. One source, of literary character, may be assumed to lie behind the famous prologue to the Gospel (1:1-18), but even its importance rests on certain symbols—Logos, light, life, and truth—which suggest the revelatory function of Jesus. It is difficult, if not impossible, to identify this symbolism with specific religious groups, for the symbols employed represent the stock-in-trade of the syncretistic cults of the era. And they had not been absent from one phase or another of the Christianity before John.

In addition to Logos, light, life, and truth, the Gospel presents us with a variety of symbols:[23] Christ, Son of God, Lamb of God, Son of Man, Savior, Lord, the Way, the True Vine, the Good Shepherd, the Door, Teacher, the Holy One of God, Prophet, King, Judge, Spirit, wine, bread, water. Each of these is brought into relation to Jesus so as to suggest some function or quality. The over-all effect of this symbolism is to produce in the reader a mood of devotion. The Gospel is to literature what a great cathedral is to architecture; it engenders a mood

---

[23] The term "symbol" is used broadly to include titles applied to Jesus.

28

of exaltation, elevating the spirit to the level of devotion. Streeter has put it well: "It belongs neither to History nor Biography, but to the Library of Devotion." [24]

Progression of thought within literary units. The present writer is of the opinion that one of the most fatal errors in interpretations of the Fourth Gospel is failure to read each natural unit of material *in toto* to determine its major stress. Stories are constructed in such a manner that a verse-by-verse interpretation results in misinterpretation. Ideas are frequently interjected which are far removed from the evangelist's normative teaching; indeed, they may be crassly materialistic for the simple reason that they serve as foils for "higher" teaching finally to emerge. We may assume that these "lower" ideas are representative of views which exist within Judaism or the church. The evangelist is not knocking down straw men, but is attacking what he believes to be serious misconceptions of religion.

This principle could be illustrated by any of the "sign plus dialogue" sections of the first twelve chapters. Ch. 6, however, offers the most pertinent example because of the tendency to find normative teaching in the sacramentalism of vs. 53. If the discourse on the Bread of Life is viewed as a whole and the progression of thought followed to its climax, the teaching becomes, instead, anti-sacramentalism.[25]

If one studies the Gospel carefully, certain normative teachings emerge.[26] These may be used as control ideas, aiding in the determination of the stress of individual pericopes. These normative concepts may be stated as follows: (a) There are two worlds: one that is above and spiritual, the other that is below and material. The first is the realm of God and the true believer; the second is the order of flesh and unbelief. (b) The

---

[24] *Op. cit.*, p. 365.

[25] Colwell and Titus, *op. cit.*, pp. 53-56.

[26] The term "normative," as used here, is descriptive of the evangelist's fundamental religious views as contrasted with inferior positions which he attacks. This distinction is important, since these inferior positions may easily be identified with the intended (normative) teaching of the evangelist. This is a common error on the part of commentators.

spiritual world is that into which the believer is born by belief in Jesus, and his participation in it constitutes eternal life. When "life" is mentioned, it is this eternal life which is the evangelist's ultimate concern. (c) Life in the Spirit is gained by an intimate, personal association of the believer with Jesus, i.e., by the inner core of reality experienced through the Abiding Presence in the community. (d) The Spirit thus experienced is creative energy; it is characterized by spontaneity rather than by predictability. (e) Revelation is a function which belongs solely to Jesus; to "see" Jesus or to "know" him means that one experiences God himself, and there is no other avenue to this experience.

When these fundamental teachings are contradicted, we may be sure that the contradictions are due to the employment of specific literary techniques. They are intended to represent the "lower" teaching of the Jews, or of still unenlightened disciples, or of Jesus himself, who projects a materialistic concept only to refute it, i.e., it becomes a foil for normative Gospel teaching.

Literary opportunism. This forms a small but definite part of the literary phenomena of the Gospel. It is expressed in the tendency to make an assertion which is of value for the immediate context but which must be denied in the light of a wider perspective. It is therefore characterized by the element of contradiction.

Perhaps the clearest example of this is to be found in Jesus' success in outbaptizing the Baptist (3:22-26). The relationship between Jesus and John is such that in no way is the latter a successful competitor of Jesus. Even on John's own grounds Jesus is superior. This superiority is at every point zealously guarded. Yet, because of the evangelist's view of baptism, he cannot permit his Jesus to baptize in mere water. Consequently, he corrects the impression by stating clearly that Jesus himself did not baptize, but only his disciples (4:2).

Other illustrations of this feature may be noted: (a) In connection with belief which is not real because it is not abiding (2:23-25; 11:45; 12:19, 42). The writer's view of Jesus is so exalted that he cannot permit the pall of unbelief to dominate entirely a given scene. (*b*) In connection with the problem of the Messiah's origin, the evangelist fluctuates between two views: the Messiah is to come from Bethlehem, David's home, and is to be a descendant of David (7:41-42); the Messiah's origin is unknown (7:26-27). This fluctuation is due to the demands of the contexts.

The "sign." Of paramount importance to the interpreter of John is a grasp of the nature of the "sign" ($\sigma\eta\mu\epsilon\tilde{\iota}o\nu$). Dodd fittingly calls the section, 2:1–12:50, "The Book of Signs." [27] He recognizes, however, the sign character of material extending beyond ch. 12.

Commentators frequently have held that John's choice of signs has conformed to the perfect number "seven." The seven are "The Changing of the Water into Wine," "The Healing of the Official's Son," "The Healing of the Man at the Pool," "The Feeding of the Five Thousand," "Jesus Walking on the Water," "The Giving of Sight to the Blind Man," and "The Raising of Lazarus." This restricted list ignores instances such as "The Cleansing of the Temple" and "Jesus Washing the Disciples' Feet," which certainly display characteristics of the sign. It is doubtful that the number "seven" has controlled the evangelist's thinking in this connection.

The sign must be viewed as an integral aspect of John's philosophical, religious, and literary approach. When we consider his peculiar kind of flesh-spirit dualism, his love for words with "lower" and "higher" meanings, his interest in Jesus as "seen" in two dimensions (externally and inwardly), it is not surprising that this tendency should find expression in a complex literary vehicle. So basic is this way of thinking to his mind that one might suspect the entire human career of Jesus to be a gigantic sign, seen only in its external aspects by the unbelieving Jews, but conveying to the believer the reality of God's love for the world. So viewed, the Gospel would have much in com-

[27] *Op. cit.*, p. 289.

mon with the mythologizing tendency in early Christianity (e.g., Phil. 2:5-11) and the Mystery cults. The highly artificial character of the career of Jesus in the Fourth Gospel indicates that its author's real concern was with that which lay beyond history, with the cosmical meaning of the Incarnation; this concern determines to a large extent his selection, arrangement, and composition of material.

It is well known that Paul had stressed the Christ of experience to the virtual exclusion of the Jesus of history. He expresses his view succinctly: "Even if we had known Christ as a human being (κατὰ σάρκα), we no longer know him that way" (II Cor. 5:16). It has been suggested that Mark's Gospel represents a reaction to this tendency to remove Jesus from history.[28] But if this is true for Mark, it is certainly not true for John. John continues Paul's emphasis in spite of the fact that he structures his message in the form of a Gospel. The effect of the gospel literary form is to give concreteness to the church's testimony. But by emphasizing the element of mystery (men see Jesus externally, but they do not "see" him inwardly), and by carefully planned literary techniques, John has accomplished in terms of a "life" what Paul did by discursive writing: in the Fourth Gospel it is still the exalted being who appears before our eyes.

This feature is not absent from the Synoptics as recent studies stress.[29] But it is highlighted only at certain points; in the transfiguration story, for instance, where the glory of the resurrection faith casts its light back upon the ministry; in Mark, the humanity of Jesus still shines through. But it is different with John; here, the interest in the heavenly being is never slackened. Jesus as the Son of God appears from the start bearing all the radiance of the heavenly world, never losing it for an instant,

[28] "Mark's Gospel may be understood as a reaction to that emphasis in the early Church on the Risen and Exalted Christ to the neglect of the historic ministry," Paul E. Davies, "Mark's Witness to Jesus," Journal of Biblical Literature, LXXIII, Part IV (December, 1954), 197-202.

[29] See, e.g., F. C. Grant's article in The Interpreter's Bible (New York and Nashville: Abingdon Press, 1951), VII, 629-47. Grant's article is concerned with Mark, the point at which the problem is most acute.

and marches triumphantly to embrace the cross as the instrument of his glorification.

Nevertheless, for all his concern with the exalted Christ, the fourth evangelist was compelled to allow some place for the historical person. As the present writer sees it, John assumes that Jesus was born of human parents, had real brothers, lived with the family at Nazareth (until his ministry began), and was in appearance like other men. But with the descent of the Spirit—the point of the Incarnation—that humanity ceased to operate, except in terms of the physical organism: he walked about, used the voice mechanism, etc., but the mental and spiritual qualities were no longer those of a man. From the point of the Incarnation, the continuum of the human element remained only in the minds of the Jews, who, from the nature of the case, saw merely a Jewish boy from Nazareth, now grown to manhood, making fantastic claims to divinity.

The point to grasp in all this is that the whole Gospel is structured on the dualistic principle. What the reader sees at first glance is the life story of a Galilean Jew, a miracle worker and teacher. But a second glance reveals something far deeper: the story of the Divine Redeemer whose actions and words are intended to penetrate the deep spiritual darkness which envelops the world.

The Johannine sign is to be understood against this background. The sign is an act of extraordinary and usually miraculous character intended to reveal the spiritual qualities of the performer; it takes place on the historical level, and is capable of being construed in a purely material sense. The relationship between the sign and the thing signified is not always obvious, being dependent on religious meaning which custom has vested in certain key symbols (e.g., wine, bread, sight, life), and on the development of thought in dialogue based on the act, or it may depend on both in combination.

The sign, as John conceives it, represents the third stage of development through which the miracle stories passed. Certain

33

of the Synoptic stories of this sort were motivated by the compassion of Jesus for unfortunate people. In these stories, faith is the prerequisite of healing. On this level we are probably close to history; that is, we may suppose that Jesus of Nazareth was the kind of person to be motivated by compassion. This is the first stage in the development of this type of traditional material.

A second stage of development is also present in the Synoptics. At this point the miracles become evidential: they demonstrate the power of the performer.

The Fourth Gospel has moved beyond both stages, although an element of the evidential remains. But in John neither the quality of compassion nor evidence of power is the important consideration: the miracle is merely the vehicle by which Jesus as revealer of God is disclosed—it reveals his glory (δόξα). Now the most dominant characteristic of this glory is not power, but life, a quality which is apparent behind each of the particular stories and symbols employed. In the last analysis they are all concerned with Jesus as Lifegiver. That is why eternal life is the Johannine equivalent of the Synoptic kingdom of God. To possess eternal life is salvation. The signs are therefore attempts of the Johannine Jesus to disclose this divine quality to the world.

The use of symbolic characters. The symbolic interest of the evangelist extends to his selection of individuals; they are not historical personages, but symbolic types. Nathanael is the type of the true Israelite, "in whom there is no deceit"; the woman at the well in Samaria is a type of the Samaritan nation; the beloved disciple is a type of the true disciple; the "Greeks" symbolize the non-Jewish world; Mary of Bethany symbolizes the devout believer; Thomas symbolizes the believer whose stress is on external evidence as to Jesus' divine nature. The individuals introduced in no sense emerge as strong, independent persons, but as devices to facilitate the well-defined teachings which the book presents.

Unconscious testimony to Jesus. The clearest example of this is the oracular utterance of Caiaphas (11:49-52), a cryptic

34

declaration that Jesus' death is to result in the uniting of the "children of God." [30] Another example of unconscious testimony is given in the account of the Crucifixion, when Pilate places the inscription on the cross: "Jesus of Nazareth, the King of the Jews" (19:19). In this case, however, the unconscious element may be somewhat weakened by the fact that Pilate is as much a protagonist of Jesus as an antagonist. Yet it can scarcely be meant that Pilate comprehended the full meaning of what he had written. The unalterable truth of Pilate's words is graphically underscored by his answer to the protesting Jews, "What I have written I have written" (19:22).

Sometimes this unconscious testimony is given in the form of reflection by the Jews on the words of Jesus. Two such instances appear in connection with Jesus' allusions to "going away." In the first instance the Jews wonder if Jesus may mean that he is going to the Diaspora to "teach the Greeks" (7:35). In the most obvious and superficial sense of their statement they are wrong; but in the sense that Jesus' Spirit will be universalized and given to the Greeks they are quite correct. The second instance represents the Jews as reflecting on the possibility that Jesus' reference to "going away" means that he intends to kill himself (8:22). Again, they are wrong in their literal reference to suicide, but right in relating the allusion to his death. Furthermore, his death is predetermined though not premeditated in the sense in which we associate it with suicide. But it is clear that both propositions—his going to the Greeks, and his going to his death—contain fundamental truths.

The use of "stupid" characters. This is one of the most frequently employed devices; it is used to facilitate the development of the normative teaching of the Gospel. The Jews, Nicodemus, the Samaritan woman, and the disciples, all fulfill this role. The pattern is the same in each case; cryptic remark by Jesus, uncomprehending response by an individual or group, development of normative teaching by Jesus.[31]

[30] Dodd, op. cit., p. 368.
[31] Colwell and Titus, op. cit., pp. 43-44, 56-58.

Employment of dramatic technique. This feature comes most clearly into play, naturally enough, in connection with the passion narrative. Pilate, for example, places Jesus on the judgment seat and makes the dramatic proclamation, "There is your king!" Pilate, the judge, is himself being judged. In another instance, Pilate questions Jesus about his claims to kingship. Standing in the presence of the king of the realm of Truth, he asks the age-old question, "What is truth?"

These are but two examples of the dramatic element. The Gospel abounds in illustrations: the contrast between light and darkness, belief and unbelief, the apparent and the real, life and death; dramatic stories such as The Raising of Lazarus, Jesus Washing the Disciples' Feet, The Anointing, The Betrayal.

In order to feel the full force of the high drama of the Gospel, the reader must understand the glory of the revelation of God in Jesus, and the deep tragedy of its rejection. The ignorance and stupidity of men are shown in active opposition to the redemptive work of God. But the tragic element is deepened by the fact that man's vision is so limited that, in his blindness, he cannot distinguish good from evil (9:40-41; 16:2). When the full radiance of the heavenly world penetrates the darkness, men set themselves in opposition to it and seek its destruction. This opposition culminates in the crucifixion of God's own Son.

This means that the dramatic element is fundamentally related to the author's dualism. The lower world stands in opposition to the higher, the apparent to the real, the temporal to the eternal, darkness to light, unbelief to belief, death to life. This consistent dualism constitutes the framework of the Gospel's story of God's redemptive contact with human history.

The rabbinical method. C. H. Dodd believes that the Fourth Gospel shows affinities with rabbinic Judaism. He discusses the problem under three heads: (a) the Torah, (b) the Messiah, and (c) the name of God.[32] It is not our purpose to discuss

[32] *Op. cit.*, pp. 74-96.

here the problems dealt with by Dodd, but instead to give two examples of the evangelist's use of the principles of rabbinical method.

The first example has to do with the problem of Jesus healing the crippled man on the Sabbath (7:21-24; cf. 5:2-9). The argument advanced rests on the fact that circumcision was permitted on the Sabbath, if the day for circumcision (the eighth day) were to fall on a Sabbath. Jesus claims that, since this is the case, it must be permissible to heal a *whole* man on the Sabbath. Dodd asks why the reference is to the whole man, and quotes R. Eliezer as follows:

> Circumcision repels the Sabbath. Why? Because on its account one makes oneself guilty of annihilating the Torah if it is not carried out at the appointed time. And is not an inference from the less to the greater permissible? For the sake of one member he repels the Sabbath, and shall not the whole of him repel the Sabbath? [33]

Dodd finds in this example evidence of John's knowledge of current rabbinical thought. The connection, however, is not altogether clear. It may be that John argues simply on the grounds that if it is permissible for circumcision to take place on the Sabbath, i.e., to mutilate *part* of a man, how much more permissible should it be to heal a *whole* man on the Sabbath.

The second example is more obvious. The Jews accuse Jesus of blasphemy because he, a man, claims to be a god (10:33). Jesus then appeals to Ps. 82:6, "I said you are gods," and argues that since men were called gods in the scripture, how much more does he have the right to the title "Son of God" (10:34-36). Here we see at work the casuistry of the method. On the face of it, at least, the argument is hardly a valid one. The logic would be that since men were called gods in the scripture, Jesus likewise has the right to be called a god. But the logic is broken by the introduction of a special category, "Son of God," which has nothing to do with the scripture cited.

[33] *Ibid.*, p. 79.

The argument is admittedly *ad hominem* and indeed is little better than a play on words, for Jesus claims to be the "Son of God" in a very different sense from that in which the judges of Israel are "children of the most high." But the analogy of the use made of O. T. quotation by Paul and in the Epistle to the Hebrews makes it quite credible that in John's time such arguments may have been used against the Jews to defend the divinity of Christ.[34]

Use of words with a double meaning. Sometimes the possibility of a double meaning is due to ambiguity in the word itself. The classic example of this is the word ἄνωθεν (3:3), which means both "again and "from above." Both meanings are intended. Nicodemus, according to plan, seizes upon the lower meaning thereby giving Jesus opportunity to develop the notion of birth from above.

A second example of ambiguity is found in the use of the word πνεῦμα, which can mean both "wind" and "spirit." Its usage in 3:8 involves a play on words.

Certain verbs contain the same feature of ambiguity. A good example of this is the verb ὑψόω, "to lift up," or "to exalt." It is used in 3:14 of the lifting up, i.e., exaltation of Jesus on the cross.

The verb ἀναβαίνω (7:8) has a similar ambiguity. On the surface it simply refers to the proposed visit of Jesus to Jerusalem, but in a deeper sense to his ἀνάβασις, i.e., his return to the Father.

In some cases the double intent is due to the use of a word in religious vocabulary. The word "night" is a good example of this. Nicodemus comes to Jesus in the night (3:2), where "night" means more than time of day; it signifies the spiritual darkness in which Nicodemus dwells. Judas goes out into the night, signifying that he has forsaken the Light of the World (13:30).

In conclusion it may be pointed out that the Fourth Gospel shares in the creative process in operation in the oral period

[34] G. H. C. Macgregor, *The Gospel of John* (New York: Harper & Brothers, 1929), p. 243. Used by permission.

and which extends to the literary era. Factors in this process may be summarized as follows:

i. The stature of Jesus of Nazareth as a religious figure must be considered basic. He was vividly remembered by those who had known him intimately in Galilee and Judea. This memory of Jesus, what he was, did, and said, constitutes the historical base of all future "sayings" of Jesus, as well as of his "deeds" and pronouncements as to his nature. It is difficult to conceive that if Jesus had been an *average* or *typical* Jew the subsequent development could have taken place.

ii. Legendary material tends to accumulate around any outstanding figure. This observation scarcely needs elaboration. Even in modern times it takes the careful historian to distinguish between fiction and fact when dealing with the life of a Washington or a Lincoln.

iii. The practice of pseudonymous writing, current in antiquity, helps to place the character of the tradition in better perspective. In view of the generally accepted practice, the question of the ethics of the procedure is not pertinent. The vast pseudonymous literature is ample evidence that the phenomenon of the Gospels is not an isolated one.

iv. The immediate followers of Jesus inherited certain patterns of thought. They tended to interpret Jesus in terms of these thought-patterns. Basic among them was *the hope for national deliverance*. This hope had assumed at least two forms in the first century: (a) The restoration of the Davidic kingdom by means of revolution led by God's Messiah. (b) The termination of the age of evil by a supernaturally initiated cosmic cataclysm. According to this view, the Son of Man would operate as God's agent. This messianic hope undergoes radical adaptation in the non-Jewish world.

v. The rise of Gentile Christianity presented an array of fresh categories for the expression of thought. Among these we may note sacramentalism and metaphysical considerations generally. So terms emerge like "Logos," "Son of God," and "rebirth."

39

vi. "Spiritism" meant that the Christian community kept in continuous contact with Jesus. This contact resulted in the creation of new tradition related to the needs of a developing church (See Acts 1:24; 9:5, 17; 16:7; I Cor. 2:11; 5:4; 12-14; Gal. 1:12; Mark 13:11; John 14:26; 15:26; 16:13; etc.).

vii. The treasure house of Old Testament "predictions" was made applicable to the career of Jesus by the belief that Christianity was the New Israel. The authoritative scriptures create events of the career; conversely, the career illuminates the meaning of the scriptures.

viii. The need for authority inspired interest in the words of Jesus. The Apocalypse of John, for example, presumes to carry the words of Jesus no less than the Gospels.

ix. The evangelistic and edificatory work of the early Christian preachers called for illustrations drawn from the career of Jesus. Indeed, some scholars believe that the preaching function accounts for the preservation and development of the tradition.

x. Strained relations with Judaism assumed different forms of literary expression, among these the attitude of Jesus himself toward the Jews. Two aspects of Jesus' career, in particular, were emphasized because they lent themselves readily to an anti-Jewish point of view: (a) Jesus' attack on Jewish religious leaders, especially the Pharisees. In expanded form this anti-legalistic material became an anti-Jewish attack. (b) The death of Jesus was interpreted so as to rid the Romans of responsibility and place it entirely on the shoulders of the Jews.

xi. The expansion of Christianity within the Roman Empire demanded an apologetic which would render the movement politically innocuous. This tendency is broken in the New Testament only by the book of Revelation where a hostile attitude toward the state is assumed. Christian apologetic, in this connection, centers largely around the problem of the Crucifixion, but is reflected also in the Christian attitude toward taxation and in loyalty to the emperor generally (Note Mark 12:13-17; Rom. 13:1-7; I Pet. 2:13-17).

xii. Embarrassing aspects of the known career of Jesus called for especially elaborate interpretation. There were three of these in particular: his lowly birth, his baptism at the hands of the Baptizer, and his death by crucifixion. These were dealt with in such a fashion as to remove all stigma.

xiii. Unknown areas of Jesus' life tended to be filled in with events congruous with his exalted position in the thought of the church. This tendency is .best illustrated by the infancy gospels, but is also evident in the birth stories of Matthew and Luke, and in the Lucan story of Jesus in the temple (Luke 2: 41-51).

xiv. Christianity's close environmental association with other religious movements called for relevant apologetic and polemic. Hellenistic religions, Judaism, and the movement of John the Baptist were all involved. The last mentioned called for special attention since the historical association of Jesus with John could scarcely be denied. The problem was solved largely by the identification of the Baptizer with Elijah (in the Synoptics), and by the witness device (in the Fourth Gospel).

xv. The growth of schismatic tendencies in the church demanded authoritative control in the direction of Christian unity. Various parties came to vie with one another as representatives of the true faith. Chief among these were the Judaizers, Pauline Christianity, and special groups like the Docetists. Perhaps the best single plea for unity is in the form of a prayer attributed to Jesus by the fourth evangelist (17:1-26).

xvi. The development of an increasingly complex ecclesiastical institution created the need for an appeal to authoritative words of Jesus on matters of practical concern such as ethics, discipline, and hospitality (See Matt. 18:15-20; Luke 10:5-7).

xvii. Perhaps one would be correct in saying that experience was the most important single factor in the development and creation of tradition. Hence, for Paul, interpretation of Jesus revolved around the central axis of his revolutionary experience (conversion). Men saw Jesus in terms of their own religious genius. This "seeing" was not objectively historical, but nonetheless religiously valid.

While these seventeen points relate primarily to the growth of oral tradition, we can see the same forces at work in the development of Gospels. In most cases the Fourth Gospel reflects the tendencies indicated.

The preceding pages have indicated the major literary features of the Gospel. It cannot be stressed too strongly that a grasp of the message of the Fourth Gospel is dependent on a knowledge of this literary method. It has also been suggested that many features of the literature are dependent on forces at work in the Christian community. While some of the literary techniques are peculiar to the fourth evangelist, the problems are those of the community, and in the general tendency toward theological reconstruction he does not stand apart.

CHAPTER II

The Logos

HOW DID THE AUTHOR OF THE FOURTH GOSPEL VIEW JESUS?
This is the all-important question facing the interpreter of the
Gospel. The problem is not a surface one involving the question
of the Jesus of history versus the Christ of faith; that question
has been largely settled in favor of the latter. Nor is it a question
of the choice of one among the many titles given to Jesus by
the evangelist. The problem reduces itself to this: Did the author
of the Gospel intend his Jesus to be understood in terms of the
Logos concept? In the area of interpretation this is the Johannine
problem.

An answer to the problem is not easy. An assessment of
scholarly studies in Johannine literature in this century discloses
that relationships between Johannine thought at this point and
Hellenistic religions and popular philosophies apparently are
manifold. Rabbinic Judaism, Hellenistic Judaism (especially
Philo), Hermeticism, Stoicism, Gnosticism, the Mysteries, and
even Mandaeism are alleged to have made their individual con-
tributions to John's Jesus conceived as Logos. Yet the striking
fact is that Logos as a title for Jesus is used only four times
in the Gospel, and these four usages are confined to the first
fourteen verses, three-fourths of them being contained in the
first verse.

This fact alone should raise a question as to the importance
of the Logos concept in the Gospel as a whole. But there are
additional factors which cast serious doubt on the centrality of
the Logos doctrine. In the following pages these will be listed
and discussed.

1. The Logos material of the Fourth Gospel may be viewed

43

as one of several examples of such material to be found in the New Testament. It is well known that Paul, in Colossians, makes use of the Logos concept, but it could scarcely be said that this concept controls his view of Jesus. Indeed it is just this philosophical tendency in Colossians which has raised questions as to the authenticity of the epistle. The most that can be said is that the Logos doctrine is tangential to the thought of Paul and represents his most philosophical attempt to meet a local emergency in the church at Colossae.

If the concept is tangential in Paul it is hardly less so in the homily known as Hebrews. In the latter there is a striking resemblance between the writer's usage and that of the fourth evangelist. For one thing, it forms an introduction to his work in a manner similar to the Prologue of the Gospel. Yet there is little relationship between the introduction and the body of the work; Jesus, in Hebrews, is not Logos but priest. It is true that there is a strong philosophical undercurrent throughout the work, and that the eternal high priest must be seen in relation to it, but the fact remains that the connection between him and the creative Logos of the first four verses is not close.

The use of the Logos concept in Hebrews and in the Fourth Gospel seems to represent a literary pattern useful in relating Jesus to the eternal order, but not presented as a basic theme strictly to be developed.

Of course there can be little doubt that Hellenistic modes of thought were making important inroads on primitive Christianity. All three writers mentioned make some use of the Logos concept. And in other and far more important ways they reveal that they had drunk deeply of the fountain of Hellenism. But there is room for doubt that any of them had organized the elements of the Christian faith around a single Hellenistic concept; the general practice was to employ a variety of categories useful in the communication of religious meaning.

2. There is considerable doubt as to the originality of the Prologue. This is not intended to imply that the Gospel once existed apart from the Prologue; rather, that the evangelist saw

in a contemporary Logos document a source upon which he could draw. Whether this document was identical with our present Prologue, without the alleged interpolated verses, or more extensive, we cannot say.

Now the use of a document like the one described would be quite in keeping with the writer's literary method. The Synoptics provide us with information regarding his treatment of sources: he never hesitates to delete or interpolate details which are irrelevant, though it cannot be said with certainty that all irrelevant elements are deleted from his Synoptic source. There is no reason to think that he would hesitate to treat other sources in the same fashion. This suggests three possibilities in the writer's treatment of the original Hymn: (a) he might interpolate material; (b) he might delete material; (c) he might allow some irrelevant or, at least, neutral material to remain. A fourth possibility that he would leave the source intact is dismissed as improbable.

If the Prologue was originally a non-Johannine hymn to the Logos, Gnostic or Stoic (and most commentators do not rule out the possibility), it is important to grasp the point that the rules which the evangelist applies to his sources generally also apply here. Seen in this light the awkward John the Baptist passages of the Prologue become understandable. A source is utilized because of its symbolic possibilities. However, the symbols of a given source do not necessarily become central to the total message, though contributory to it. Frequently a symbol has central importance *only in its relation to the immediate picture drawn*; the evangelist is a literary opportunist!

The title "Lamb of God," employed only twice (1:29, 36), and placed on the lips of John the Baptist in both instances, is a case in point. Of course no literary source can be identified, though the writer seems to be indebted to the tradition for the title (I Cor. 5:7; Rev. 5:6, 8, 13; 6:1; etc.). "Lamb of God" is, to be sure, related to the account of Jesus' death (Jesus dies at the time of the slaying of the Passover lamb), but it would be entirely unwarranted to interpret the Jesus of the Fourth

45

Gospel in terms of the Lamb symbolism of ch. 1. In spite of a certain fundamental unity, the Gospel consists of a series of still pictures any one of which could stand alone.

"Logos" is no exception to this rule. That the evangelist had no aversion to the term is demonstrated by its presence in the text. But the fact that it does not occur beyond the Prologue is evidence that his use of this title does not differ from other cases. The chief value of "Logos" seems to lie in its ability to suggest that Jesus was pre-existent, that he was one in nature with God, and to support the general theme of revelation.

The Prologue does supply some important ideas which are utilized in the Gospel proper: the notion of rejection, the concept of rebirth, the emphasis on Light, Life, Truth, and on revelation. How many of these concepts may have been in the original Hymn we cannot say. But it is noteworthy that certain ideas do not reappear: the concepts of World-Creator, Fullness, and Grace. This rejection and selection of concepts contained in sources is typical of the evangelist's method.

The view is misleading which assumes that the Prologue's origin in a source has no bearing on the Logos problem. For it is possible that the evangelist's selection of his source was due to an interest in symbols other than Logos. Inasmuch as the concepts of Light, Life, and Truth pervade the Gospel, while Logos as a title does not appear beyond the Prologue, it is reasonable to conclude that this trilogy constituted his chief interest.

3. The problem of the relation of the Logos to the Gospel may be studied in terms of literary balance. If the Logos controls the Christology of John, then the reader would expect an epilogue to balance the thought of the Prologue. But no such epilogue appears; instead, we find a balancing of ideas in terms of the descent and ascent of the Spirit. Why, then, not make the Spirit the controlling idea? From the point of view of the church the central datum of its experience was the unseen spiritual Presence. This datum of experience needed to be

explained, both in terms of its relation to the historical event of Jesus' career, and, back of that, to the eternal God.

There was precedent for this view of the Spirit. A certain segment of the tradition had early begun to go in the direction of making the Spirit paramount. The Synoptic stories of Jesus' life had given a prominent place to the coming of the Spirit upon him. This idea would be still more attractive to a man who had no interest in the concept of the virgin birth. Even the Gospels of Matthew and Luke seem to make the point of real beginnings, not at the birth, but at the baptism. Paul, moreover, had emphasized the Spirit to an amazing degree. It gave him the experiential element in salvation, though he was hindered from going all the way by the current eschatology. But the fourth evangelist knew no such limitation. Freed from the shackles of an imminent eschatology he could give full rein to his interpretation of Jesus as the Spirit-filled Christ, who, by his death, had made himself available forever.

The place of the Spirit in the Gospel will be considered at length below. For the present it is sufficient to point out that there is no counterbalance of prologue with epilogue, of the Logos become flesh with the discarnate Logos; the balance occurs in terms of the descent and ascent of the Spirit.

4. The evangelist's thought regarding the Incarnation has a bearing on the question of the Logos' centrality. If Jesus is the Logos, when and by what means does the Incarnation take place? We are thrown back upon two possibilities. Either it occurs in terms of the natural processes of birth or we must assume that the writer accepted the doctrine of the virgin birth.

As to the first, it seems inconceivable that the author of the Gospel could embrace it. He asserts emphatically, "that which is born of the flesh is flesh," and that is to relate natural birth to the lower world. There is no reason to attribute this position to him, unless we concede to him the theory that Jesus was poured through Mary's womb as water through a tube. But, of course, that is out of the question!

Scholars who are content to affirm that Jesus was the divine

Logos from the beginning, and let it go at that, bypass this all-important question of how and when the Incarnation took place. Their position would be understandable if John's picture of Jesus were that of a man who by virtue of his moral and spiritual excellence caused men to recognize him as one sent from God; that would make his divinity to be grounded in his humanity. But this is not the case in the Fourth Gospel. In this Gospel, Jesus is a god, not a prophet (in spite of the application of the term to him); in fact the ethical element is almost entirely absent. Divinity does not arise out of humanity; the human tends to obscure the divine. If Jesus is the Logos, he is "veiled in flesh."

The Jesus of the Fourth Gospel is divine, not through moral struggle, but because of a power which comes on him *from without*. Even Mark, whose picture of Jesus at times approaches the prophetic, feels called upon to explain Jesus in terms of an infusion of Holy Spirit which made him God's adopted Son. Whatever the phrase "And the Logos became flesh" may mean, it does not mean that Jesus was a man in the sense, for example, that Peter was a man. We can conclude only that the process of natural birth is not a satisfactory explanation of how our author accounted for the Incarnation.

That the evangelist held the theory of the virgin birth of Jesus is likewise excluded. He is mentioned as Jesus of Nazareth, the Son of Joseph (1:45); he has brothers (7:3 ff.); and the reference in 7:40-52 rules out any belief that Jesus hailed from Bethlehem.

It is misleading to say, as some do, that the evangelist had no interest in the virgin birth, for that might be construed to mean that his attitude toward the problem of origins was a casual one. That this was not the case is demonstrated by the pervasive concern regarding this matter, summed up in the question, "You know me, and you know where I come from?" John's lack of reference to the virgin birth indicates a lofty disdain for a theory which would limit the Incarnation to a semiphysical process. To assert the possibility that he held this theory is to misunderstand his teaching on the sarx-pneuma dualism and to underestimate it. His insistence is that real life cannot possibly emerge from the physical.

5. When the Logos concept is made central, a confusion emerges at the point of the farewell addresses in connection with Christ as Logos and the Spirit which is promised. In one breath Jesus declares that he will send the Spirit and in the next that he himself will come. If, indeed, the Logos-Christ is speaking, then the Spirit as an independent reality would seem to be irrelevant. Commentators have felt this and have gone so far as to declare that John's concept of the Spirit is superfluous.[1]

The total impression of the Fourth Gospel is against a distinction between Christ and the Spirit. It will not allow many roads from heaven to earth. There is but one avenue of the divine life: Jesus himself is the Way. But as the Spirit he is experienced in the church. If it is maintained that the Spirit, not the Logos, is the controlling concept of the Gospel, the confusion largely disappears. Long ago, Origen, one of the Fourth Gospel's early interpreters, wrote a word of warning regarding the use of the title "Logos." He lists the titles applied to Jesus in the Fourth Gospel: Son of God, Light of the World, Resurrection, Way, Truth, Life, Door, Good Shepherd, Christ, Master, Lord, King of the Jews, True Vine, Bread of Life. He argues that the same principle of interpretation which is applied to each of these titles ought to govern the interpretation of "Logos" also:

What caprice it is, in all these cases, not to stand upon the term employed, but to inquire in what sense Christ is to be understood to be the door, in what way the vine, and why He is the way; but in the one case of His being called the Word, to follow a different course.[2]

---

[1] E. F. Scott, The Spirit in the New Testament (New York: George H. Doran Company, 1923), pp. 205-8.

[2] Commentary on John I. 23.

49

Origen's advice is well taken. But if we dismiss the notion that Logos is the Gospel's controlling idea, does this mean that the Gospel is devoid of any unifying principle? This is by no means the case. The position advanced in these pages is that the unifying principle is the concept of the Spirit. The Spirit doctrine involved has its basis in the traditional Christian belief as reflected in the Synoptic Gospels, Acts, and especially Paul's letters, but has been modified considerably by Hellenistic influences "atmospherically" mediated. To a consideration of the Johannine view of the Spirit we now turn our attention.

CHAPTER III

The Spirit

THE JESUS OF THE FOURTH GOSPEL MUST BE STUDIED IN RELATION to two points of origin, the earthly and the heavenly. First of all, the writer of the Gospel holds that a child was born in Nazareth of Galilee. The name of his father was Joseph. From the Gospel itself there is no hint as to the name of his mother, and unless we had access to other tradition the name "Mary" would not present itself to our minds. The evangelist holds also that Jesus was one of several children born to this couple for he speaks of Jesus' brothers (2:12; 7:3, 5).

This Nazareth boy, according to the author, is later remembered by his fellow Jews. When Jesus makes a claim to heavenly origin, they exclaim, "Is not this Jesus, the Son of Joseph, whose father and mother we know?" As they remember him in the family setting, there is nothing about him to warrant claim to an unusual origin.

Loisy has correctly pointed out that Jesus appears in the Gospel "as a member of a family, is reputed son of Joseph and has a mother and brothers." He states further that

the book, in the form in which it has come down to us, seems to attribute to the Christ an existence completely human, assigning him a real birth followed by an integral human life up to the age of thirty after which his ministry, as divine revealer of a mystery, begins and lasts for about three years.[1]

But Loisy does not think of this human element as having been a part of the original Gospel:

[1] Alfred Loisy, The Origins of the New Testament, tr. L. P. Jacks (London: George Allen and Unwin, Ltd., 1950), p. 25. Used by permission.

51

Not only is this in violent and consciously intended contradiction to the Synoptics but is an addition and a contradiction to the fundamental idea of the fourth Gospel itself, the idea namely of a divine incarnation for the manifestation and fulfilment of human salvation, the said manifestation having no need to pass through preparatory stages while concealed under a developing human envelope.[2]

Retreat into this kind of explanation is too easy a solution. One can very readily cut the Fourth Gospel to fit his own pattern. What is needed is a theory, not necessarily orthodox, which will allow these intricately interwoven elements of the Gospel to remain as part of its total fabric. In this case it is precisely the "human envelope," with which the Jews are acquainted, that causes them trouble. The tension thus created between the appearance and the real, the outer and the inner, the human and the divine, the flesh and the spirit, is too inextricably a part of the total fabric for it to be extracted without reducing the Gospel to a shred.

The Jews of the Fourth Gospel, from beginning to end, view Jesus as merely a Nazareth product with false pretensions to extraordinary powers. At the beginning of his career they think of him as Joseph's boy from Galilee and when he hangs upon a cross they view him as a defeated aspirant to national leadership. Jesus of Nazareth, king? Impossible! They have no king but Caesar (19:15). All this moves on a completely historical level. This is one aspect of the drama of the Fourth Gospel and failure to recognize it results in a one-sided and hence perverted interpretation. This side of the picture must be held in mind when Jesus as the divine being, the Gospel's ultimate concern, is contemplated.

But there is a second vantage point from which to view the Jesus of the Fourth Gospel. Here, we must begin with the heavenly realm, with God and his concern for the salvation of mankind. As we take our stand here we see God sending forth his Spirit into the world so that he might take up his abode

[2] Loc. cit.

in human life. *But, being in Jesus of Nazareth, he never ceases to be the divine being who was with the Father.*

The divine Spirit merges with the man from Nazareth at the time of its descent; this is the point of the Incarnation (1: 29-34). This merging of the two (Spirit with flesh) accounts for the element of Jewish misunderstanding, for the Jews cannot see beyond the familiar external features of the human Jesus. They see Jesus, son of Joseph, but they cannot "see" Jesus, Son of God. When the divine Spirit merges with the historical Jesus, Spirit is, in a sense, submerged; that is, it is not apparent to the physical eye as the Jesus of history is; to see Jesus as the Spirit requires the eye of faith. This the Jews do not possess; hence, the conflict.

The event of the Incarnation is attested by the Baptist who views it in retrospect. The account stands near the beginning of the Gospel proper (1:29-34). Earlier, John has been introduced; first, by a series of negatives: John is not the light (1:8), he is not the Christ (1:20), he is not Elijah (1:21), he is not the prophet (1:21); and, secondly, by reducing him to a mere function: a voice crying in the wilderness (1:23). The "voice" of John is raised in testimony: "Jesus of Nazareth is the Chosen One of God, for God's Spirit has come upon him." John's testimony is not based on any chance incident in his career; he has been sent by God for the purpose of bearing witness to the event (1:33). This is the sole function of John in the Fourth Gospel. There is no evidence that he baptized Jesus; instead, Jesus is baptized with the Spirit. John's baptism with water provides the setting for Jesus' baptism with the Spirit. One can see behind this, of course, the baptism stories of the Synoptics, but the embarrassment caused by Jesus' baptism at the hands of John is removed.

In his discriminating treatment of church and gnosis, F. C. Burkitt presents a similar position. According to him, the Prologue introduces John to the readers of the Gospel, and mentions a mysterious person known as Jesus Christ. But the latter is mentioned in a manner which makes an introduction necessary. This introduction is contained in 1:19-34. It is given in the form of a testimony by the Baptist. In the first place, John testifies that he himself is not the Christ or Elijah or the prophet, but that he is the Voice whose function is to identify the mysterious Coming One. John's testimony in the second part is prompted by the appearance of Jesus who is acclaimed by John as the Lamb of God. How does he know this? He had learned by inspiration that God's Spirit would rest upon the One who would baptize with Holy Spirit. John, in testimony, now declares that he had seen the Spirit descend upon Jesus. Jesus, therefore, is the Chosen of God (ὁ ἐκλεκτὸς τοῦ θεοῦ). This means that John had witnessed the Incarnation!

Burkitt says:

From the moment of the Descent Jesus can say, "I and the Father are one" (ἓν ἐσμεν, x 30: cf. I Cor. iii 8): what He says is creative and authoritative, because it is of the same nature as the Divine Voice of which we read in the opening chapter of Genesis. In the terminology of Pistis Sophia, Jesus has become the Master of the ineffable Mystery: "He is a man in the world, but He towereth above all angels and will tower still more above them all; He is a man in the world, but He is King in the Light." And, just as in Pistis Sophia, the true Life consists in knowing Him.[3]

This presentation of the descent of the Spirit as the method of the Incarnation seems to have had its roots in Synoptic and perhaps in Gnostic thought. The connection with the Synoptic story seems obvious; the narratives have the following points in common: the quotation from Isa. 40:3 (John 1:23; cf. Mark 1:3; Matt. 3:3; Luke 3:4); the reference to John as baptizing in water, and Jesus, by contrast, baptizing in the Holy Spirit (John 1:33; cf. Mark 1:8; Matt. 3:11; Luke 3:16, 22).

An important difference, however, between John and the Synoptics is that in the former there is no voice from heaven announcing that Jesus is God's Son. But the change of setting

[3] Church & Gnosis (Cambridge: The University Press, 1932), pp. 99-100. Used by permission.

makes that impossible since the Baptist is testifying to an event which has already taken place. But there is a substitute for this omission in the words of John's testimony: "I have seen and borne witness that this is the Son of God" (1:34). Henceforth, "Son of God" becomes the most characteristic title for Jesus in the Gospel.

It is not easy to demonstrate that the Fourth Gospel is indebted to Gnosticism at this point. Certain factors, however, make it a possibility. In the first place, this problem is part of the larger one of the relation of the Fourth Gospel as a whole to Gnosticism, a relationship which, whatever form it may assume, cannot be denied. The fact, objectively determined, that the Gnostics used the Fourth Gospel in the second century was due to the Gospel's intrinsic character. What they could see in it, of course, was its emphasis on salvation by gnosis. And while, as Dodd has pointed out,[4] there are real differences between John's thought and that of the advanced Gnostic systems, it is still true that there are congenial points of contact between them.

One of these points of contact is the concept of Jesus as an emanation from deity. He is spoken of many times in the Gospel as "one sent" from God. To interpret this, as Dodd does,[5] in terms of the prophetic model is entirely to miscomprehend the Johannine view of Jesus. The ascribing to Jesus of a prophetic sense of mission, even ideally conceived, is completely out of place in the Fourth Gospel. The evangelist's Jesus is not one who starts at the human level and because of a sensitive inner life submits to the call of God. Instead, he begins in close relation to God in heaven, and is then sent out from God into the world. No prophet, however ideal, could ever say, "I have come down from heaven," or "I and the Father are one." The real ego of Jesus did not proceed by way of the womb, but through the descent from heaven. The ego of Jesus in John is the Spirit, not the human person in whom the Spirit became

[4] Op. cit., p. 114.
[5] Ibid., p. 255.

55

incarnate. When the Spirit merges with the son of Joseph, the latter is canceled (or perhaps elevated and merged with the divine Spirit) except in terms of bodily presence—a fact which tends to obscure the Spirit's presence.

This idea of Jesus as a divine emanation had been suggested by Paul. In Colossians he writes: "In him all the pleroma was pleased to dwell" (1:19). In more developed form this idea appears in the Valentinian Marcus according to Irenaeus as follows:

And on His [Jesus'] coming to the water [of baptism], there descended on Him, in the form of a dove, the Being who had formerly ascended on high, and completed the twelfth number, in whom there existed the seed of those who were produced contemporaneously with Himself, and who descended and ascended along with Him. Moreover he [Marcus] maintains that that power which descended was the seed of the Father and the Son, as well as that power of Sige which is known by means of them, but cannot be expressed in language, and also all the Aeons. And this was that Spirit who spoke by the mouth of Jesus, and who confessed that He was the Son of Man as well as that he revealed the Father, and who, having descended into Jesus, was made one with Him. . . . He [Marcus] maintains, therefore, that Jesus is the name of that man formed by a special dispensation, and that He was formed after the likeness and form of that [heavenly] Anthropos, who was about to descend upon Him. After He had received that Aeon, he possessed Anthropos himself, and Logos himself, and Pater, and Arrhetus, and Sige, and Aletheia, and Ecclesia, and Zoe.[6]

When due allowance is made for the idiosyncrasies of the complex Valentinian system, this statement from Irenaeus leaves us with a variation of Paul's view: in him the whole pleroma was pleased to dwell. Gnostics of the Valentinian variety, such as described, would find in the Fourth Gospel an attractive picture of Jesus. Here they would read of the Spirit descending on Jesus in all its fullness so that he became Son

[6] *Against Heresies* I. xv. 3.

of God, Son of Man, Savior, Life, Light, Truth, as well as Logos—terms which played an important part in the Gnostic system of emanations.

It is misleading to view the Fourth Gospel, in its relation to Gnosticism, either in terms of the Synoptics conceived as normative or from the vantage point of the so-called orthodoxy of Irenaeus. The Gospel's milieu is fluid, being constrained neither by a primitive "orthodoxy" nor by that of the late second century. The fourth evangelist feels free to depart from the past; and as for the future, that is in the making; its direction has not yet been determined. He feels equally free, therefore, to accept or reject Synoptic and Pauline elements on the one hand, and Gnostic elements on the other.

It may safely be said that the Fourth Gospel writer was Gnostic enough to assert the doctrine of salvation by gnosis, to use a Gnostic hymn to the Logos, and to employ the Gnostic mechanism of emanation. But his Gnosticism was not sufficiently advanced (measured against the developed systems of Valentinus or Basilides) for him to depart from certain elements contained in Paul's letters and the Synoptics. In particular, the Pauline doctrine of the Spirit had made a strong impression upon him. Experientially for Paul the Spirit is important, but he cannot quite square it with his doctrine of the Last Things. He speaks of it as the "guarantee" of the future life (II Cor. 1:22; 5:5). But it is more than a guarantee for the fourth evangelist! Unhindered by the eschatological problem he represents the Spirit as bestowing eternal life now. His view represents a development of the Pauline concept, and is largely due to a radically different view on eschatology.

The merging of the divine Spirit with the human Jesus raises the question of the relationship between the two. Does the divine Spirit obliterate the human Jesus? To what extent, if any, is the Jesus of the Fourth Gospel, beyond the point of the Incarnation, a human being? The whole matter of the sarx-pneuma dualism comes to its sharpest focus at this point.

In a sense, the Spirit is submerged by the Incarnation. Jesus as the Spirit, as has been said, becomes "veiled in flesh." This submergence expresses itself in two ways. First, Jesus appears no different in form from what he was in his role as son of Joseph. Secondly, the evangelist never says, "The Spirit said," with reference to a pronouncement of Jesus. Strangely enough, perhaps, he still uses the name "Jesus." But numerous other titles come to the fore, all of which are designed to express aspects of the Spirit's nature or function. It is as though the Spirit were a powerful life-giving fluid compressed and imprisoned within a vessel awaiting the moment of release, at which time it can become powerfully effective. Its potent properties may be suggested by various titles or labels, but no one of these exhausts its meaning. Spirit, as has been said, is submerged. We would have no right to say this except that the submerged Spirit rises gloriously to the surface at the Cross and in the giving of the Spirit to the disciples (20:22). That the author was conscious of possible misunderstanding at this point is evident from the well-known passage, "Now this he said about the Spirit, which those who believed in him were to receive; for as yet the Spirit had not been given, because Jesus was not yet glorified" (7:39). This passage is like an explanatory note. It is like saying, "Be informed that what I am talking about in these pages is that Jesus has the Spirit, but it cannot be released until he dies on the cross." But in spite of the author's warning note, readers down to the present day have failed to understand. In this sense, sarx has obscured pneuma.

This is a strange development when one considers that the major, almost exclusive, concern of the evangelist was with Jesus as the Spirit, not as a flesh person. Some commentators, having seen this, have held that the physical aspect of Jesus was, for the author, only an appearance.[7] But this judgment is unwarranted. While undue emphasis should not be placed on such items as the weariness of Jesus at the well, his tears, and

[7] Guy M. Davis, "The Humanity of Jesus in John," *Journal of Biblical Literature*, LXX, Part II (June, 1951), 105-12.

his thirst on the cross, these are nonetheless descriptions of human behavior. And the inability of Jesus' would-be captors to seize him is due simply to a "higher determinism" which guides his destiny until the appointed hour. The Jesus of the precrucifixion period is no ghost who, on that account, eludes his pursuers.

Nevertheless, the flesh of Jesus is not the evangelist's principal concern. If the words of the Prologue, "and the Logos became flesh" (1:14), are to be taken as in any sense thematic for the whole Gospel, they must be explained in the light of its interpretation of flesh. The translation of ἐγένετο as "became" is itself defective. The Logos still continues to be the Logos as 1:14b indicates. Men are invited to see beyond the flesh of Jesus to what he really is—the Son of God. The reference to the Logos become flesh, when interpreted in terms of the Gospel as a whole, can scarcely be understood as meaning more than that the divine Spirit descended on Jesus in the manner suggested above.[8] If so, the emphasis is still on Logos, not on flesh. For to see Jesus as flesh is to see him externally, even as the Jews see him. And for men to see only the physical form denotes spiritual blindness.

But the evangelist, unlike the Gnostics, does not think of the flesh per se as evil. While flesh, unregenerated by the Spirit, is alienated from God, it is still true that it is capable of a congenial relation with the Spirit. Jesus accordingly performed signs while in the sarx-soma-pneuma state. This means that the Fourth Gospel is not otherworldly: men may possess eternal life now because the Spirit can interact with flesh so as to lift them above mortality. So far as this world is concerned, then, a real optimism is affirmed. The Gnostic doctrine that the body is the tomb of the soul is not true for our author. Of course, his concern is not for a "natural" spirit liberated from a fleshly body, but for the divine Spirit which infuses men and lifts them above the fleshly level. That is to say, his concept of rebirth is

[8] Supra, pp. 51-54.

that it is from outside, from above, and that it may take place before the fleshly body dies.

What is true for men, in general, was true for Jesus also, only he was a special case: through him the divine Spirit was made available to men. Here we see the wide sweep of the evangelist's imagination. What he does is to relate a reinterpreted Synoptic baptism story to a reinterpreted Synoptic passion account: at the baptism, Jesus receives the Spirit without measure, during his career it remains in him and him alone; he is the storehouse of the spiritual life: he offers wine, water, and bread—food and drink to sustain the inner life of men; then, at the Crucifixion, all this spiritual wealth is poured out and made available to those who believe. Hence, the Crucifixion is related to the Incarnation and again to the experience of the abiding Presence in the Christian community.

It is no wonder, then, that the Gospel anticipates the Crucifixion from the outset, viewing it as Jesus' "hour," his "glorification," his "going away." And it is easy to understand why references to the Spirit become more numerous as the reader approaches the drama of the cross: the purpose of the Incarnation is nearing its fulfillment. The radical interpretation of the Crucifixion offered by the Fourth Gospel is that it liberated the Spirit, thereby making the cross absolutely essential to the drama of redemption.

A tendency to make a distinction between Jesus and the Spirit has been responsible, in part, for failure to recognize the unitive function which this doctrine of the Spirit provides. The references to the Spirit and to the Paraclete in the Discourses become meaningful only when they, together with Jesus, become identified as the same thing. This is done in one passage: "I will ask the Father, and he will give you another Helper [Paraclete], that he may be with you always, the Spirit of Truth, whom the world cannot receive, because it neither sees him nor knows him; but you know him, for he abides with you, and he is in you" (14:16-17). This is like saying, "I, Jesus, will ask God for another Paraclete to be with you after

I am gone. The world cannot recognize this Paraclete, but you are able to recognize him for I am talking about myself dwelling in your midst, and I will be with you as the indwelling Spirit of Truth."

The phrase, "*another* Paraclete," is the main source of the difficulty, for it seems to differentiate between Jesus and the Paraclete whom the disciples will receive. A sufficient explanation is found in the difference between the Spirit incarnate in Jesus of Nazareth and the discarnate Spirit of the church. That the author had this distinction in mind is clearly shown, first, by the repeated reference to "a little while" (7:33; 13:33) and, secondly, by the Thomas story (20:24-29). The cross draws a line between Jesus capable of being seen in two dimensions and the Jesus who can be seen in one dimension only. To say that the Father "will send another Paraclete" is the same as saying, "I will come to you," a statement which Jesus makes in the verse immediately following the above quoted passage (14:18). Verbal distinctions between Jesus (Christ), the Spirit, and the Paraclete become unimportant when the thought of the Discourses is viewed as a whole and in the light of the total function of Jesus from the Incarnation to the giving of the Spirit. The stream of divine spiritual life passes from the eternal God through Jesus and on into the church where it takes up its abode.

We may conclude, then, that not Logos but Spirit is the concept which binds the elements of the Gospel together into a meaningful unity. The Spirit's descent, its expression in the signs, the promise of its coming in the Discourses, and its bestowal in the Johannine "Pentecost" of ch. 20, all combine to produce an over-all unity which is not adequately cared for by the Logos approach.[9] Moreover, this stress on the Spirit as the

[9] There is a current tendency to find a close connection between the religious community of Qumran and that which produced the Fourth Gospel. Dupont-Sommer quotes K. G. Kuhn of Göttingen as follows: "The parallels with the teaching of Jesus and the Synoptic tradition are numerous and significant. But the profound relationship with the Gospel of John seems to be even more important. . . . We succeed in reaching in these new texts the native soil

controlling idea meshes most naturally with the concept of eternal life, the possession of which the evangelist equates with salvation; from the point of view presented here, the Spirit is the rich source of this life.

(Mutterboden) of the Gospel of John" (*The Jewish Sect of Qumran and the Essenes*; tr. R. D. Barnett; New York: The Macmillan Company, 1955, p. 151). This view of the relationship between John and the sect of Qumran is unconvincing; the sect is ascetic and moralistic while John is not; the sect considered water baptism important, John minimizes it. The alleged similarity between the Logos passage of John and the Divine Thought passage of the Manual of Discipline does no more than reinforce the notion that the concept of an intermediary as the agent of creation was widespread. John still stands as a Greek Gospel.

PART II

THE COMMENTARY

The Prologue

1:1-18

THE MAJOR EMPHASIS IN THIS CHRISTIANIZED HYMN TO THE Logos[1] is on the idea of revelation. Indeed, it appears that this was the author's main reason for choosing the Hymn as an introduction. The interpolated passages (those which have to do with John the Baptist, and those which are obviously Christian) betray the author's real interest; they support the concept of revelation already present in the Hymn, and help accommodate it to the evangelist's point of view.

The details of the Prologue support the position that revelation is its main concern. The pre-existence of the Logos, his intimate association with God, life manifested as light, the witness of the Baptist, rejection of the Logos by his own people, the Logos become flesh, superiority of the Logos over the Baptist and Moses—each of these underscores the idea of revelation.

With the exception of "Logos," these ideas appear in the body of the Gospel. Pre-existence is implied in many places, especially in those passages where Jesus speaks regarding his origin; for example, "I am the living bread which came down from heaven" (6:51); and is explicitly claimed in two passages: "Amen, amen, I tell you, I existed before Abraham did" (8:58), and more plainly still in the prayer for Christian unity: "And now, Father, glorify me in your presence with the glory

---

[1] The term "Logos," conventionally translated "Word," has a wide variety of meanings: "Reason," "Thought," "Word," a discourse, a saying or expression, an account or reckoning, etc. Perhaps the Prologue means to equate the Logos with ultimate reality, with the Truth ($\dot{a}\lambda\dot{\eta}\theta\epsilon\iota a$), which it considers is revealed in Christ. "Reason" in the Stoic sense is certainly not intended, and "Word" presents too restricted a meaning. "Word" and "Thought" are closely related, since in the Hebrew tradition the spoken Word may represent the projected thought of God. In view of the impossibility of giving the term adequate translation in a single English expression, it seems better to leave it untranslated.

which I had in your presence before the world existed" (17:5).

Closely related to the concept of pre-existence is that of the Logos' intimate association with the Father. Jesus, who was with God (πρὸς τὸν θεόν) in the beginning, is the bearer of "heavenly" things" (3:12). He is able to tell of the glory which he had with God before the world began. This is more than a prophet could ever do, for at best he only comprehends the "outskirts of his ways." But Jesus had been in "the bosom of the Father," and so is able to reveal him as no other can.

Not only is the Logos in close relationship with God, but he *is* God (θεός), i.e., he shares in the divine nature (1:1).

Intimate pre-existence of this divine being with God enables the fourth evangelist to attribute an absolute authority to Jesus' words. His authority is not adulterated by an admixture of human error with prophetic inspiration. His words come directly from the source of all wisdom. The words attributed to the Baptist express this clearly:

He who comes from above is above all others. He who originates from the earth belongs to the earth, and speaks of it. He who comes from heaven is above all others. He testifies to what he has seen and heard, and no one accepts his testimony. He who accepts his testimony certifies that God is true. For he whom God has sent speaks God's words; he does not give the Spirit sparingly. The Father loves the Son, and has surrendered everything into his hands. (3:31-35.)

This means that the utterances of Jesus in the Fourth Gospel are never of the nature of casual conversation. When Jesus speaks, his words are "spirit and life"; they are the projected thoughts of God himself, and so are powerful and life-giving.

Pre-existence and intimate association of the divine Logos with God, taken together, make possible a kind of revelation incapable of being superseded. It is no wonder, then, that revealers like the Baptist and even the great Moses are given the status of inferiors. As early as the Prologue the evangelist

66

prepares the way for the reduction of the Baptist to a "voice" (1:23), and of Moses to one who merely wrote about Jesus (1:17; cf. 5:46).

In vs. 4 the Logos is said to possess life, and that this life manifests itself as light—the light of men. "Light" is the subject of vss. 5-9, and is, perhaps, the dominant symbol of the Prologue. Possibly one should distinguish, in this connection, between the thought of the original Hymn and that of John. It is probable that the author of the Hymn was much more interested in philosophical and cosmological speculation than the fourth evangelist. In his thought of light he may well have shared in that widespread speculative tendency which expressed itself in the quasi-philosophical outlook of a Philo. But the fourth evangelist was above all a religionist, and the subtleties of Hellenistic speculation seem foreign to his mind.

It is improbable, therefore, that the allusion to light means much more than Paul had in mind when he wrote, "For the God who said, 'Let light shine out of darkness,' is he who has shone in our hearts, to give the knowledge of God's glory in the face of Christ" (II Cor. 4:6). In the case of both Paul and the evangelist, the concept of Jesus as light is related to their doctrines of the Spirit. The passage from Paul quoted above, for example, is placed in the context of the new order of the Spirit as contrasted with that of death (II Cor. 3:7 ff.). The Fourth Gospel's concept should be related in the reader's mind to the all-important event of the descent of the Spirit (1:29-34).

The notion of rejection, so fundamental to the evangelist's thought, is likewise related to the problem of revelation. Rejection of the Logos means the rejection of Jesus. This concept is a monumental feature of the Gospel, providing the element of tragedy. The tragic elements as they relate to Jesus as a person are removed from this Gospel's story of the Crucifixion. Instead, we are left with the cross as the instrument of Jesus' glorification. Tragedy enters with rejection of the light. The Jews reject, and so abide in darkness. Alienated from the light of the Spirit's reality, they are doomed to the lower world of darkness and unbelief. The dark tragedy of rejection is the measure of the greatness of the revelation.

The incarnation of the Logos, indicated by the words, "And the Logos became flesh" (1:14), focuses the revelation on the scene of history where it properly belongs. It now becomes historically located, so that men may see in it the glory of God himself. This item (1:14) has often been the basis for the argument that the Fourth Gospel is antidocetic. Viewed in relation to the Gospel as a whole, the problem has to do with the connection between *the Spirit* which descends upon Jesus and the human organism of the *man* Jesus. Does the Spirit so change Jesus that he can no longer correctly be called a "flesh person," or does the Spirit simply dwell within the organism without any transmutation of his flesh? An answer to this question is important to an understanding of the character of the revelation.

It appears at times as if Jesus were incapable of being seized by human hands. Men try to arrest him, but cannot (7:30). A second arrest is attempted but does not succeed (10:39). It is to be noted that in the first instance the explanation of their failure to arrest Jesus is that "his hour had not yet come," and in the second instance that "he escaped from their hands." What "escaping from their hands" might mean is not clear. But if we were to read it elsewhere, it is doubtful if we would see more in it than that Jesus eluded his enemies. However, the author makes it quite plain that the Jews had encircled Jesus (10:24), thereby heightening the marvelous, if not miraculous, nature of the escape. The other explanation (7:30), that of the immunity of Jesus from capture, is of a different order. There is no hint of clever action on his part. His immunity is due simply to the fact that his hour to die has not arrived. When he is seized it will be for the purpose of glorification on the cross. The explanation here must be that Jesus is protected until the appointed time by a "higher determinism"; seizure can take place only when God wills it.

There is no indication, then, that the Jesus of the pre-crucifixion period was a noncorporeal being. Certainly the Jews had no inkling of it, for his familiar appearance constituted the great barrier to belief on their part (e.g., 6:41-42). On the other hand, the resurrection appearances present an entirely different picture. Mary Magdalene fails to recognize Jesus at the tomb (20:14): and Jesus appears to the disciples "the doors being shut"—a twice repeated phrase (20:19, 26). The Jesus of the resurrection appearances is a ghostly figure, while he of the earlier period is not.

But it would be a mistake to assume that the Jesus of the Fourth Gospel is, on that account, an ordinary human being. The body is at the most an instrument whereby the Spirit becomes functional in history. Whatever else the reference to the Logos become flesh might mean, it certainly does not lead us in the direction of the discovery of the Jesus of history.

It seems that the Fourth Gospel is not at all concerned with the docetic problem. Passages which are called in to support an antidocetic position can all be explained on other grounds. The weariness of Jesus at the well in Samaria is a device to initiate a dialogue between him and the Samaritan woman; the tears of Jesus at the time of Lazarus' death represent the sorrow of God in the presence of unbelief; the thirst of Jesus on the cross is in fulfillment of scripture; the invitation of Jesus to Thomas to touch him (never carried out) becomes the foil for the Gospel's ultimate teaching: "Blessed are they who have not seen, yet believe," a teaching that is more docetic than antidocetic.

What we may say is that the phrase "And the Logos became flesh" forms a part of the general theme of the Prologue, namely, that of revelation. Light, life, and truth became incarnated and hence localized in Jesus. The Gospel affirms that belief in Jesus as light, life, and truth gives men eternal life, i.e., salvation. Seen in this light, the Prologue prepares the way for the unfolding drama of divine revelation which is the heart of the Fourth Gospel.

The Question of John's Identity
1:19-23

Two kinds of assertions are made in this passage regarding John the Baptist. The first deals with what John is not, the second with what he is. Already, in an interpolated section of the Hymn to the Logos, we have been told that John was not the true light (1:8). Here, by a series of negatives, three important special categories are denied him: he is not the Christ; he is not Elijah; he is not the prophet. These denials would be meaningless apart from the assumption that claims to a special status for the Baptist were being advanced in the area where the Gospel was written. The first chapter of Luke's Gospel strongly suggests the possibility that in certain circles John had been given messianic status (Luke 1:5-24, 57-80). The same possibility is reflected in a second Lucan passage:

As the people were in suspense, and all men questioned in their hearts concerning John, whether he were the Christ, John answered them all, "I baptize you with water; but he who is stronger than I is coming, and I am not important enough to untie his sandals; he will baptize you with the holy Spirit and with fire." (3:15-16.)

In Acts, John is credited with the denial of a messianic role: "What do you suppose that I am? I am not he. No, but one is coming after me, and I am not worthy to untie the sandals of his feet" (Acts 13:25). Christian apologetic is obviously at work here, but apologetic is itself based upon factors current in the environment, in this case belief in the Baptist as the Messiah. The correctness of this claim the fourth evangelist vigorously denies.

Not only so; for he goes on to assert that a claim to Elijah's function is likewise false. This differs from the messianic claim, for it had been supported by the Christian church itself. Indeed, Jesus himself was supposed to have believed it:

Amen, I tell you, among those born of women no one greater

70

than John the Baptist has appeared; yet he who is of least importance in the kingdom of heaven is greater than he. From the days of John the Baptist until now the kingdom of heaven has been taken by force, and men of force seize it. For all the prophets and the law prophesied until John; and if you are willing to accept it, he is Elijah who was to come. (Matt. 11:11-14; cf. Mark 9:13; Matt. 17:13.)

Even tradition ascribed to Jesus is refuted! [2]

So far, the evangelist has informed his readers that John was not the Messiah, and that he was not Elijah. Now, he goes further and asserts that he was not "the prophet." One thing is clear regarding this enigmatic title: it stands alongside the two terms "Messiah" and "Elijah." This would suggest that "the prophet" is a term of similar import. And since the emissaries are Pharisees, it is likely that its frame of reference is as Jewish as "Messiah" and "Elijah." The most probable reference is to the prophet of Deut. 18:15 (cf. Acts 3:22; 7:37, where this concept is accommodated to a Christian frame of reference), in which the prophet referred to is Moses. This position is set forth by Bultmann in his commentary. However, he goes on to suggest that the term "the prophet" may not stem from orthodox Judaism, but from heretical syncretistic circles in which "the prophet" was applied to one of the aeons, and that at the time when the Gospel was written members of the Baptist sect called their master by that name.[3]

Other passages complicate the issue still more. A series of names appears in the Synoptic accounts of the Caesarea Philippi

---

[2] This refusal on the part of the fourth evangelist to allow an important item of Christian tradition to stand unchallenged illustrates his willingness to strike out in new directions. He stands out as an independent spirit, willing and eager to blaze new trails in his interpretation of the story of Jesus.

[3] Rudolf Bultmann, *Das Evangelium des Johannes* (Göttingen: Vandenhoeck and Ruprecht, 1950), pp. 61 ff. It is interesting to note that H. A. Fischel argues for a Rabbinical-Gnostic background for the term. He points, for instance, to the Gnostic idea of the true prophet as one repeatedly incarnated in the great prophets of all ages, a figure or power proceeding from the World of Darkness into the World of Light, H. A. Fischel, "Jewish Gnosticism in the Fourth Gospel," *Journal of Biblical Literature*, LXV, Part II (June, 1946), 157-74.

incident bearing a striking resemblance to that in John 1:20-21. Jesus, it is thought, may be Elijah, Jeremiah, one of the prophets, or even John the Baptist (Matt. 16:14; cf. Mark 8:28-29; Luke 9:7-8). That the fourth evangelist had Jeremiah in mind is doubtful, but the combination "Jeremiah or one of the prophets" is interesting. Matthew and Luke mention the prophets in general but omit any reference to Jeremiah. The fact that all three Synoptics have a special category, "the prophets," in a list so similar to that in the Fourth Gospel sounds suspiciously like some kind of dependence. All categories which had been associated with Jesus (Christ, Elijah, one of the prophets) are now denied the Baptist. But it is clear that the third category is given a different meaning in John by the use of the definite article. It is at this point that it has become assimilated to the Deuteronomy passage, possibly with the heretical sectarian twist suggested by Bultmann.

But the emphasis on what John *is not* now gives way to what he *is*. He is "a voice of one calling in the desert, 'Make straight the way of the Lord,' as the prophet Isaiah said." This traditional Christian accommodation of the Isaiah passage must be interpreted in terms of the Johannine concept of the Baptist's function. Certainly it does not mean that John was a preparer of the Messiah's way in the sense that he was Elijah. That idea has already been denied. The emphasis in the Isaiah quotation is mainly on John as a "voice." The "Lord" here must be Jesus rather than God. To make straight the way of the Lord can mean no more in the Johannine context than the Baptist's proclamation, "This is he," for identification of Jesus as the Son of God is clearly his function.

The Question of the Baptist's Credentials
1:24-28

THE MESSENGERS ARE REPRESENTED AS BEING ἐκ τῶν Φαρισαίων (literally, "out of the Pharisees"). It is probable, however, that the writer meant to indicate Pharisees who were concerned about the technicalities of John's practice of baptism. It is like the present concern for proper ordination to the ministry which alone gives one the right to administer the sacraments. The inquiry of the messengers is equivalent to the question, "Why do you baptize if you do not have the proper credentials?" The Baptist's reply is to contrast the inferiority of his own baptism with that of the Coming One. He needs no official credentials since his baptism is only in water; the Coming One will baptize in the Holy Spirit, and, since he is the Christ, he has the best possible credentials. This minimizing of water baptism has a profound relation to the evangelist's thought on the sacraments of the church. Water baptism is an unofficial act and the person performing it needs no accreditation. Spirit baptism, on the other hand, is the divinely authorized function of the Christ.

The Incarnation
1:29-34

HERE WE FIND THE TRUE BEGINNING OF THE GOSPEL'S STORY about Jesus as the Son of God. All that is past is prelude to this all-important event! For the first time in the Gospel Jesus appears on the scene. John the Baptist sees him coming and now makes his momentous declaration: "There is the one I have been speaking of. I was present when God's Spirit came upon him, and by supernatural revelation I was told its meaning. Now it is my task to proclaim it: I was a witness to the Incarnation. This is God's Son!"

The Baptist now introduces Jesus as the Lamb of God who bears away the sin of the world. The title "Lamb of God" is used only here and in 1:36. Its use in the Fourth Gospel presents somewhat of an enigma since the Johannine interpretation of Jesus is not in sacrificial terms. That there is a deliberate tie-in with the crucifixion story, however, seems certain in view of the placing of Jesus' death at precisely the time of the slaying of the

sacrificial lamb and the refusal to break his legs in accordance
with scripture (19:31-33). What seems to be suggested is not
that Jesus is a sacrifice which men offer to God, but that he is
God's gift to men. This is in keeping with a recurring theme of
the Gospel, which is that God out of his great love sent Jesus
into the world to save it (e.g., 3:16; 6:38-39; 10:15; etc.).

The two great events of the drama, the descent of the Spirit
and the Crucifixion, are united by the lamb symbolism because
in them God's love is actualized. The giving of the Spirit means
that the divine life enters the world through Jesus, becoming in
him like good wine and sparkling water. Then, the Crucifixion
makes this gift universal. These events represent two aspects of
the "givingness" of God.

The Lamb of God is described here as the one who bears
away the sin of the world. It is important to note that "sin"
is in the singular. The fourth evangelist ignores the moralistic
problem, so does not write about "sins" as did Paul and the
Synoptists. Sin, for him, consists of one thing: failure to believe in Jesus. Yet the connection between the lamb symbol and
the bearing away of sin must be intentional. If the cross is not
viewed in sacrificial terms, as is most certainly the case, it still
must have power to remove sin. How is this effected? The answer
seems to be this: God gives his Lamb for the world; and the
attraction of this demonstration of divine love is so strong that
unbelief is dispelled: "And when I am lifted up from the earth,
I will draw all men to myself" (12:32).

John is represented in this passage as baptizing in water. The
term "water" is used in two senses in the Fourth Gospel. In
connection with baptism its importance is minimized. In Jesus'
conversation with Nicodemus (3:5 ff.) it is noteworthy that
water as a medium of rebirth is subordinated to the Spirit. In
a later incident, Jesus and John are baptizing contemporaneously
in Judea. The evangelist relates that John was baptizing at
Aenon because there was plenty of water there, as if to underscore the fact that John's baptism was only in water. But right
away he hastens to add that Jesus himself did not baptize, but

only his disciples (4:2). The literary opportunism of the author permits him to have Jesus outbaptize John, that is, to beat him on his own terms, and so satisfy the demands of the immediate context. But he does not wish to give the impression that this was really Jesus' mode of operation, so he hastens to make the correction.

Water is also used as a symbol of the Spirit. This is its meaning in the story of Jesus at Jacob's well (4:7-42). Water, in this case, is spring water, a fact which gives it rich symbolic value (much like "wine") and is intended to suggest the quality of life bestowed by the Spirit (cf. 7:37-39).

Now it is significant that two baptisms are placed in juxtaposition in the narrative of the Incarnation. Water baptism is John's baptism (1:31). Jesus, on the other hand, baptizes with the Holy Spirit (1:33). Baptism in water is patently inferior to baptism with the Spirit. The former is important only as a setting for the Incarnation. It would be quite inappropriate to have Jesus, in whom are fountains of living water, submit to John's baptism. And, by the same token, it would be altogether unnecessary for Jesus to advocate mere water as the medium of regeneration. The water of life flows directly from him to the believer.

According to the Baptist's report of the Incarnation, the Spirit descended on Jesus and remained on him. The twice-repeated word "remained" (1:32, 33) accounts for one difference between Jesus and the prophets: whereas it came upon the prophets intermittently, it came upon Jesus to abide permanently. A second difference is due to the fullness of the Spirit which Jesus received. A later passage states that he received the Spirit without measure (3:34). These two factors (the coming of the Spirit in its fullness and its abiding presence) made Jesus Son of God in a unique sense. This uniqueness is summed up in the term μονογενής (1:14, 18; 3:16, 18) sometimes translated "only begotten." What the term conveys, however, is the concept of uniqueness. "Son of God" becomes the most representative title for Jesus in the Gospel, not because it stresses the idea of divine begetting, but because the title was already in common usage in the church, and its connotations of dearness and nearness served the purpose of the evangelist admirably (cf., for example, Matt. 21:33-41). It had also appeared prominently in all three Synoptic accounts of Jesus' baptism to which the present passage is so deeply indebted (Mark 1:11; Matt. 3:17; Luke 3:22).

This account of the Spirit's descent is the closest approximation in John to a substitute for the virgin birth stories of the two earlier Gospels. It is frequently asserted that the Prologue is this substitute. But the Prologue is in no sense a description of the mode of the Incarnation. It simply announces that it had happened. It is different with the passage under discussion. The Baptist sees Jesus walking toward him and is prompted to report what he had seen take place. In fact, up to this appearance of Jesus, complete dependence has been placed on the verbal testimony of John. Now, when Jesus appears, John can point to him and say, "This is the one I have been speaking of." The actual event has occurred in the past, and John views it in retrospect.

The First Three Disciples

1: 35-42

THE PASSAGE DEALING WITH THE "CALL" OF THE DISCIPLES EXtends from vs. 35 to vs. 51. However, it has seemed advisable for purposes of interpretation to break it after vs. 42. Each division of the "disciples" passage makes a distinct contribution to the Gospel writer's thought, so requires separate consideration.

Ch. 1, thus far, has stressed the role of the Baptist. The passage before us is concerned with John also, but in such a way that, logically, he should disappear from the story. Jesus actually takes over John's disciples (at the suggestion of the latter), as if the work of the Baptist were now completed. But the fourth evangelist is not consistent, for John appears later still baptizing in water and making disciples (3:22 ff.). The continuing presence of the Baptist is due to his importance as a witness to Jesus as the Spirit-filled Christ, and underscores the fact that logical consistency must, for our writer, give way to other considerations.

The section (1:35-42) deals with the first three disciples. Two are disciples of John, the third is Simon. With identification of Jesus as the Lamb of God by the Baptist, the two disciples leave John and follow Jesus. There is no hint of conflict or competition between Jesus and John. The latter by his announcement, "There is the Lamb of God!" actually suggests that his two disciples leave him and become followers of Jesus: this is assumed to be completely normal procedure.

Of the two disciples of John, one is identified as Andrew. The second disciple is anonymous. In tradition he has become identified with John the son of Zebedee, and modern scholarship has frequently supported this theory. Since in the Synoptics two pairs of brothers are mentioned in the same context in which Jesus calls disciples, these pairs being Simon (Peter) and Andrew, James and John (Mark 1:16-20; Matt. 4:18-22; Luke 5:1-11), and since the former of these pairs forms an element in the Johannine account, it is assumed that the unnamed disciple is one of the second pair. The honor always falls to John! He figures prominently in the Acts account in close association with Peter, and late second-century tradition ascribes the writing of the Gospel to him. This tradition also involves the identification of the unnamed disciple with the "beloved disciple" who first appears, as such, in the story of the washing of the disciples' feet (13:23).

In all probability too much has been made of this anonymous disciple. There is a strong possibility that the fourth evangelist is indebted for his two disciples of the Baptist to Luke's account of the embassy of two *disciples* sent to Jesus by the Baptist with the question, "Are you he who is to come, or shall we look for another?" (Luke 7:18-20). On this assumption he changes this incident in such a manner that all doubt on the Baptist's part is removed. Instead, he announces Jesus as the Lamb of God with the clear implication that it is his disciples' new role to follow Jesus. It is to be noted, moreover, that the second of the two disciples is not identified as Andrew until the evangelist is ready to introduce Simon. Apart from this link between the two disciples, the identification of Andrew as one of them would serve no particular purpose in the preceding portion of the narrative. The anonymous disciple is not identified for the simple reason that he has no further function in the story; his function has been served when John's disciples follow Jesus and abide with him, refuting the Lucan incredulity.

It is important to note that Jesus does not "call" these disciples. They are attracted to him in much the same way that bits of steel are attracted to a magnet. They find out where Jesus is staying (ἦλθαν οὖν καὶ εἶδαν ποῦ μένει: "So they went and saw where he was staying") and remain with him for the day. One suspects that there is a much deeper meaning here than the surface one that they were Jesus' guests for a day. That meaning probably is that they learn where Jesus really dwells, that is to say, in the realm of eternal life, and they associate themselves with him in the sense that they are no longer of "this world" (cf. 17:14). It may be significant that the word used to indicate where Jesus is "staying" is μένω, the same verb used to show that the Spirit came to abide permanently (1:32, 33).

Significantly, the first words uttered by Jesus in the Fourth Gospel are, "What do you seek?" (1:38). In a real sense they raise the fundamental religious problem, both of the Gospel itself and of human experience generally. By accepting Jesus' invitation to go with him to his abode (1:39), the disciples have discovered (or are in the process of discovering) the goal of their religious quest.

Something of a climax seems to be reached in the Simon episode (1:40-42). Andrew calls his brother and announces simply, "We have found the Messiah." No questions are raised by Simon; he readily accepts the implications of Andrew's momentous declaration. Perhaps there is some affinity between

Andrew's announcement and Matt. 16:17-18, where Peter makes his famous confession of faith, "You are the Christ, the Son of the living God," although a closer Johannine equivalent is given later: "Lord, to whom shall we go? You have words of eternal life, and we have believed and are sure that you are God's Holy One" (6:68-69). At least, it is closer in that it comes from Peter himself and is a messianic confession.

But dependence on Matthew seems almost certain in view of Jesus' act in renaming Simon, "Cephas," which, the evangelist hastens to explain, means "rock." [4] The passage reads:

Blessed are you, Simon, son of Jonah, for flesh and blood has not revealed this to you, but my Father who is in heaven. And I tell you, you are Peter, and on this rock I will build my church, and the gates of Hades shall not prevail over it." (Matt. 16:17-18; cf. I Cor. 15:5.)

However, in the Fourth Gospel any reference to Peter as the foundation of the church is conspicuous by its absence. There seems to be a general tendency to minimize Peter.

Interestingly enough, Andrew does not introduce Peter to Jesus. Instead, Jesus looks at him and announces, "You are Simon the son of John." There is no need for an introduction. Jesus knows him already! Supernatural knowledge regarding his disciples is a distinct feature of ch. 1, the second instance appearing in the Nathanael story when Jesus says to Nathanael, "I saw you when you were under the fig tree, before Philip called you" (1:48).

Philip and Nathanael
1:43-51

THE STRESS OF THIS PASSAGE IS ON THE CONVERSATION BETWEEN Jesus and Nathanael. Before examining it, attention must be given the transition verses (1:43-45).

---

[4] There is a play on words here. The Aramaic "Cephas" and the Greek "Peter" both mean "rock."

One of the problems is identification of the subject of vs. 43. Is it Andrew, Simon, or Jesus, who decides to go into Galilee? An attractive theory would be that we have the sequence: Andrew finds Peter; Peter finds Philip; Philip finds Nathanael. This kind of sequence appears in 12:20-22, a passage concerned with the coming of the Greeks who want to see Jesus; "Philip went and told Andrew; Andrew and Philip went and told Jesus."

It is more likely, however, that the pronoun "he" in vs. 43 refers to Jesus. In the preceding verse Jesus has spoken to Simon, and it is likely that he forms the subject of the sentence under discussion. Furthermore, the decision to go to Galilee is more in keeping with the role of Jesus than of the disciples. Jesus makes the decisions in this Gospel, not the disciples. This conclusion is supported by the sequel, which shows that Jesus went to Galilee so that Philip and Nathanael might become disciples. This means that 1:43-51 is a continuation of the ingathering of the disciples, which is concluded with the coming of Nathanael. The Gospel assumes from this point on that the circle of disciples is complete.

It is likely that the evangelist means to suggest that Philip, as well as Nathanael, became a disciple in Galilee, although the plural, "We have found" (1:45), links him with Andrew and Peter (1:44). It could also be argued that Jesus' injunction to Philip, "Follow me," means no more than "Come with me" (Goodspeed), but its dependence on the familiar Synoptic command to discipleship prevents so commonplace a meaning. It could be that "Follow me" has the dual meaning for the evangelist (a) "Come with me to Galilee," and (b) "Be my disciple."

In any case, Nathanael is located in Galilee, and his meeting with Jesus forms the major emphasis of this section. Philip, duplicating the role of Andrew in relation to Simon, finds Nathanael and announces to him an amazing discovery, "We have found the one of whom Moses wrote in the law, and of whom the prophets wrote, Jesus, son of Joseph, who is from Nazareth" (1:45). This is an odd introduction of the Promised

One. Andrew's announcement had been more direct, "We have found the Messiah" (1:41). But the reason for describing Jesus in so truly historical terms becomes evident with Nathanael's response, "Can anything good come out of Nazareth?" (1:46). It is as if the evangelist deliberately introduced the historical fact that Jesus was from Nazareth, so that he could have Nathanael make the natural response, in effect, "What you are saying is ridiculous!" Then the evangelist is free to rest his case about Jesus on experience itself (the ultimate basis for Jesus' claims in the Gospel). This is expressed in Philip's invitation, "Come and see." Nathanael accepts, with the result that he confesses Jesus as the Son of God and the King of Israel (1:49).

The meeting between Jesus and Nathanael is of special interest. Jesus greets Nathanael with the words, "There is a genuine Israelite in whom there is no deceit" (1:47). The words signify to Nathanael that Jesus already knows him. This occasions surprise: "How do you know me?" (1:48). Jesus' reply implies his own possession of supernatural knowledge. That is the point of this part of the story. Jesus has come to Galilee for the very purpose of meeting Nathanael. Even before Philip called Nathanael, Jesus had seen him "under the fig tree," i.e., at his home. The action of Philip in finding Nathanael is really superficial, since Jesus has already included the latter in the circle of disciples.[5]

This supernatural knowledge calls forth the great confession of Nathanael. But to Jesus this kind of knowledge is an inferior basis of faith. Nathanael will see greater things than these; he

[5] "Is it conceivable that the phrase 'under the fig tree' indicates something far more prosaic [than study of the Law by the Rabbis or than peace and plenty], namely, accurate knowledge of a person's whereabouts and movements?" C. F. D. Moule argues for this position, citing the *History of Susanna* which suggests to him that "Under what tree?" was a stock question—a proverbial expression, and that "the Johannine phrase might mean quite simply, that Jesus knew all about Nathanael, as though he had watched his every movement, as the heart of Elisha watched Gehazi in II Kings 5:26." (C. F. D. Moule, "A Note on 'Under the Fig Tree' in John 1:48, 50," *Journal of Theological Studies*, V, Part 2 (October, 1954), 210-11).

will "see the heaven opened and God's angels ascending and descending upon the Son of Man."

What is the significance of this promise to Nathanael? For one thing, there seems to be a clear allusion to the Jacob story of Genesis. Nathanael is characterized as an Israelite free of deceit in contrast to Jacob before he became Israel. The reference to the angels of God ascending and descending upon the Son of Man is reminiscent of the ladder which Jacob saw reaching to heaven at Bethel (Gen. 28:12): "And he dreamed that there was a ladder set up on the earth, and the top of it reached to heaven; and behold, the angels of God were ascending and descending on it."

The value of the Jacob story to John lies partly in its concept of Jacob transformed so as to gain the name Israel (Gen. 32:28), and partly in its assertion that heaven has drawn near to earth (Gen. 28:12). These ideas are readily applicable to John's position: (a) Nathanael is Israel (Jacob transformed, i.e., without deceit), or, better yet, he is a type of the New Israel, the People of God, who see, not as in a dream but in reality. (b) In Jesus the gate of heaven is thrown wide open. This feature of the story is given the more weight. One would expect it to be so, since the Gospel is largely dedicated to the proposition that the glory of the heavenly world has now been revealed.

The title "Son of Man" now appears for the first time (1:51), and may be dealt with most extensively at this point. Few terms have provoked so widespread an investigation as this one. Though exceedingly widespread in the speculative thought of the first century of our era, its origin is obscure. Some scholars trace the ultimate origin of the anthropos myth to Iranian sources, others to Babylonian mythology. Here, we must be content to determine the thought of the fourth evangelist on the title in terms of its function in the Gospel, and then to relate that function to the passage under consideration.

The Fourth Gospel uses the title thirteen times.[6] The refer-

[6] There is a variant in the manuscripts at 9:35, some of them reading "Son of

ences are: 1:51; 3:13; 3:14; 5:27; 6:27; 6:53; 6:62; 8:28; 9:35; 12:23; 12:34 ("Son of Man" is used twice in this verse); 13:31. An analysis of these passages reveals that they fall naturally into categories dealing with revelation, life, judgment, and glorification (crucifixion).

Passages dealing with the concept of revelation are 1:51 and 3:13; those dealing with Jesus as giver of life are 6:27 and 6:53; the idea of glorification is set forth in 3:14; 6:62; 8:28; 9:35; 12:23; 12:34; and 13:31; the notion of judgment is indicated in 5:27 and 9:35. These categories, however, tend to merge with one another. One gains the distinct impression that, in the final analysis, they have to do either with the descent of the Son of Man (i.e., as the Spirit) or with his ascent (i.e., with his glorification through crucifixion).

There is little reason to go far beyond the Christian tradition for the Johannine meaning of Son of Man. It finds its roots in the Synoptic concept, is perhaps modified by Paul's Heavenly Man (I Cor. 15), and certainly by the fourth evangelist's creative mind, freed from the restraining effects of an imminent eschatology. It is possible that the Gnostic emanation concept influenced his thought also.

The Synoptic Son of Man is a glorious being who is to appear on the clouds of heaven at the end of the age (e.g., Mark 14:62; Matt. 26:64; Luke 22:69). But in the Fourth Gospel the Son of Man has already come; he has descended from heaven (3:13; 6:62). If we are correct about the Incarnation, the coming of the Son of Man must be identified with the descent of the Spirit. The evangelist has transferred the event from its traditional association with a future cosmic cataclysm to the point of the Incarnation. For him the new age arrived with the coming of Jesus, and the glorious attributes of the Son of Man belonged to Jesus during his earthly career.

The judicial function of the Son of Man, which is plain in

God," instead of "Son of Man." If this variant were granted as original, the cumulative picture of Jesus as the Son of Man in the Fourth Gospel would not be changed.

the Synoptics (e.g., Luke 21:36, and especially Matt. 25:31-46), is found in the Fourth Gospel as well. It is true that Jesus says he has not come to judge the world, but to save it (3:17), but this reference is to judgment in its more conventional sense. It is a mere signature of the older point of view—a point of view which must undergo radical change. The nature of this change is suggested by the term "life" in the passage: "For just as the Father has life in himself, so also he gave the Son to have life in himself. And he gave him authority to exercise judgment, because he is the Son of Man" (5:26). Son of Man and judgment are brought together here. Yet the reference to life gives to judgment an inner, mystical quality not associated with eschatological judgment.

The fact is, since the Son of Man has already come, and since he is the embodiment of the eternal order of reality, men stand in judgment in their response to him: they are being judged now.

But this present judgment is related primarily to the Crucifixion, for in that event the revelation of God comes to its most luminous expression. That is the reason why the writer has Jesus say when the Greeks come to see him, "The judgment of this world is now. The ruler of this world shall be cast out now" (12:31). The context of this passage is Jesus' approaching death on the cross. The cross is the sign of all signs! If the glory of the Spirit is not revealed in it, then men stand under condemnation, for by their own response they have condemned themselves.

This kind of judicial function is a far cry from that of the transcendental Son of Man, but it is the genius of the fourth evangelist that he is able to assimilate a concept's inner core of meaning to his own religious perspective.

It is also possible that the author of the Fourth Gospel was indebted to Paul for his concept of the Son of Man. While Paul does not use the title in his letters, in I Corinthians he sets forth his notion of Jesus as the Heavenly Man (I Cor. 15:44-50). This concept, it must be remembered, forms a part of his argument relative to the problem of the resurrection of the dead. The central element in his argument is contained in vss. 44-50:

If there is a physical body (σῶμα ψυχικόν), there is also a spiritual body (σῶμα πνευματικόν). Thus it is written, "The first man, Adam, became a living being" (ψυχὴν ζῶσαν), the last Adam, a life-giving spirit (πνεῦμα ζωοποιοῦν). But it is not the spiritual which is first, but the physical, then the spiritual. The first man is of the dust of the earth; the second man is from heaven. As is the man of dust, so are those who are of the dust; and as is the man of heaven, so are those who are of heaven. Just as we have borne the image of the man of dust, we shall also bear the image of the man of heaven. I tell you this, brothers: flesh and blood cannot inherit the kingdom of God, nor does the perishable inherit the imperishable.

The contrast which Paul makes here is between the earthly man and the heavenly man. The former is a living being merely; the latter is life-giving spirit. Paul is talking to believers, so he points out the fact that the image of the man of dust will yield to the image of the man of heaven, that is to say, flesh will give way to spirit.

This element in Paul's thought is part of his mysticism. It is this background in Christian thought which helps the fourth evangelist accommodate the earlier Son of Man concept to his view of Jesus. In the discourse on the Bread of Life he represents Jesus as offering to the Jews the flesh and the blood of the Son of Man (i.e., his own flesh and blood), which, if eaten, will give them life. But in the end it turns out that Jesus is not talking about flesh and blood as material substances, but of the Spirit which gives life, for "flesh is of no account." *To eat Jesus' flesh is to participate in the life which his death effects.* In the Fourth Gospel Jesus as the Son of Man who came down from heaven is equivalent to Paul's Heavenly Man; that is to say, he is life-giving spirit.

We cannot say, of course, that the fourth evangelist was indebted to Paul in the precise sense that he wrote with this section of Paul's letter before him. It is more likely that he wrote his Gospel under the general, but nonetheless powerful, impact of the thought of Paul which he had fully assimilated.

The introduction of the title "Son of Man" in Jesus' words to Nathanael (1:51) becomes understandable when viewed against this background. The promise to Nathanael is a promise of the revelation in Jesus of the heavenly realm. The Man from heaven carries in himself the priceless gift of the Spirit, a gift ultimately to be bestowed through the cross to those who believe in him. Nathanael, as representative of the New Israel, will see the things to be revealed and receive the gift of life.

The Wine of the Spirit
2:1-11

THE STORY OF THE WEDDING AT CANA PRESENTS US WITH THE first of the Johannine "signs." Cana is represented as the locale for the performance of a second sign also, the healing of the official's son (4:46-54). Cross references in the second account indicate that the evangelist held the story of the wedding in mind while writing about the healing (4:46, 54). It is noteworthy that no element of hostility is associated with either of these Cana signs.

The first four verses of the first Cana incident need to be considered separately. They form an introduction to the main part of the narrative, but in addition have importance in their own right. The stress of the passage falls on Jesus' response to the suggestion implicit in his mother's words, "They have no wine." By his reply, "Woman, what have we in common? My hour has not yet come," Jesus makes it plain that he is no longer subject to parental authority. This is, in effect, a declaration that he is on a superior level of being as compared with people generally—his own mother being no exception. Relationships which were taken for granted in family life prior to the descent of the Spirit no longer obtain. He is no longer son of a mortal woman; he is the Son of God.

86

This interpretation suggests the folly of the frequent attempts to soften the word γυνή on the grounds that it is too harsh a word for Jesus to have used when addressing his mother. But the Jesus of the Fourth Gospel is not a Jesus of tender compassion. Jesus' words here constitute a rebuke, the rebuke of a divine being whose nature is quite unknown to his mother, for she is unaware that the Incarnation has taken place. In external appearance the same, Jesus, son of "Mary" (the name does not occur), has yielded his identity as a person to the divine Spirit.

These introductory verses also serve as a point of departure for the first of the signs proper, the changing of the water into wine. Jesus' mother is represented as concerned over the circumstance that the supply of wine has been exhausted. She says simply, "They have no wine." Her concern over the lack of wine places her in the same category with the materialistic Jews of the Gospel. But for Jesus the words, "They have no wine," have another meaning; he takes them to mean, "They do not have the Spirit." This makes meaningful the reference to Jesus' hour ("My hour has not yet come"), since the "hour" is the Crucifixion, at which time the Spirit is to be given to the world. His reply to his mother might be paraphrased as follows: "Why do you tell me what to do, since you no longer have authority over me? As to the giving of the Spirit, that cannot take place until I am lifted up on the cross" (cf. Goodspeed, "Do not try to direct me. It is not yet time for me to act").

In the sentence, "They have no wine," "wine" equals "the Spirit" in the mind of Jesus. Ordinarily, in the Fourth Gospel, it is Jesus who projects a symbol which can be interpreted on two levels. But this is not always the case, as is proved by 4:31-34, where the disciples offer Jesus food and he replies that he already has food to eat; his food is to do the will of God.

But while Jesus cannot give the Spirit until he dies, he nevertheless proceeds to perform a sign. He changes a great quantity of water (120-130 gallons) into wine, signifying the ultimate transformation of the water of Judaism into the intoxicating wine of the Spirit. It is beside the point, and quite impossible, to see here wine which is nonintoxicating. The point of the story is that it *is* intoxicating! The wine which Jesus gives parallels the "good wine" which the manager of the banquet declares is customarily served first. This is the wine which makes men intoxicated; and so with the Spirit! The religion of the Spirit is intoxicating, it endows men with a vitality and power which a legalistic religion cannot give.

Some scholars (Loisy, for example) hold that this story has been borrowed from the religion of Dionysus. This is unnecessary, although the general association of wine with deity and its general use as a religious symbol would help infuse with meaning the evangelist's use of the term. But that is only to say that John is himself a product of Hellenistic culture and expresses himself in terms of it. The more immediate background, however, is to be located in the Hebrew-Christian tradition itself. In primitive Christian times possession of the Spirit had expressed itself in actions that could be construed as the result of "intoxication." One has only to read the Pentecost story of Acts to understand this (Acts 2:1 ff.). And it may well be that the Pentecost story is the literary antecedent of this first of the Johannine signs. In the earlier story occur the mocking words of the people, "They are filled with new wine." To this accusation Peter replies, "They are not drunk as you think. What you see is a fulfillment of Joel's prophecy, that in the last days God will pour out his Spirit upon all flesh." For the fourth evangelist this is happening in Jesus. The sign which Jesus performs anticipates the Johannine Pentecost-equivalent (20:22). It anticipates his death, as the words "My hour has not yet come" indicate. It may be that the number of water-pots (six) carries a symbolic reference to the hour of Jesus' death at the sixth hour (19:14), i.e., noon (cf. 4:6); at this hour the Spirit is to be released.

A feature of the Cana story (easily overlooked) is that no "Jews" are present. The group is composed of Jesus, his mother, his brothers, and his disciples. Others, with the exception of characters such as the manager of the banquet and the servants (who are necessary details of the story), have no place in the account. This is a story with meaning for believers. The fact that those invited constitute a select group accounts for the lack of the element of hostility. Its result is belief *on the part of the disciples* (2:11).

Vs. 11 makes it clear that the purpose of the sign is the manifestation of Jesus' glory, that is, his divine nature as the Spirit. It should be kept in mind that in the Fourth Gospel attention is always centered on *Jesus*. The church's possession of the Spirit is a reality only because Jesus himself first possessed it and gave it to his own.

The Sign of Jesus' Authority

2:12-25

THE MOST OBVIOUS FEATURE OF THIS STORY IS ITS NEW SETTING at the beginning of the ministry. This is important if for no other reason than that it sheds light on the evangelist's willingness to depart from the pattern set by Mark. His interest is religious, and any pattern or tradition is subservient to it.

In the Synoptics, the Cleansing of the Temple is the incident which incites the Jews to put Jesus to death (Mark 11:15-17 Matt. 21:12-13; Luke 19:45-46). This function is served in the Fourth Gospel by the story of the Raising of Lazarus. Instead of discarding the story of the Cleansing of the Temple, the evangelist adapts it to his own outline of the ministry.

His method of adaptation is most interesting. Most of the new material introduced is from earlier tradition. The demand for a sign (2:18) is apparently based on Mark 11:27-33 and parallels. But the allusion is complex, for there is also an affinity with Matt. 12:38-42. Both passages seem involved. The former raises the question of authority, which is certainly implicit in the Johannine narrative. The latter makes a natural point of contact with John's thought because of its use of the word "sign" ("We wish to see a sign from you"), and because it connects Jesus' resurrection with the sign. This, as we shall see, is the point of the Johannine account.

The allusion to the destruction of the temple (2:19) is probably indebted to Mark 14:58, but is given a peculiar meaning in John, perhaps under the influence of Mark 11:18 (the scribes sought a way to destroy Jesus).

Even the statement that the Resurrection generated in the disciples' belief in the scripture and in the words of Jesus (2:22) has a natural base in Luke 24:24-27.

Possible sources for the "whip" (2:15) and for the "forty-six years" (2:20) are more difficult to determine, though the former may be a messianic symbol.[7]

There is little doubt that the story of the Cleansing of the Temple had messianic significance for the Synoptists. This meaning is continued by the fourth evangelist and strengthened by the addition of the whip and by the quotation from Ps. 69: 9, "Zeal for your house will devour me." The sequel to the cleansing proper (2:18-20) must therefore be seen against the background of the act of Jesus so conceived. But the Jews, who are not at all convinced of Jesus' messiahship, need some evidence of his authority or official right to do this deed. The act of "cleansing" therefore becomes the springboard for the sequel where the central thought of the passage is located.

The sequel begins with the Jews' request for a sign which will convince them of Jesus' right to act in this manner. Jesus' reply (2:19) is characteristically enigmatic: "Destroy this temple, and I will raise it up in three days." Characteristic, also, is the Jews' failure to grasp the hidden import of Jesus' words. The Jews think he is speaking of Herod's temple. But the evangelist informs us that Jesus was speaking of the temple of his body. This is clearly an allusion to his death and resurrection. Jesus' authority, then, will be revealed in the fact that he will rise from the dead. In other words, the sign of Jesus' messianic au-

---

[7] Macgregor, The Gospel of John, pp. 57-58.

thority is his death and resurrection. This reflects early Christian thought on the relation of his messiahship to the Resurrection, and is supported by the statement (made in 2:22) that the disciples became aware of what Jesus meant only when he was raised from the dead. The sign of Jesus' messianic authority is the Resurrection (cf. 8:28: "When you have lifted up the Son of Man, then you will know that I am he").

This shift of attention from Jesus' act of cleansing the temple to the identification of his body as the temple is facilitated by an interesting literary device: the use of two different words for temple, one, ἱερός, signifying the temple generally, and the other, ναός signifying the sacred inner sanctuary. Ἱερός is used through vss. 13-16, ναός in the remaining verses. Appropriately, Jesus introduces the term ναός in the sentence, "Destroy this temple and in three days I will raise it up." It is significant, perhaps, that Paul uses ναός in those passages which speak of the body as the temple of God (I Cor. 3:16, 17; 6:19; II Cor. 6:16; cf. Eph. 2:21). In Colossians, he sets forth the proposition that the entire *pleroma* settled bodily in Christ (Col. 2:9). Jesus is the sacred temple in which God's Spirit dwells!

It may be said that the first two incidents, the Wedding at Cana and the Cleansing of the Temple, anticipate the great events of crucifixion and resurrection. The Wedding at Cana anticipates the giving of the Spirit through the cross; the Cleansing of the Temple suggests that the great sign of Jesus' messianic authority is death and resurrection. But even the disciples must wait until these events take place before they can fully understand. By its pervasive reference to the end events of Jesus' life the Fourth Gospel is, in a sense, a passion narrative from beginning to end. We must hasten to add, however, that the term "passion" is not entirely accurate when applied to our evangelist's view of these end events. The cross does not cast a shadow backward over the pages of the Gospel; it is more correct to say that it floods those pages with its light.

Vss. 23-25 set forth a persistent feature of the Gospel, namely, belief on the part of the people which is not real, i.e., not abiding.

91

In the present passage there is a play on words; the verb πιστεύειν ("to believe")

occurs in successive verses with quite different meaning: The Jews believed on Jesus, but Jesus did not trust himself to the Jews. The author of the Gospel knew that a secondary meaning of πιστεύειν is "to entrust oneself to" when the pronoun repeats the subject. He used it because he wanted to focus attention on the nature of the belief.[8]

One suspects that the reason for this element of belief which is not true belief is that, on the one hand, the picture of Jesus presented is such as to make him (from the author's point of view) irresistibly attractive, and, on the other hand, the evangelist is confronted with the historical fact of the Jewish rejection.

The Birth from Above
3:1-21

IN FORM, THE MEETING OF NICODEMUS WITH JESUS IS MUCH like the Johannine sign, containing incident plus discourse. In this case, the sign-equivalent is the dialogue, strictly speaking, which is set forth in vss. 2-10. Vss. 11-21 are an elaboration of the major idea stated in the dialogue, namely, that eternal life comes as the result of birth from above.

At the point of vs. 11 the change from the singular to the plural shows that, unconsciously, the author has merged his representation of the thought of Jesus into that of his own second-century group—a very understandable error in view of the fact that his Jesus is, from beginning to end, a mouthpiece for one variety of second-century Christology. A similar lapse is to be found in 17:3, where there is a shift from the first to the third person in the phrase, "And *Jesus Christ* whom thou hast sent."

Nicodemus is represented in this story as (a) a Pharisee (literally, "out of the Pharisees"); (b) a leader of the Jews (a

---

[8] Colwell and Titus, *op. cit.*, pp. 58-59.

characterization designed to give him status); (c) the teacher of Israel (the article here is important for it serves to give Nicodemus added status, and to make him a fitting representative of the Jews; this he becomes in vs. 11). The closest Synoptic counterpart to Nicodemus is the Rich Young Ruler (Mark 10: 17), although Gamaliel of Acts 5:34-39 reminds one of Nicodemus in his second appearance in the Fourth Gospel (7:50-51). In the third and final appearance of Nicodemus in our Gospel, he, in association with Joseph of Arimathea, brings about one hundred pounds of myrrh and aloes for purposes of embalming Jesus' body (19:39). Perhaps Nicodemus is a composite of the Jews generally, of the Rich Young Ruler, and of Gamaliel. These would correspond to representations (a), (b), and (c) above, respectively.

The account tells us that Nicodemus came to Jesus *by night*. Numerous explanations have been given this, as, for example, that Nicodemus did not wish his fellow Jews to know of his contact with Jesus, or that, in his enthusiasm, he could not wait until morning to meet Jesus. There is in fact some warrant for the former of these possibilities. Joseph of Arimathea appears in 19:38 as a disciple of Jesus, "but secretly, for fear of the Jews." But this possibility assumes less importance when one becomes familiar with the evangelist's method of employing striking contrasts. In this instance, Nicodemus comes to Jesus in spiritual darkness. That is where he actually is as he approaches Jesus who is the Light of the World. A ruler, a teacher, a respected person in the religious life of the community, Nicodemus walks in darkness; it could almost be said that he *is* darkness, just as Jesus *is* light (ch. 8 gives a most discouraging view of Judaism, and this must be taken as normative of the evangelist's position). A similar use is made of "night" in 13:30. In the latter instance, Judas leaves the Light of the World, whereas Nicodemus comes to the Light. In spite of his status as a leader and teacher, however, he does not yet know in whose presence he stands.[9]

[9] Nicodemus later becomes a disciple (19:39-40).

Nevertheless, Nicodemus' cultural level stands him in good stead; he has a degree of awareness never equaled by other Jews in this Gospel. In contrast to them (cf. 6:42; 10:20), he sees in Jesus more than the son of Joseph, merely, or a demon-possessed person. He greets Jesus with the words, "Rabbi, we know that you are a teacher who has come from God, for no one is able to perform these signs which you are doing unless God is with him." This is right so far as it goes. Jesus has been sent by God; his teachings are divinely given. But the statement does not go far enough; it is weak because of what it does not say. Jesus is more than a teacher—even one who is God-sent. He is God's only Son, and, as Nicodemus will soon hear, he will bestow the life-giving Spirit on all who believe.

What is the logical connection between Nicodemus' initial statement (3:2) and Jesus' reply (3:3)? The reply seems to require some such question as "What must I do to see the kingdom of God?" (cf. Mark 10:17: "What must I do to inherit eternal life?"). Given that kind of question the answer seems perfectly logical: To see the kingdom of God you must be born ἄνωθεν.[10] Or, to argue from Nicodemus' initial statement, the logical response would be something like, "Yes, you are right, or partly so; I have been sent from God, and I teach as he commanded me, but I am much more than a teacher— I am the Son of God." But, of course, no such logical connection occurs—at least not on the surface.

The break in logical connection is due to an apparent shift of the subject from Jesus in vs. 2 to men in general (ἐὰν μή τις γεννηθῇ ἄνωθεν, οὐ δύναται ἰδεῖν τὴν βασιλείαν τοῦ θεοῦ: "Unless one is born again he cannot see the kingdom of God") in vs. 3. But this change in subject is more apparent than real. The connection between vss. 2 and 3 must lie on a deeper level than a surface reading would give. Jesus' answer that the requirement for entrance into the kingdom of God is rebirth, must be equivalent to what he says in vs. 12: "If I tell you of things of earth and you do not believe, how will you believe if I tell you of things

---

[10] The word ἄνωθεν has a double meaning: "again" and "from above."

of heaven?" That is, Jesus is in effect saying to Nicodemus, "You are saying something about me when you are in no position to make a judgment. I belong to God's Kingdom, and to understand what I am you must be born from above. Since you have not had this rebirth you take me to be a teacher like you. If you would understand the things of heaven you must become a citizen of that realm." So understood, Jesus' answer is directed to the inadequacy of Nicodemus' description of him. This description is an inference drawn on the basis of the signs and is shown to be inadequate. A true disciple of Jesus, one born from above, would "see" the kingdom of God, and confess Jesus as God's Son.

The heart of the section comes in vss. 5 and 6. Two literary devices are employed to set it forth. In the first place, Nicodemus is given the role of a "stupid character." [11] This gives Jesus opportunity to develop his message. Secondly, words with a double meaning are employed: ἄνωθεν, meaning "again" and "from above," and πνεῦμα, meaning "wind" and "spirit." These two devices are inseparably related; the "stupid" Nicodemus grasps the lower meaning while Jesus expounds in terms of the higher.

The major emphasis of the passage is on the birth from above, which is contrasted sharply with birth which is purely biological. Human nature, untouched by the Spirit, is part and parcel of the lower world—the world of flesh. That which is born of the Spirit is spirit; the one is of earth, the other is of heaven; the one is temporal; the other is eternal.

One must feel the full force of this emphasis on the Spirit if he is to appreciate Jesus' function as the author of eternal life. The importance of this passage, therefore, can scarcely be overestimated. In a sense it sets the pattern for the Gospel's dualism: the phenomenal world versus the unseen world of the Spirit. While the fourth evangelist does not think of the flesh per se as evil, since it is a part of the world of matter it is subject to death and decay. The paramount importance of the second,

[11] Colwell and Titus, op. cit., pp. 43-44.

spiritual, birth makes it entirely possible for the evangelist to assume a natural birth for Jesus. The second birth conquers the mortality of the first (biological) birth. The evangelist's only aversion to flesh is when it is not indwelt with the Holy Spirit. Spiritual birth gives meaning to biological birth. This means that eternal life may be a present possession while one is in the flesh. There is, therefore, a fundamental optimism in the message of the Fourth Gospel.

This Spirit concept differs from the Hellenistic mystery notion of sacramental rebirth. Jesus' statement, "The wind blows where it chooses and you hear its sound, but you do not know where it comes from or where it is going. It is like this with every one who is born of the Spirit," recognizes the spontaneous character of the Spirit's operation.[12] No sacramentalist could talk like that!

On the other hand, a problem is presented by the reference to "water" along with "Spirit" in vs. 5: "Unless one is born of water and Spirit he cannot see the kingdom of God." Three possibilities present themselves as accounting for the inclusion of "water": (a) the evangelist has in mind the dual baptism of water and the Spirit as described in Acts (Acts 2:38; 8:14-17; 10:44-48; 19:1-7); (b) the two words "water and" are a gloss whose purpose was to bring the crucial passage into conformity with later Christian practice; and (c) "water" must be interpreted in the light of its development as a symbol as in the story of Jesus and the Samaritan Woman (4:7-42) and its explicit identification with the Spirit in 7:37-39.

[12] It is possible that the translation of vs. 8 as given here is incorrect; that the analogy of the wind is not intended. If so, the translation would be as follows: "The Spirit breathes where he chooses, and you hear his voice, but you do not know where he comes from or where he is going. It is like this with every one who is born of the Spirit." This translation has much in its favor, when one considers Jesus' role as the Spirit-filled Christ who ultimately breathes the Spirit on his disciples (20:22). Furthermore, the words, "you do not know where he comes from or where he is going," are harmonious with the Gospel's emphasis on Jesus' mysterious origin and destiny (e.g., 8:14); men are mystified by his allusions both to "where he comes from," and "where he is going." It is quite possible, however, that, in view of John's method, both meanings are intended, and that its full force is felt only by a reading of the Greek text.

As to the first, it should be noted that the evangelist dismisses the water baptism of John as an inferior baptism, soon to be superseded by the baptism of the Spirit (1:31-33). The question is whether or not our evangelist could subscribe to a water baptism accompanied by Spirit baptism which would, by virtue of the combination, elevate the former to a level superior to John's water baptism. We may be sure that the Gospel writer would never say, "Unless one is born of water he cannot see the kingdom of God." It is possible, however, to put it another way. Could the writer have omitted "water" so that the statement would read, "Unless one is born of the Spirit he cannot see the kingdom of God"? To this question there is but one answer, and that is an emphatic "Yes!" If this explanation is to be at all satisfactory the two elements, water and spirit, must stand together.

In a later scene, on the other hand, Jesus himself is baptizing in competition with John the Baptist (3:22-23). This is, admittedly, a difficult passage. Goguel has argued cogently that a source lies behind this section.[13] He believes that the source originally had to do with a discussion between John and Jesus over the matter of purification. The evangelist changed the wording so that, as it now stands, the dispute is between John's disciples and a Jew. But it should be pointed out that the problem of purification still remains in the account as the fourth evangelist uses it. In the verses which follow, however, the Baptist's testimony falls back on the view, earlier expressed, that Jesus is the Spirit-filled one and so can bestow the Spirit, i.e., baptize with the Holy Spirit (3:25-36; cf. 1:33).

The evangelist, being a literary opportunist, uses his source to show that Jesus could outmatch the Baptist on his own level, but immediately proceeds to give Jesus a higher function, namely, the giver of the Spirit. That such a correction was deemed necessary is proved by the clumsy statement in 4:2: "Although Jesus himself did not baptize, but only his disciples."

[13] Maurice Goguel, The Life of Jesus, tr. Olive Wyon (New York: The Macmillan Company, 1944), pp. 271-75.

Dodd feels that this is the work of a redactor, on the grounds that the parenthesis ruins the sentence.[14] But if we take Goguel's position it is easy to explain the clumsy character of the parenthesis as an attempt on the part of the evangelist to make a source, fundamentally alien to his own thought, conform to the ideational pattern of his Gospel. This means that Jesus did not baptize, though the evangelist was well acquainted with the practice of the church: the disciples did baptize.

The possibility that the words "water and" constitute a gloss must not be ignored. The passage would be better understood without them in view of the fact that the whole development of thought is in terms of Spirit-birth; to be born from above is to be born of the Spirit. This is the position taken by Bultmann. He considers the two words an interpolation by an ecclesiastical redactor in the interests of the sacraments.[15]

The third explanation of the reference to water in vs. 5 presents a live option. "Water" is used in two senses in the Fourth Gospel. In a lower sense it is used to describe John's baptism (1:26, 31) and the Jewish ceremonial religion (2:6). But on a higher level "water" is what Jesus gives: Whoever drinks of *this* water will never thirst again for it will be a spring of water— the water of eternal life (4:14). It is certain that what the evangelist had in mind here (4:14) was water as a synonym for the Spirit. The sequel to the well episode of the story of Jesus in Samaria makes it plain that "God is spirit" and that worship must be "in spirit." Dodd points out that this worship is the correlate of birth ἐκ πνεύματος ("of the Spirit").[16] Furthermore, it is made very clear that water symbolizes the Spirit (7: 37-39).

The interpreter of the Fourth Gospel has to ask whether or not it is likely that the evangelist would introduce an intermediate view of "water," signifying Christian baptism as a lower but important correlate of baptism with the Spirit. This seems

[14] *Op. cit.*, p. 311, n. 3.
[15] *Op. cit.*, p. 98, n. 2.
[16] *Op. cit.*, p. 314.

unlikely, since an admission of the legitimacy of water baptism of any sort would tend to offset his emphasis on the impotency of John's baptism; and, on the other hand, it would weaken his position on the all-important baptism with the Spirit. It is more reasonable to assume that the original distinction, so clearly put—John's baptism is in water; Jesus' baptism is in the Holy Spirit (1:31, 33)—holds true for the entire Gospel.

If this is so, then vs. 5 (which, it should be remembered, is dealing with the central message of the book) makes no compromise with water baptism, but holds rigorously to the function of the Spirit as the medium of regeneration. "Water" and "spirit," conjoined, have the same kind of relationship one to the other as "spirit" and "life" in 6:63. If this is the case, then the stress on the Spirit in contrast to that on flesh falls naturally into place. The phrase ἐξ ὕδατος καὶ πνεύματος could be translated "out of water, even spirit" from this point of view. It would be strange for this Gospel to conceive of its central figure as advocating water baptism as a prelude to baptism with the Spirit. It does not temporize with orthodoxy (if such there could have been), but blazes a new trail, completely free of the restraints of external rites and ceremonies, whether Jewish or primitive Christian.

The series of ideas set forth in 3:1-21, in addition to the central idea of the birth of the Spirit discussed above, may be listed as follows: (a) Jesus, as the Son of Man, descended from heaven, is the sole bearer of the knowledge of heavenly things (3:12-13). He is therefore divine revealer. (b) The gift of eternal life is contingent on Jesus' death on the cross: the Son of Man must be lifted up (ὑψόω means both "to lift up" and "to exalt," an obvious play on words: 3:14-15). (c) The nature of God's love is demonstrated by the fact that he gave his only Son for the salvation of the world (3:16). The same idea was suggested by the title "Lamb of God" in 1:29, 36, but is made more intimate and tender here by the use of the phrase "only Son." (d) Judgment is automatic; it is implicit in the kind of response men make to Jesus as the Light (3:17-21).

The Baptist's Final Testimony
3: 22-36

AS HAS BEEN SUGGESTED,[17] IT IS PROBABLE THAT A SOURCE LIES behind this section and continues through 4:3. The source contained an account of a dispute between John's disciples and Jesus (or perhaps between disciples of John and disciples of Jesus) over the question of baptism. The fourth evangelist has utilized this source to stress the superiority of Jesus over John. Instead of Jesus' great success provoking in the Baptist a spirit of contention, it elicits his final, most comprehensive, and enthusiastic testimony about Jesus as possessor of the Spirit. This seems to be the import of the passage viewed as a whole.

The first readers of the Gospel must have wondered how John would react to the report of his disciples: "Rabbi, he who was with you across the Jordan, to whom you have testified, here he is baptizing, and all are going to him" (3:26). His answer had, of course, been anticipated in ch. 1 (1:19 ff.). John is not at all offended by Jesus' greater success. This is how it should be, for in relation to Jesus, John is as a friend to a bridegroom: Jesus, not John, has the bride (the Spirit?); John as the friend of the bridegroom rejoices in the latter's success. Jesus' fame must grow while that of John must die out (3:27-30). This is consistent with the role of John in the first chapter; and the two accounts are related by a cross reference: "You yourselves bear witness to me that I said, 'I am not the Christ, but I have been sent before him'" (3:28; cf. 1:20, 23). The reason for Jesus' superiority over John is that God has "surrendered everything into his hands" (3:35). In the words of 3:27, "A man is unable to receive anything unless it is given to him from heaven." [18]

[17] Supra, pp. 97-98.

[18] This passage reflects the Synoptic question put to Jesus himself: "By what authority are you doing these things?" and his counterquestion, "Was the baptism of John from heaven or from men?" (Mark 11:27-33). The import of this Marcan incident is that Jesus' authority has a heavenly origin.

It is a mistake to assume, as some do, that 3:31-36 represents a dislocation of the text, and that it consists of misplaced words of Jesus or reflections of the evangelist. The message of Jesus and the message of the evangelist are identical. Jesus says what the evangelist wants him to say; that is, the evangelist speaks through Jesus. Furthermore, what the Baptist says in testimony about Jesus is what the evangelist would say. The words of the evangelist, of Jesus, and of John, have the same content; they are all words of faith about Jesus as the one sent from heaven. On the other hand, what the Jews say is not the message of the evangelist, but a foil for the superior utterances of Jesus, i.e., for a presentation of the evangelist's normative teaching.

If the section 3:31-36 is conceived as representing the Baptist's viewpoint, it must be a continuation and elaboration of the testimony already begun in vss. 27-30. In this section of his testimony, John affirms that Jesus comes from heaven, a fact which accounts for his superiority. Since Jesus is from heaven, he speaks of heavenly things, though men of earth cannot understand him. This point has already been made in the dialogue between Jesus and Nicodemus (3:11). Stated differently, since Jesus possesses the Spirit without measure, his words are divine utterances (3:34). Belief in Jesus as this Spirit-filled Son of God issues in the possession of eternal life; failure to believe in Jesus as God's Son means that God's anger remains upon men. Belief gives the abiding Spirit, while disbelief gives the abiding anger of God. The issue is clearly drawn.

Jesus in Samaria

4:1-42

THE STORY OF JESUS IN SAMARIA FALLS NATURALLY INTO FIVE parts: (a) the setting (4:1-6); (b) Jesus as the source of living water (4:7-15); (c) the spiritual nature of true worship (4:16-26); (d) the readiness of the harvest (4:31-38); (e) Jesus recognized by the Samaritans as the Savior of the world (4: 27-30, 39-42).

The function of 4:1-6 is to move Jesus from Judea to Samaria and, specifically, to locate him at Jacob's well. The reference in vs. 1 to the Pharisees' knowledge of Jesus' action in out-baptizing the Baptist probably implies hostility on their part. He therefore leaves Judea for Galilee. This movement makes possible Jesus' work in Samaria and, subsequently, in Galilee (4:43).

The statement to the effect that Jesus had to pass through Samaria on his way to Galilee (4:4) is not historically true. Jews moving from south to north could, and usually did, use the route east of the Jordan and so avoided contact with the obnoxious Samaritans. But history has no place here. Of course, the more direct route between Judea and Galilee was through Samaria, and this fact gives the impression of credibility to the statement. There may also be a secondary meaning in the words, in that they give expression to the divine intention of Jesus: the Samaritans *had* to be evangelized.

The specific setting for the dialogue is a Samaritan city called Sychar, and, even more specifically and conveniently, beside Jacob's well, located on the historic site of Jacob's gift of land to his son Joseph (Gen. 33:19). The reference to the time of day, "It was about the sixth hour" (4:6), in all probability refers symbolically to the hour of Jesus' death. Through his death the Samaritan nation will be given the water of life (cf. the reference to six waterpots in 2:6, and the exact correspondence of phrasing between 4:6 and 19:14b: "It was about the sixth hour").

Much has been made of the reference to the weariness of Jesus (4:6), especially as antidocetic propaganda.[19] The fact is that it is difficult to find strong indications of the humanity

[19] E.g., Macgregor, *op. cit.*, p. 96. An examination of Macgregor's references reveals their weakness as evidence for his position. The two references (11:35; 19:28) can be explained on other grounds. See *supra*, pp. 58-59. In addition, Macgregor commits a major error in method when he interprets the mind of the Fourth Gospel in the light of I John. This fallacy is perpetuated by Howard in *The Interpreter's Bible*, Vol. VIII (New York and Nashville: Abingdon Press, 1952).

of Jesus in the Fourth Gospel. The present passage is a device which the writer employs to initiate the dialogue between Jesus and the woman. On the face of it, all that Jesus wants is a drink of water from Jacob's well. But that he received the water is never reported. The weariness of Jesus is lost in the larger issue of Jesus as giver of eternal life. When all is said and done, it is rather odd to speak of the humanity of one who changes water into wine, restores health to a dying boy, walks on water, gives sight to the blind, and raises the dead. It appears that an appraisal of the evangelist's views on the docetic problem leads to the conclusion that he betrays no dismay whatsoever over docetism, and that his total picture of Jesus brings him dangerously near the docetic viewpoint.[20]

The second division of the story (4:7-15) has Jesus as the source of living water as its main theme. Jacob's well provides the point of reference. The literary devices are the familiar ones: a symbol capable of spiritual as well as literal meaning (in this case "water" is the symbol), and a "stupid character," whose inability to get beyond the literal meaning makes it possible for Jesus to "correct" her literalism in terms of a higher meaning.[21] The woman of Samaria is important only for the lesson which the evangelist wishes to teach. When that has been done she fades from sight never to reappear.

The crux of the teaching comes in vss. 10 and 14: "If you knew God's gift, and who it is that said to you, 'Give me a drink,' you would have asked him, and he would have given

[20] Supra, pp. 68-69.

[21] The inability of the woman to grasp what Jesus is talking about (the language being intentionally veiled) provides a thread of continuity which runs throughout the story (4:15, 28-29, 39). In vs. 15 she expresses her lack of comprehension in the words: "Sir, give me this water, so that I may not be thirsty, nor come out here to draw water." Jesus then deliberately shifts the conversation to another subject—the woman's domestic life, and, at the same time, reveals his supernatural knowledge. This item is picked up in vs. 29 where the woman tells the people, "Come and see a man who told me all I ever did." Then, after the Samaritans have had Jesus as their guest for two days, they tell the woman that their belief is based on a more solid foundation than her testimony to Jesus' supernatural knowledge; they have heard for themselves and know on that basis that Jesus is the world's Savior (4:39-42).

you living water"; "Anyone who drinks the water which I shall give him will never be thirsty. The water which I shall give him will become within him a spring of water gushing up for eternal life." So far the teaching is plain. Jesus supplies living water which is superior to the well-water which the woman has come to draw.

But the meaning of the symbol "water" is not made clear. The clue to its meaning is found in its description as a spring of water gushing up for eternal life. Jesus is the source of this water. All who drink from this source themselves possess a perennial source of life. What can this be but the Spirit which Jesus possesses? Later in the story God's nature is defined as spirit (4:24), and worship of God must therefore be in spirit and truth. One is reminded, too, of the great invitation of Jesus in 7:37-38 which could be considered a succinct summary of this part of our story: "If any one is thirsty, let him come to me, and let him drink who believes in me. As the scripture has said, 'Out of his belly shall flow streams of life-giving water.' " The evangelist then goes on to identify this life-giving water with the Spirit which Jesus will give through his glorification (7:39).

The import of the third division (4:16-27) is clear, although the passage contains certain obscure allusions. The obscurities are contained in the references to the five husbands (4:18), and to the woman's paramour who is described as "not her husband" (4:18). These allusions may have been introduced only to suggest Jesus' supernatural knowledge and so lead to the woman's response, "Sir, I see that you are a prophet" (4:19). However, the number "five" (4:18) seems too specific for that. A persistent and likely interpretation is that the five husbands refer to the gods of II Kings 17:24, 28-30 (cf. Josephus *Ant.* ix. 288-91).

But what can be said of the man who is not her husband? Some commentators see here an allusion to the God of Israel whom the Samaritans worship in a way all their own. Dodd finds in the reference to the five husbands and the paramour

104

a reference to popular syncretistic cults of Samaria, which combined Yahwism with pagan elements.[22]

It is possible that the evangelist is influenced by events of the Samaritan mission as recorded by the writer of Acts, especially by the story of Simon Magus and his attempt to purchase with money the power of the Holy Spirit (Acts 8:5-24). Two verbal similarities between Acts and the Fourth Gospel tend to support this position. In the Acts story of the Samaritan mission, Philip goes down (from Jerusalem) to a city of Samaria, $\epsilon i s \ \tau \grave{\eta} \nu$ $\pi \acute{o} \lambda \iota \nu \ \tau \hat{\eta} s \ \Sigma a \mu a \rho \acute{\iota} a s$ (8:5); in the Fourth Gospel, Jesus goes to a city of Samaria, $\epsilon i s \ \pi \acute{o} \lambda \iota \nu \ \tau \hat{\eta} s \ \Sigma a \mu a \rho \acute{\iota} a s$ (4:5). In Acts, Peter speaks of the Holy Spirit as the gift of God, $\tau \grave{\eta} \nu \ \delta \omega \rho \epsilon \grave{a} \nu \ \tau o \hat{\upsilon} \ \theta \epsilon o \hat{\upsilon}$ (8:20); in John, Jesus speaks of the gift of God, $\tau \grave{\eta} \nu \ \delta \omega \rho \epsilon \grave{a} \nu \ \tau o \hat{\upsilon} \ \theta \epsilon o \hat{\upsilon}$ (4:10), undoubtedly a reference to the Spirit which is indicated by the symbol "water."

Second-century Christianity, certainly from the time of Justin Martyr, tended to identify Samaritan religion with the false religion of Simon. Indeed, he becomes the father of heresy. It matters little whether or not the Simon of Acts was the same as the Simon of the gnostic cults. The important thing is that second-century Christians identified them, so that Samaria becomes almost a synonym for false religion.

But it must be added that the fourth evangelist is interested not merely in refuting a specific Samaritan religion, no matter how false. His genius is such that he employs a source or a tradition only to move from it to a universal frame of reference. So his concern here is really not with Samaria, but with the replacement of all false religion with the religion of the Spirit. But Samaria serves as a good foil for this teaching.

As was true in the dialogue between Jesus and Nicodemus, so here the dialogue between two individuals becomes one between representatives of groups. This change occurs at vs. 20. It is, at first glance, the religion of Mount Gerizim versus the religion of Jerusalem. From the woman's perspective this is

[22] Op. cit., p. 313.

exactly what it is. But this is not really the case. We are already acquainted with the evangelist's evaluation of Judaism. It is made clear that salvation is not to be found in Judaism: it comes from Judaism (4:22). Jerusalem worship and that of Mount Gerizim will both yield to a religion not at all dependent on place. It will be a religion in harmony with the nature of God himself (4:21-24). So the comparison is between false religion, as represented by Samaria, and Christianity, the true religion of the Spirit.

The interesting climax of this episode is contained in vss. 25-26. In response to Jesus' pronouncement on the nature of true worship, the Samaritan woman declares, "I know that Messiah is coming. When he comes he will explain everything to us." It is as if she has caught in the words of Jesus about God and the nature of true worship a hint of the long-hoped-for revelation in the Messiah. Jesus makes his meaning plain in memorable words, not easy to translate without loss of simple directness, ἐγώ εἰμι, ὁ λαλῶν σοι: "I am he; he is speaking to you" (4:26). The new era in religion, of which Jesus has been speaking, is summed up in him. The religion of Judaism in the first place (1:1-11), and now the false, syncretistic religion of Samaria, must yield to the new and superior spiritual religion which comes through Jesus.

Vss. 27-30 serve as a preparation for the final episode. The disciples, who had gone into the city to purchase food (4:8), now return. At this point the woman leaves for the city to report to the people there concerning Jesus' supernatural knowledge. The people leave the city and start toward Jesus. The narrative is now interrupted by the fourth division of our story, namely, the readiness of the harvest (4:31-38). The account of the meeting between Jesus and the Samaritan people and its consequences is renewed after this interlude and forms the story's climax.

The closely knit character of the narrative is shown by the incident of the return of the disciples with the food procured in the city. As early as vs. 8 the purpose of their errand had been stated. Their absence made possible the private conversation of Jesus and the woman. Now, with their return, a second purpose is served, for "food" immediately suggests a deeper meaning, just as "water" did at the beginning of the story.

The movement of thought is from food which is bought (4:31) to food which Jesus has, unknown to the disciples, and identified as Jesus' obedience to the will of God and the completion of his work. The word "complete" refers to Jesus' death (5:36; 17:4; 19:28, 30). Strategically placed between the clear statement that the Samaritans were on their way out of the city to meet Jesus (4:30) and the final section in which these people confess him as the Savior of the world, the passage contemplates this movement of the people as fields already white for harvest (4:35). Its source seems to be the Synoptic saying of Matt. 9:37-38 and Luke 10:2, possibly combined with the parable of the sower (Mark 4:3 and parallels). Luke's passage may have special relevance, since it is given in the setting of the journey of Jesus and his disciples through Samaria.

If all elements of the passage are considered, the import seems to be this: The food which Jesus has is the carrying out of God's will; first, in terms of the performance of the signs and by his teachings, and, secondly, by going to his death on the cross, bringing the work of God to completion. Putting it plainly, the disciples do not begin and complete the process of sowing and reaping. All they can do is gather the harvest. The seed itself has already been sown in the appearance, career, and death of Jesus. As Jesus later says, when the Greeks come to see him, "Unless the grain of wheat dies when it falls into the ground, it remains a single grain. But if it dies, it bears much fruit" (12:24). Or to put it in still other words: when Jesus is lifted up on the cross he will attract all men to himself (12:32). Attention is centered on Jesus, not on the arduous work of the disciples in evangelist effort; that kind of effort would be doomed to failure apart from the work of God in Christ which is already in process.

The final section of the Samaritan episode is contained in

vss. 39-42, with an anticipatory introduction in vss. 27-30. Vs. 30 left the reader with the knowledge that the Samaritans were advancing toward Jesus. Their interest, so far, is based on the woman's words, "Come and see a man who told me all I ever did" (4:29). On this basis many of the Samaritans come to believe in him (4:39). But this is a secondary basis for belief. Now, when Jesus himself comes to live with them (4:40), they believe, not on the grounds of indirect testimony, but because of personal experience (4:42). So enthusiastic is their belief in Jesus that they hail him Savior of the world!

Jesus' Own Country
4:43-45

THESE VERSES PROVIDE A TRANSITION FROM THE SAMARITAN STORY to the account of the second sign performed at Cana. They contain a special problem, however, so will be treated separately.

In vs. 44 reference is made to a declaration of Jesus that a prophet has no honor in his own country. In the following verse it is said that when Jesus came into Galilee he was welcomed by the people. This implies that Galilee, for the author, was not Jesus' own country. In the Synoptic accounts, the proverbial saying, of which John 4:44 is a variant, is based on the assumption that Jesus is a Galilean (Mark 6:4; Matt. 13:57; Luke 4:24). Indeed the Lucan narrative is even more specific; it locates Jesus in Nazareth where he utters the proverbial saying (Luke 4:16).

It must be kept in mind that Jesus had merely passed through Samaria on his way from Judea to Galilee. Vs. 54 shows clearly that the writer was concerned, not with Samaria, but with Judea and Galilee: "Now this was the second sign which Jesus performed when he had come from Judea to Galilee." So identification of Jesus' own country is not dependent upon a choice among Judea, Samaria, and Galilee; the choice is between Judea and Galilee. Since there has been opposition to Jesus in Judea,[23]

[23] This is implied in 2:24-25 and again in 4:1-3.

the natural inference is that Judea is substituted for Galilee by the fourth evangelist as Jesus' own country. Judea is the place where Jesus is not honored. So he goes to Galilee where he is welcomed by the people.

The problem finds solution only as we keep in mind the various levels of meaning which the evangelist delights in finding almost everywhere. On one level (the lowest possible), Jesus is indeed from Nazareth. Philip, a disciple of Jesus, makes that clear (1:45). The tradition of the Bethlehem origin of the Messiah confuses the people who otherwise might believe in Jesus; they know he comes from Galilee (7:40-44). His brothers are located in Galilee. They are represented as urging Jesus to reveal himself in Judea if he would be known openly (7:1-9). The Jews of Capernaum know his father and mother (6:42). In 7:52 the Pharisees imply that Nicodemus, since he attempts to mediate a dispute in favor of Jesus, must be from Galilee too. A large part of the problem of the Jews of the Gospel is due to the fact that they know too well the obscure Galilean origin of Jesus (e.g., 7:27).

However, the train of thought which makes Jesus a Galilean is largely submerged by another which locates his origin in heaven (6:42; 7:28, etc). Biologically speaking his father is Joseph and he hails from Galilee, but spiritually speaking, his Father is God and he comes from heaven. For our author the real Jesus belongs to this second plane. When the Spirit descends upon Jesus, the Galilean connection ceases to have importance; he repudiates parental authority (2:4),[24] cutting ties which relate him to a human life. While those who have known him look at him and say, "There is Jesus of Nazareth," Jesus himself must always insist, "I have come down from heaven."

Now this divine being, whose homeland was heaven, belongs properly to the holy city Jerusalem, not to obscure Nazareth, during his life on earth. Macgregor has noted this with reference to the difference in the setting of Jesus' ministry when compared with the Synoptics:

[24] Supra, pp. 86-87.

Allowance must be made for the idealistic tendency of our Evangelist, who desires to show that Jesus, so far from being an obscure teacher in such an outlying region as Galilee, taught and died at the headquarters of the national religion.[25]

Recognition of this tendency ought to dispose of the notion that the fourth evangelist had access to non-Synoptic, historically reliable, tradition concerning Jesus' career. Even if this had been available, his method would not permit him to squeeze the portrait of his subject into a rigidly historical frame. Since Jerusalem and Judea is where the Christ belongs, then there he must be placed, historical facts to the contrary notwithstanding.

Jesus belongs to Jerusalem, moreover, because there he must be glorified. It is misleading to say, merely, that Jesus must die in Jerusalem. The place where one is imprisoned and executed as the result of religious and political intrigue is enemy territory and would be so construed if, on historical grounds, it could be shown that the victim came from elsewhere. This could have been done in the case of Jesus. But the meaning of the death of Jesus is reconstructed so that all elements of tragedy are removed. The cross signifies life not death! It is impossible to think of the work of the Jesus of our Gospel as in any sense efficacious apart from its story of the cross. The cross is the fulfillment of all that precedes it, and with it comes the full flood of the life of the Spirit. Jesus does not shrink from Jerusalem, he embraces it, for in the purpose of the Father that is where he belongs; the land of rejection is also the land of glorification!

On the lower level, then, Jesus is the man of Nazareth, and on the higher level he is the man of heaven; but while he tarries for a short time on earth, the man of heaven fittingly embraces the holy city and the land of the Jews as his own country.

[25] Op. cit., p. xiv.

Distance Transcended

4:46-54

THE SOURCES BEHIND THIS STORY ARE MATT. 8:5-13 AND LUKE 7: 1-10. The statement in vs. 53, "He and his whole household believed," seems to show dependence on Acts (Acts 16:15, 31, 34; 18:8).

The story in the Fourth Gospel, however, shows certain differences when compared with the Synoptic accounts. In John, Jesus is in Cana, not Capernaum, when he performs the miracle; the father's rank is that of a royal official, not a centurion; the one who is healed is the official's son, not his slave; all specifically Jewish elements are absent from the Johannine account; cross references in John relate the story to the first miracle at Cana.[26]

The point of this story seems to be centered in vs. 50, with Jesus' words, "Go, your son will live," and its confirmation in vs. 53 where it is said that the father knew that the healing had taken place at the exact time when Jesus had uttered these words. This element of the story comes into John from Matthew's account where Jesus says to the centurion, "Go; be it done for you as you have believed." "And," the evangelist adds, "the servant was healed at that very moment" (Matt. 8:13). Nothing is made of the exact time of the healing in Luke (cf. Luke 7:10).

The most frequent interpretation of this passage is that it sets forth the superiority of the man's faith. But there are many elements in the story which seem to be at least as important as this, though there is more to the story than a general interlocking of meaningful symbols. Since its stress falls naturally on the moment when Jesus spoke the words, "Your son will live," attention is directed not only to the man's faith, but also to Jesus who makes the boy well. In fact, vs. 48 seems to cast doubt on the genuineness of the man's faith prior to the healing. It is strange, on the face of it, that Jesus' response to the man's pleading request for help should be, "Unless you see

[26] Colwell and Titus, op. cit., pp. 37-39.

111

signs and wonders you will not believe." But this strangeness disappears when we remember that the evangelist's real interest is not in the recovery of the dying boy, but in evidence of the life-giving power of Jesus. The statement about signs and wonders then becomes a means of directing attention to belief in Jesus. Belief on the part of the official and of his household comes at the end of the story, after the healing has been accomplished. The function of signs (and this one is not an exception) is to create belief; belief is not the precondition of healing.

Since Jesus is the center of attention in the story the question now becomes one of its meaning in relation to him. When Jesus utters the words, "Go, your son will live," it is as if a strange power goes out from him to make direct contact with the boy so as to revitalize his body. The statement, "Your son will live," is a signal that this has happened. Later the father knows that the healing took place *at that precise moment*. This knowledge leads to belief on his part and that of his family. The distance from Cana to Capernaum serves to emphasize the greatness of this strange power.

The nature of Jesus' power is clarified by the cross reference in vs. 46. The setting for this healing is Cana, the place where he had made the water wine. The same power is in operation a second time.[27] We have seen that "wine" in the first Cana story is a symbol of the Spirit.[28] But in that story there was no indication of the functional abilities of the Spirit beyond what is suggested by the symbol "wine." But with this second Cana miracle there begins a cycle of signs which illustrate the power of the Spirit. They culminate in the greatest of them all, the Raising of Lazarus (11:1-44), which shows Jesus to be the victor over death itself. In fact, Jesus as Life-giver seems to be the dominant theme of the whole cycle of signs: he gives life to a dying boy; he restores strength to a man crippled for thirty-eight years; he provides life-giving bread; he gives sight to a

[27] Dodd, op. cit., p. 319.
[28] Supra, pp. 87-88.

blind man; and he raises a dead man to life. These are all activities revealing the power of the life-giving Spirit, which the first miracle at Cana prefigures, and which is still to find its most dramatic and saving expression in the cross. The specific function of this incident, therefore, is to portray Jesus as the possessor of God's Spirit which is powerful and life-giving, reaching across the miles to effect its healing work.[29]

The Divine Claims of Jesus
5:1-47

THE STORY RELATED IN VSS. 1-9 IS IMPORTANT LARGELY BECAUSE of the discussion to which it gives rise. This discussion deals basically with the problem of Jesus' claims to divine prerogatives. But, like all the Johannine signs, the miracle per se has a message to relate.

The setting of the story is Jerusalem at the time of a feast, or, if the article is allowed, the feast, in which case the Passover is probably intended.[30] The great amount of attention which commentators have given to the passage in relation to chronology is unwarranted. The various feasts of John's Gospel have dramatic value; they provide appropriate settings for symbolic, literary reconstruction. It is barely possible that there is literary dependence on Nehemiah at this point as the possible reference to the sheep gate (?) of vs. 2 might suggest, and that the feast is the Feast of Booths (Tabernacles) celebrating the reading of the law by Ezra the scribe (Neh. 8:16-18). This would fit well with the symbolism of the five porches (John 5:2) as referring to the five books of the law. If the evangelist had this very important historical event in mind, the symbolism assumes

[29] It is helpful to note in this context that just as space is no obstacle to Jesus' spiritual presence, so time provides no barrier to those who would believe (20:29). Space and time are both transcended in him.

[30] It can be argued, to the contrary, that the feast of the Jews was Tabernacles not Passover (see "Sukkoth," *Universal Jewish Encyclopedia*). The fact that the Feast of Tabernacles is mentioned explicitly in 7:2 need not be construed as weakening the possibility that the feast of 5:1 is Tabernacles; the Fourth Gospel is built more on the basis of artistic than historical arrangement.

added meaning: the great crowd of blind, lame, and paralyzed people lying within the confines of Judaism, with the Torah offering its supposedly life-giving advantages. The one man singled out is representative of the whole. He has not taken advantage of the pool, that is to say, he has not grasped the meaning of the law. That meaning (if we interpret the incident in terms of its sequel) is found in these words: "For if you believed Moses you would believe me, for he wrote about me. But if you do not believe what he wrote, how will you believe my words?" (5:46-47). The Torah by itself is impotent, though rightly understood, it points to the living water, that is, to Jesus.

It is difficult to suppose that the author would have used the symbolism of the healing water of the pool without some such idea in mind. It is certain, in view of his general appraisal of Judaism, that he would reject the notion that Judaism by itself healed men. But Judaism (Torah) as a "pointer" would be consonant with his view and use of the scriptures. A true grasp of their meaning would point men to Jesus as the living water.

But the cripple, who had not been thus enlightened by the law, is confronted by Jesus himself without the benefit of the testimony of the law. The presence of the one to whom the scriptures point means that the prior testimony may be bypassed. Jesus has only to speak the word and the man is healed.

Dodd, however, sees in this another meaning:

There lies the healing water, but the cripple remains unhealed: so that Torah promised life to men, but the Gospel tradition knew of "publicans and sinners" for whom it did nothing: the sick who needed a physician (Mark ii. 16-17). Of them the cripple of Bethesda may serve as representative. But how, it may be said, could the Torah, beneficent as it was, benefit those who refused to make use of its means of grace? The man might have been healed long ago, perhaps, if he had stepped down into the pool. Precisely; and that is why the first word of Jesus is, "Have you the will to become a healthy man?" The reply is a feeble excuse. The man has not the will. The law might show the way of life; it was powerless to create

114

the will to live. The will to live, together with the power to live, is given in the word of Christ.[31]

The importance which Dodd gives to the man's lack of will is interesting homiletics, but it is doubtful if it is good interpretation. The man's reply that he cannot get into the pool is not so feeble an excuse if we remember that he is a cripple. Furthermore, Jesus himself apparently thought his answer sufficient, for he uttered life-giving words which gave the result the man had hoped for over a period of thirty-eight years. For Jesus, the man's answer was the same as a categorical "Yes," and he proceeded to act on that basis.

The story was apparently constructed from the Christian belief in the crippling effects of Judaism as a religion, combined with legendary and superstitious notions of the healing properties of water. This would make the "water" element of the story only superficially important. The writer's real intent is to show the superiority of Christianity over Judaism.

We are told in vs. 9 that the healing took place on the Sabbath. This information comes as a surprise, and must be understood as a device for purposes of transition. From now to the end of the chapter the problem becomes one of Jesus' claims to divine authority. This is set forth under two main questions: (a) What right does Jesus have to break the Sabbath? (5:16); (b) What right does Jesus have to claim equality with God? (5:18). The former is discussed in vss. 9b-17; the latter in vss. 18-30. Vss. 30-47 deal with the problem of witnesses to Jesus' divine claims, and are intended to support what he has said about his right to work on the Sabbath and his claims to divine sonship.

The Sabbath question begins with the transition passage, 5:9b. Ultimately, the problem relates to Jesus as a Sabbath-breaker, but is preceded by the Jews' accusation that the man is breaking the Sabbath by carrying his mat. Immediately, however, the burden of responsibility is placed upon Jesus, since he had

[31] Op. cit., pp. 319-20.

THE MESSAGE OF THE FOURTH GOSPEL

told the man to take his mat and walk (5:11). Vs. 13 makes it clear that the latter did not know it was Jesus who had healed him. This is an example of healing without belief. The man had simply made it clear that he wanted to be healed. The expected source of healing was Torah, but, instead, he had found it in Jesus.

The fact that Jesus finds the man in the temple (5:14) suggests that Jesus is in full command of the situation, not a fugitive from justice. It also makes possible the identification of Jesus as the man who had presumably violated the Sabbath (5:15). Vs. 16 is an historically accurate observation: "For this reason the Jews persecuted Jesus, because he did such things on the Sabbath."

Jesus' words, "My Father is working until now, and I am working also," are given in the form of a reply to the unexpressed thought lying behind vs. 16. This thought, when put into words, would be, "Why do you break the Sabbath?" (cf. Mark 2:24; 3: 2). The answer of Jesus in vs. 17 is interesting for two reasons: (a) it assumes the recognition in rabbinic circles of the Sabbath work of God;[32] and (b) it identifies the work of Jesus as at one with the work of the Father, and leads to the accusation that Jesus makes himself God's equal (5:18). It should be noted that in vs. 18 the two problems of the discourse are clearly summarized: "So for this reason the Jews sought all the more to kill him, because he not only broke the Sabbath, but even called God his own Father, making himself equal with God."

The assertion, "My Father is working until now, and I am working also," means that God's creative work continues in Jesus. The Jews know that if this were true an attack on Jesus would be an attack on God himself. Jewish circles had to admit that God never ceased from his work, a fact which the Rabbis tried hard to explain. Later (7:22-23) Jesus bases his right to heal on the grounds that it is more important to make a man's whole body well on the Sabbath than to mutilate him as the Jews would do were the time for circumcision to fall on a

[32] Philo, Leg. Alleg. I. 5; Shem. R. 30.

116

Sabbath. But the present passage grounds Jesus' activity in the fact that he is God's Son and that he does what he sees the Father doing (5:19). Thus are anticipated the future declarations: "I and the Father are one," and "He who has seen me has seen the Father." There is unity of *being* between Jesus and God. The Jews make this inference and feel that it violates the monotheistic principle and is blasphemous. The charge of blasphemy comes to its clearest expression in 10:33: "We do not stone you for a good work, but for blasphemy, and because you, a man, make yourself a god."

This becomes the dominant theme of vss. 19-30, although reference to the Sabbath problem is not lacking (5:19-20). When the concept of the close relation of Jesus to the Father is in the evangelist's mind, he tends to use the term "Son," and that is true in this instance. The Father has bequeathed to the Son his own creative prerogative, even to the extent of giving life to the dead (5:21). There is parallelism here: God works on the Sabbath, so Jesus works on the Sabbath; God gives life to the dead, so Jesus will cause the dead to rise. The emphasis on life-giving is prompted by the healing of the man at the pool, but in a deeper sense it springs from the evangelist's conviction of the true meaning of the Incarnation.

Very naturally the concept of Jesus as life-giver passes over into the theme of judgment. All judgment has been given the Son by the Father. This judgment is inherent in the fact of Jesus' presence in the world. The great test comes in the response which men make in his presence—belief or unbelief. If one hears Jesus' message, accepts it, and believes in him as God-sent, he meets the test and passes from death to eternal life. Not that Jesus is the ultimate object of belief; the author is very careful to guard himself at that point. To believe in Jesus is to believe in God. God and Jesus represent a continuum of spiritual life. It is precisely because the Jews fail to see this that they accuse him. They think of him as a man making a claim to the status of deity. And even if they could concede reasonable grounds for his claim, their problem would remain, since the ancient monotheistic doctrine would be in jeopardy. But Jesus as divine Son is not Jesus as an independent deity. The divine involvement includes God and Jesus, the Father and the Son, an involvement which in ch. 17 is extended to embrace the beloved community, the church, as well (e.g., 17:10). But the ultimate object of belief is God.

The remainder of the chapter, vss. 31-47, is designed to support Jesus' right to claim divine authority. Vs. 31 assumes the accusation, "You are testifying about yourself; your testimony is not true" (cf. 8:13). This is based on the legal stipulation that the testimony of a witness with respect to his own case was invalid. In 8:14 Jesus asserts that his testimony is true even though he may be his own witness. This assertion is made on the grounds that he knows his divine origin and destiny and so has the right to speak on his own behalf. However, he accommodates to the common legal custom, and calls other witnesses on his behalf.

The witnesses are four in number: the Baptist, the works, the Father, and the scriptures. The reference in vs. 32 to "another" witness might be construed as the witness of John. It is more likely that it is a reference to the supreme witness of the Father, who is himself responsible for the testimony of John, the works, and the scriptures. The witness of the Father contrasts sharply with that of John who is represented as the burning and shining lamp (not "light"), destined to throw but a fleeting light of testimony across the darkness and then to disappear. It is a legitimate testimony so far as it goes, but it is not continuous. Possibly the tradition of John's imprisonment and death lies behind the suggestion of the transitoriness of his witness.

More important than the testimony of John is that of Jesus' works. The function of Jesus is to bring to completion the works which the Father has given him. The term translated "works" ($\check{\epsilon}\rho\gamma\alpha$) refers not only to the signs ($\sigma\eta\mu\epsilon\hat{\iota}\alpha$), but also to the whole divine vocation of Jesus culminating in his death and the release of God's Spirit into the world; the individual works make up the whole work of redemption.

The testimony of the Father is indirect; he testifies through the works and through the scriptures. Direct testimony seems to be suggested in vs. 37. But it must not be supposed that the evangelist held to the concept that a theophany was possible apart from Jesus. He says plainly in the Prologue that no man has ever seen God; it is the function of the Son to make him known (1:18). It is only through Jesus that God reveals himself and utters his testimony. In this sense the witness of the Father is united with the witness of the scriptures. The scriptures do not contain the words of God (i.e., the words of eternal life: 5:39) apart from their testimony to Jesus. The law of Moses standing by itself is invalid; its validity lies in the recognition of its complement, which is Christ. This view makes Judaism a truncated religion apart from Jesus as its fulfillment. The object of man's existence is the gaining of life—and this Judaism is powerless to give (5:40). Yet the scriptures, rightly understood, point to Jesus as the sources of life (5:39-40). This whole section, 5:31-47, points up the religious exclusiveness of the Fourth Gospel.

Life-giving Bread

6: 1-71

IT IS IMPORTANT TO KEEP IN MIND THAT CH. 6 CONSTITUTES A literary unity. The breakdown given here is purely for purposes of analysis. The chapter as a whole moves on three levels: (a) the purely materialistic level where "bread" is provided hungry people miraculously; (b) the level where "bread" signifies the flesh of Jesus, still materialistic, but representing a development over the allusion to mere bread of the first level; (c) the level of the Spirit which illuminates all that has gone before. These three levels are skillfully blended so as to result in an intricate literary pattern.

The miracle itself is based on the Synoptic stories (Mark 6: 32-44; Matt. 14:13-21; Luke 9:10-17; cf. Mark 8:1-10; Matt. 15:32-39). However, John has changed the accounts con-

119

siderably. He omits some of the details found in the Synoptic stories as, for example, the element of compassion (Mark 6: 34). In Mark the disciples remind Jesus of the lateness of the hour and of the need for food, while in the Fourth Gospel Jesus takes the initiative in this regard. Some details are added also; the boy who has the lunch, the barley loaves, distribution of the food by Jesus himself, the command to the disciples to gather up the food so that none be lost.

The story of the miracle (6:1-13) moves on the first and lowest level where the physical need of hunger is met. The account proceeds in two directions. In the first place, the people are so impressed by Jesus' ability that they hail him as "the prophet who is to come into the world" (6:14), and, on that basis, propose (as Jesus knows) to make him king by force. Jesus renounces this acclaim, and retires to the mountains. This betrays the evangelist's desire not to associate Jesus with popular messianic ideas.

In the second place, the miraculous feeding presents Jesus in the role of a provider of material necessities. Philip and Andrew are used as foils to emphasize the greatness of the miracle in this respect (6:7-8). When the crowd comes to Jesus from across the lake, Jesus sees through their zeal in seeking him out. It was not because they "saw signs" (i.e., understood the spiritual import of the feeding), but because they had eaten bread, and, like well-fed cattle, were satisfied with what they had consumed (6:26). The Greek word χορτάζω makes this meaning clear. It was used with reference to the feeding or fattening of cattle.

The inability of the crowd (which becomes "the Jews" in vs. 41) to understand the meaning of Jesus' veiled references to spiritual bread (6:27-33) leads to their request: "Sir, give us that bread always" (6:34). This is the equivalent, under the new symbol "bread," of the Samaritan woman's plea: "Sir, give me this water, so that I may not be thirsty, nor come out here to draw water."

This lowest level of materialistic interest is the base line on which further development is built. The transition from the first level to the second begins with vs. 27: "Do not work for perishable food, but for food which remains for eternal life, which the Son of Man will give you, for God has placed his seal upon him." It ends with vs. 51: "I am the life-giving bread which came down from heaven. If any one eats this bread he will live forever. And my flesh is the bread which I will give for the life of the world." In view of the highly mystical and spiritual teaching which precedes vs. 51, the reference to flesh is like a trap, baited for the Jews to spring. And spring it they do! "How can this man give us his flesh to eat?" The answer of Jesus strikes as "low" a level as can be imagined: the Jews must eat the flesh of the Son of Man and drink his blood in order to obtain eternal life. Imagine the writer of 3:6 ("That which is born of the flesh is flesh, and that which is born of the Spirit is spirit") saying that Jesus' flesh is true food and his blood true drink!

But this revision to a crassly material level is for a purpose. For one thing, it makes contact with the sacramental practice of the Christian church—a practice which the evangelist may now correct by the device of sharp contrast: "The Spirit is what gives life; flesh is of no use. The words which I have spoken to you are spirit and life" (6:63). This statement illuminates all that has gone before: "flesh" turns out not to be flesh at all. "Flesh and blood" do not refer to Jesus' body composed of material substances, but to the Spirit given when his flesh dies, when the Son of Man ascends where he was formerly (6:62).

If one keeps in mind the unity of the chapter, and that the thought proceeds from one level to another, he is saved from the fallacy of attributing ideas to the evangelist which are not representative of his thinking, but are the "baited traps" mentioned above. Specifically, the fallacy of attributing sacramentalism to him is controverted by this approach. The allusions to flesh and blood in vss. 53-56 are shown to belong to the same category as bread in vss. 33-34. To stop at the "flesh and blood" passage and assert that this represents the thought of the author is like identifying miracle per se as the reality. These things arrest the attention of the Jews. That is their literary function. But anything grasped by the Jews in this Gospel is purely materialistic, and, we may be sure, rejected by the author.

Repeatedly, the normative message of the evangelist appears:

Do not work for perishable food, but for food which remains for eternal life, which the Son of Man will give you, for God has placed his seal upon him. (6:27.)

Amen, amen, I tell you, Moses did not give you bread from heaven, but my Father gives you the true bread from heaven. For the bread of God is he who comes down from heaven, and gives life to the world. (6:32-33.)

I am the life-giving bread. He who comes to me shall never be hungry, and he who believes in me shall never be thirsty. (6:35.)

As the living Father has sent me, and I live because of the Father, so he who eats me will live because of me. (6:57.)

The Spirit is what gives life; flesh is of no use. The words which I have spoken to you are spirit and life. (6:63.)

These are passages which express the Gospel's intended message. They are all words of Jesus, not of the Jews or even of disciples, though it must be pointed out that words of Jesus, *spoken in the process of elaboration*, are frequently subject to a "lower" interpretation. But when this is the case the lower idea or symbol becomes a pedagogical device for the identification of spiritual truth. The identification of these items gives us the lesson really intended by the evangelist, and conveys the "normative" teaching of the Gospel.

Looking now at the story in the light of the developmental point of view outlined above, the following points may be noted: (a) the setting; (b) some details peculiar to the fourth evangelist's story of the feeding; (c) the function of the story of the walking on the water; (d) elements of the dialogues with the Jews and with the disciples; (e) the sequel to the dialogue with the disciples.

The geographical setting of the miracle proper (though not of the discourse) is the east side of the lake of Galilee. The temporal setting, however, is the more important; it fixes the event at the time when the Passover was near. One can visualize the crowds, normally flocking to Jerusalem, being drawn instead to Jesus. According to the account, Jesus has gone into the mountain, presumably for privacy, but when he raises his eyes the people are coming toward him. It is as though, quite unconsciously, they are being drawn to a superior source of food than the Jewish passover.[33]

It is plain that the evangelist is dealing in this chapter with the Christian eucharist. The art of the catacombs indicates that second-century Christians symbolized the eucharist by the loaves and the fishes. The loaves and the fishes of the Synoptic accounts are probably eucharistic as well, although the Synoptics use the word εὐλογέω ("to bless"), not εὐχαριστέω ("to give thanks") as does the Fourth Gospel (Mark 6:41 and parallels; cf. John 6:11; but cf. Mark 8:6; Matt. 15:36). It is worth noting, also, that the reference to barley loaves seems to be taken from II Kings 4:42-44 where there are additional similarities to the Johannine account; for example, the "servant" (perhaps the boy of the Fourth Gospel), the protest that the amount of food is insufficient for the large number of people, the miraculous feeding, and fragments left over after the feeding. The barley loaves of the Kings account represent the first-fruits, which in Leviticus are connected with the Passover (Lev. 23:9 ff.). In the Fourth Gospel there is no account of the Supper as in the Synoptics; in its place we find the story of Jesus who assumes the role of a slave (13:1 ff.). The Fourth Gospel writer has seen fit to deal with the eucharistic problem in another manner, under the symbol of Jesus as the Bread of Life. But in doing so he is not altogether at variance with the

[33] There is a reflection here (6:3) of the Sermon on the Mount (Matt. 5:1), and the mysterious mountain may suggest, as it almost certainly does in Matthew, the new Sinai where the Christian equivalent of the law is given. But while in Matthew Jesus' superior teachings supersede the Mosaic law, in John the law is superseded by Christ himself.

123

Synoptics. They had, in effect, set forth the proposition that the Jewish passover had been superseded by the Christian eucharist, and John does the same thing. But his view of the eucharist is not, on that account, identical with that held by the Synoptic writers; it is uniquely his own.

It is not at all clear that the evangelist placed value on the eucharist as an institution. His concern seems to be for an abiding personal relation between Jesus and his followers; they are to feed on him as the life-giving heavenly bread. In the same manner, the author's concept of the church is in no sense institutional. It consists of the vital relationship between the believer and God, but made possible by the work of Jesus. God, Jesus and the fellowship represent an interlocking trinity, because the fellowship is caught up in the oneness of divine life; ch. 17 makes this clear.

It may be, therefore, that the absence of the Supper points to a radical difference in the evangelist's thought about the eucharist from that current in the church. Jesus himself in his real spiritual presence constitutes the eucharist. When one feeds on him, that is, partakes of his Spirit and shares in his life, he comes to possess now and forever the life which rites, whether pagan or Christian, seek to provide. The Spirit's presence is too real, too intimately personal, to be mediated through external rites and ceremonies. This concern with the personal relation between the individual and Jesus is the burden of the discourse on Jesus as the Bread of Life (6:35-58).

Two uniquely Johannine additions to the story are of special interest. The first has to do with the distribution of the food by Jesus himself (6:11). In the Synoptics, Jesus gives the food to the disciples who, in turn, distribute it to the people (Mark 6:41; Matt. 14:19; Luke 9:16). The change introduced by John can hardly be accidental. Seen in the light of the discourse which follows, it seems to put aside any suggestion of a mediatorial element (the disciples) as existing between Jesus and the people. Jesus himself distributes the bread, thus enriching the symbolism on which the discourse is to be based.

124

Vs. 35 sums it up simply and adequately: "I am the life-giving bread. He who comes to me shall never be hungry, and he who believes in me shall never be thirsty." To believe in Jesus is to feed on Jesus, and the result is life.

A second detail worthy of attention is contained in vs. 12. It is the injunction of Jesus to the disciples to "gather up the remaining pieces that nothing be lost." On the face of it, this would mean nothing more than the exercise of care with regard to the remains of the eucharistic elements; and on the lower level of thought that is probably what is meant. But the saying is intentionally enigmatic, for in another and more important sense the words refer to the care of the disciples which Jesus exercises.[34]

This concern with the preservation of the twelve is present not only in ch. 6; it appears also in ch. 13 [35] with reference to the "chosen" ones of Jesus (13:18), again in 15:16, very strongly in the prayer for Christian unity (17:6, 9, 11-12, 15), and in 18:9. The problem is related to that of the defection of Judas, which itself demanded explanation (6:70; 13:18-19, 21-30; 17: 12). But perhaps more important still is the relation of this concern for the preservation of the disciples to the story of Jesus walking on the water. This is our next consideration.

There are three apparent reasons why the evangelist used the story of Jesus walking on the water: (a) he found it embedded in that section of the Synoptic tradition which he employed as a source (Mark 6:45-52; Matt. 14:22-33); (b) it effects the transition to the discourse on the Bread of Life by prompting the query of the Jews, "Rabbi, when did you get here?" (6:25); and (c) it makes its own peculiar contribution to the development of thought.

This contribution seems integral to ch. 6, and is not dependent for its place in John merely because of its attachment to the Synoptic source. Apparently the evangelist retained it because

[34] Edwyn Hoskyns, The Fourth Gospel (ed. F. N. Davey; London: Faber and Faber, Ltd., 1939), I, 325-26.
[35] Infra, pp. 179-88.

of its symbolic possibilities. The problem is to identify these possibilities.

The elements which appear important in the story are the darkness, Jesus' absence from the disciples, the storm on the sea, the appearance of Jesus walking on the water, fear, words of reassurance, and the quick arrival at the land. Three factors, in particular, stand out from the Synoptic counterparts. First, the reference to "the fourth watch of the night" (Mark 6:48; Matt. 14:25) is changed in John to "it was now dark," and is given a stronger emphasis by its new position at the beginning of the story. It becomes an introduction for the story: "It was now dark, and Jesus had not yet come to them" (6:17). Secondly, there is the element of the storm on the sea. And, finally, joy and safety for the disciples come with the appearance of Jesus.

The sequence of events is reduced to this: absence of Jesus, the period of distress, and Jesus' return with its attendant joy. If the unit is to be allowed a truly Johannine purpose, it must be interpreted in the light of the Gospel's concerns. It is not difficult to identify the present concern. The story is anticipatory in character, looking ahead to the time when crucifixion will separate the disciples from Jesus, and at the same time affirming the joy of the resurrection faith. That the disciples will be kept safe has already been suggested symbolically in vs. 12. The characteristic Johannine element, the reference to darkness: "It was already dark, and Jesus had not yet come to them" (6:17), may well mean the darkness which is the result of Jesus' absence (cf. 3:2 and 13:30 for the same symbolism). If this interpretation is correct, the story anticipates the "little while" of 16:16 ff. This idea is elaborated on in several passages:

Amen, amen, I tell you, you will weep and wail, but the world will rejoice; you will be sorrowful, but your sorrow will become joy. When a woman is in labor she has sorrow, for her hour has come; but when the child is born, she no long remembers the suffering in her joy that a human being has been born into the world. So you have sorrow now; but I will see you again, and your hearts will rejoice; and no one will take your joy from you. (16:20-22.)

The light is with you for a little longer. Walk while you have the light, lest darkness overtake you. He who walks in the darkness does not know where he is going. Believe in the light while you have it, that you may become sons of light. (12:35-36.)

Viewed from this perspective, the story stresses Jesus' care for his own, particularly his care for the disciples in relation to his impending death on the cross, an event which, according to Mark, struck terror to their hearts so that they forsook him and fled (Mark 14:50). But our evangelist's sense of Jesus' eternal presence will not permit him to follow Mark at this point. Jesus comes to them in their distress in a form which transcends material limitations with his words of absolute assurance, "It is I, do not be afraid." With this utterance of Jesus, the disciples "willed" (the word used in Mark 6:48 of the supposed intention of Jesus to pass them by) to take him into the boat. And they come *immediately* to the land. Thus the words of the psalm are fulfilled: "Then they were glad because they had quiet, and he brought them to their desired haven" (Ps. 107: 30).[36]

The discourse itself proceeds in terms of pairs of contrasting ideas: perishable food versus food that endures (6:27); manna versus true bread from heaven (6:31-32); Jesus, son of Joseph, versus Jesus, Son of God (6:42-51); flesh as bread versus the Spirit as bread (6:51b-63). It is to be observed that the movement is always from the lower to the higher level.

The discussion of perishable and enduring food is based on the account of the feeding as vs. 26 plainly indicates. It is given a peculiar turn by stress on the term "work" in the clause "Do not work for perishable food" (6:27). The Jews ask, "What must we do to perform the works of God?" (6:28). The answer is that the work of God is belief in Jesus. This makes clear the distinction between Christianity and Judaism;

[36] Cf. Hoskyns, *op. cit.*, I, 327.

127

Judaism was dedicated to the doing of God's will as revealed in Torah, while Christianity found the divine revelation in Jesus and stressed the centrality of belief in him. At a point like this the Fourth Gospel shows strong affinity with the position of Paul.

The reference to the manna in the desert (6:31) leads to the identification of Jesus as the life-giving bread. The manna was not true bread from heaven; the proof of this lies in the fact that the fathers ate it and yet they died (6:49). On the other hand, the true bread from heaven, which is Jesus, is authenticated by its life-giving power. Yet the Jews insist that manna fell from heaven, for so "it is written" (6:31; cf. Exod. 16:4, 15). This argument from the scriptures seems incontrovertible but is given no real attention. It is simply affirmed that not Moses but God gives the true heavenly bread, and that it is not manna but Jesus. However, identification of Jesus with the true heavenly bread is left somewhat obscure (6:33). The obscurity is intentional. Its purpose is to provoke the Jews' request, "Sir, give us that bread always" (6:34).[37] This request does not mean that the Jews now believe in Jesus. It is a statement betraying their ignorance and materialism, and belongs exactly in the same class with the Samaritan woman's request, "Sir, give me this water, so that I may not be thirsty, nor come out here to draw water" (4:15). The Jews' ignorance serves to provoke the explicit statement: "I am the life-giving bread. He who comes to me shall never be hungry, and he who believes in me shall never be thirsty" (6:35). Jesus is the true heavenly bread.

Jesus' claim that he had come down from heaven now raises the question of his origin (6:41-51). The Jews argue, "We know his parents. We know all about his origin. He

---

[37] The term χύριε, translated here as "Sir," frequently appears as "Lord" in standard translations of John. This meaning is almost certainly wrong as applied to two passages: 6:34 and 4:15. The translation "Lord" in 6:34 implies some degree of understanding and faith on the part of the Jews. But the immediate context as well as the whole Gospel fails to support this view.

might have said, 'I have come from Nazareth,' but in view of our knowledge of him, his claim to a heavenly origin is ridiculous." Jesus' reply to their incredulity is in part a reiteration of his former claim supported by the appeal to his life-giving power. But an additional element appears in vs. 44: no one comes to Jesus unless the Father draws him. Just what is involved in this being drawn to Jesus is not made clear. The evangelist perhaps feels he has left the impression that God makes himself known apart from Jesus, for he hastens to add, "Not that any one has seen the Father, except he who is from God . . ." (6:46). But the allusion to being drawn of God is clearly related to scripture (6:45), so it may mean simply that if the Jews had read it with understanding they would have been drawn to Jesus. Nevertheless, an element of determinism must be allowed the section, for the plain fact is that the Jews do not have that understanding.

The final pair of contrasting ideas begins with the startling announcement: "And the bread which I will give for the life of the world is my flesh" (6:51b). As the account reads, the allusion is to a theophagy: to obtain life one must eat the flesh of the god and drink his blood. The reaction of the disciples to this suggestion is indicated by the words: "This is a hard teaching; who can listen to it?" To them the idea is repulsive. Jesus now makes his meaning plain: "What if you were to see the Son of Man ascending where he was before? The Spirit is what gives life; the flesh is of no use" (6:62-63). It is important to get the meaning of this passage clearly in mind. What is the connection between the reference to the ascent of the Son of Man on the one hand, and the allusion to the Spirit and the flesh on the other? The thought may be expressed as follows: "Are you offended at the idea of eating the flesh and drinking the blood of the Son of Man? What, then, will be your reaction when his flesh dies? At that time there will be no flesh left to see; the Spirit alone will be left. And the Spirit is the only thing that matters; there is no profit in the flesh. But the Spirit gives life. This is the meaning of my words."

Vss. 66-71 report that the true disciples, the twelve, are screened from the total number of disciples by Jesus' harsh teachings. The Johannine equivalent of Peter's confession at Caesarea Philippi in the Synoptics is given here (6:69). It is remarkable that the title which Peter uses for Jesus is "the Holy One of God," used in Mark and in Luke by the demoniac (Mark 1:24; Luke 4:34). On the other hand, the fourth evangelist fails to identify Peter here with Satan as Mark and Matthew do (Mark 8:33; Matt. 16:23). In this omission he agrees with Luke. Our author uses the idea, however, for he speaks of Judas as a devil (6:70-71), thereby transferring the sinister description from Peter to Judas.

Polemic Against the Jews

7: 1-52–8: 12-59

CHS. 7 AND 8 SHOULD BE STUDIED AS A UNIT. THE SETTING, EXCEPT for the introductory section (7:1-9), is Jerusalem, specifically the temple, at the feast of Tabernacles. This feast provides a fitting backdrop for the drama to be enacted: The Lord whom the people were seeking came suddenly to his temple (Mal. 3:1); the customary use of water and light in the celebration of the festival find their meaning in Jesus as the source of living water —the Spirit (7:37-39) and in the great proclamation, "I am the light of the world" (8:1). Furthermore, the great historic occasion of the reading of the Torah by Ezra was on the occasion of the Feast of Tabernacles (Neh. 8:13-18). This may help explain why the most vigorous anti-Jewish polemic occurs in these chapters.

The account begins with Galilee and Judea, contrasted in terms of their respective attitudes toward Jesus. In Galilee, Jesus can go about unmolested, but not so in Judea, for there the Jews are seeking to put him to death (7:1). On the whole, in the Fourth Gospel, Galilee is friendly to Jesus (4:45), while Judea is hostile. But the hostility manifest in Judea must not be interpreted to mean that Jesus is at the mercy of the Judeans.

On the contrary, he enjoys immunity from capture until the appointed hour, an immunity which is evident on the occasion of this particular feast (7:43, 46; 8:59).

The passage opens with one of those rare occasions in our Gospel when members of Jesus' family, in this case his brothers, are present (7:3-10). His brothers' role parallels in some respects that of Jesus' mother in the first Cana episode (2:1-5); they make a suggestion which Jesus repudiates; they belong to "this world," while Jesus belongs to the higher order; finally, Jesus carries out, but in his own way, a suggestion which they have made. The mere fact that they are brothers "after the flesh" does not mean, therefore, that they have anything important in common. Since they belong to "this world" they may journey to Jerusalem knowing that they are safe. They and the Jews of Judea belong to the same fleshly order, and the kingdom of the flesh is not divided against itself. The distinction between Jesus and the world is absolute; there is no shading from one level to another through brotherly affection. This is made explicit: "For not even his brothers believed in him" (7:5). The brothers are unbelievers, and so abide like other Jews in the world of darkness. The lines are sharply drawn; blood relationship does not compensate for lack of belief. Only belief (in the Johannine sense) creates the fellowship of the Spirit.

Difficulty has been found with the reading of 7:8: "I am not going up to this feast." The difficulty is due to the fact that subsequently Jesus does go to Jerusalem (7:10). A variant reading is found in some manuscripts at this point, qualifying the negative "not" by "not yet," obviously designed to eliminate the apparent contradiction. But if one understands the fourth evangelist's literary method, the contradiction is more apparent than real. The meaning of the unqualified negative of vs. 8 is to be found in the fundamental distinction between Jesus and his brothers as belonging to two different orders of existence. For the brothers to go up to the feast means, merely, their participation as Jews in a religious festival. But for Jesus it means being lifted up on the cross, glorification, through his death.

131

Emphasis is therefore to be placed on the demonstrative adjective "this"; he will not "go up" at this particular feast. The verb "to go up," ἀναβαίνω, is in all probability an additional item intended to signify the ἀνάβασις ("the ascent") of Jesus. The implication is that he will "go up" at some future festival, which, of course, actually takes place at the Passover.

Vs. 10 shifts the scene from Galilee to Jerusalem, although Jesus himself has not yet made his appearance. The people are more concerned with the possibility of Jesus' appearance than with the events of the festival. Two appraisals of Jesus are given by them: (a) he is a good man (7:12); and (b) he misleads the people (7:12). The first is mildly complimentary, denoting the quality of belief of which some Jews were capable, but which is inadequate; the second associates Jesus with popular messianic expectations. Both views contain an element of truth: Jesus is good and he is Messiah, but the nature of his goodness and of his messiahship is completely misunderstood.

The temple becomes the setting for Jesus' appearance as a divine teacher. Here the towering figure of the One Sent from God dominates the celebration of the festival. His teaching causes the Jews to marvel: "How is this man literate when he has never had an education?" The answer is as revealing as the question in that there is no attempt to defend Jesus as the possessor of a formal educational training. Jesus' teaching is independent of the schools, for it came from God himself. In the saying "The teaching is not my own; it is from him who sent me," "my own" does not mean Jesus as a human being, a son of Joseph, but Jesus as divine, subordinate only to God (7:16; cf. 8:28). Thus, the accusation that Jesus lacked formal training is made to appear irrelevant, and the wisdom of the schools mere pedantry. In this way the writer meets the contemporary accusation that Jesus was illiterate.

But the divine origin of Jesus' teaching is not incapable of being validated. If the will of any man is in line with the will of God he will have the confirmation in himself (7:17). The ultimate test of the claims of Jesus is experience.

The events recorded in chs. 7 and 8 are dominated by controversy, first between Jesus and his brothers, and then between Jesus and the Jews. In connection with the controversy between Jesus and the Jews, the latter seize upon Jesus' question in vs. 19, "Why do you seek to put me to death?" Their desire to kill Jesus is related to the healing of the crippled man in ch. 5. There is no reason to think that this reference indicates misplacement. Jesus has interjected a reference to Moses and the law in vs. 10. It is at this point that the evangelist connects the dialogue with the incident of ch. 5. The argument runs: "Moses gave you the law. Now the law which Moses gave permits you to circumcise a man on the Sabbath if the eighth day coincides with it. Instead of cutting a man's body (as circumcision does) I made a man's whole body well, and yet you say that I broke the law and want to put me to death. You ought to judge, not superficially, but with discrimination." This represents a higher interpretation of the law than that to which its champions were willing to subscribe.[38]

This interpretation of the law leads to further speculation. First, there is the question of Jesus' freedom to speak openly. "Why do not the authorities arrest him? Perhaps they know that he is, in fact, the Christ." There is a nascent faith here, but it is not allowed to come fully to birth, for immediately doubt sets in. This man's origin is known, but that of the Christ is shrouded in mystery. The evangelist fluctuates at will between the two theories of the Messiah's origin then current. On the one hand, he uses the traditional notion that the Messiah must come from Bethlehem (7:42) based on Mal. 3:1, and, on the other hand, he resorts to the concept of a hidden Messiah 7:27; cf. Justin Martyr, *Dialogue with Trypho*, viii).

[38] One is reminded of Mark's story of Jesus and the man with the withered hand: "And they watched him carefully, to see whether he would cure him on the sabbath, that they might accuse him. And he said to the man who had the withered hand, 'Get up, and come here.' And he said to them, 'Is it right to do good or to do harm on the sabbath? to save life or to kill?' But they were silent. And he looked around at them with anger, hurt by their hardness of heart, and said to the man, 'Put out your hand.' He put it out, and his hand was restored." (Mark 3:2-5.)

In the background of the Jews' knowledge of Jesus' origin must lie the items relating to his lowly Nazareth beginning. Since they know these things, and since the origin of the Christ is unknown, the Jews hold that Jesus cannot be the Christ. In reply, Jesus says in effect: "You think you know me and my origin, but you do not. I have come from God, but, then, you do not know God either" (7:28-29).

This reply prompts the Jews to try to seize Jesus, but they cannot because his hour had not yet come (7:30). Yet an element of belief appears, though more in the form of a wistful query: "When the Christ comes, will he perform more signs than this man has performed?" (7:31). This element of belief causes an undertone of unrest among the people, and again prompts the chief priests and the Pharisees to demand Jesus' arrest. They dispatch officers to arrest him and bring him to them (7:32), but the words of Jesus about the Spirit (7:37-38) prevent the seizure. All that the officers can say in defense of their insubordination is, "No one ever spoke like this man" (7:46). Two reasons for Jesus' immunity thus appear: (a) the "higher determinism" related to his "hour"; and (b) the power of his message.

The problem of Jesus' origin and destiny is treated in the two chapters under discussion. In the earlier chapters, the problem of his origin is based largely on the misunderstanding of the Jews who invariably think of him as a Galilean, and fail to grasp the meaning of his claim to a divine origin. With ch. 7 this conflict resulting from his dual origin passes largely from the picture, and increasingly we are left with the single idea that Jesus had come from the Father and belongs to heaven. Significantly, the nearer one gets to the cross the more attention is focused on Jesus' destiny, as much an enigma to the Jews as his mysterious claims to a heavenly origin hitherto had been.

Vs. 33 introduces the problem of Jesus' destiny in words that constitute an enigma: "I am with you yet a little while, and then I am going away to him who sent me" (7:33). This causes the Jews to speculate: "Perhaps he is going to the Diaspora among the Greeks. Perhaps he will teach the Greeks." There is a similar confusion on their part in 8:21-22. In that case, Jesus' reference to "going away" leads the Jews to ask, "Will he kill himself?" In each of these speculations there is an element of truth. Jesus' "going away" will indeed bring his teaching to the Greeks (cf. 12:20-21). Similarly, his "going away" means his death, self-consciously anticipated and willingly accepted. Unwittingly, the Jews hint at fundamental truths.

One of two great proclamations of these two chapters is contained in 7:37-38; the other is in 8:12 where Jesus proclaims himself as the light of the world.

The proclamation is described in solemn fashion. On the last, the climactic day of the festival, Jesus rose up and issued his great invitation: "If any one is thirsty, let him come to me." The Johannine apocalypse provides an interesting parallel to this invitation: "The Spirit and the Bride say, 'Come,' And let him who hears say, 'Come.' And let him who is thirsty come, let him who desires take the water of life without price" (Rev. 22:17).

There is a special problem of translation at this point. The traditional rendering, for example, is followed by the Revised Standard Version: "If any one thirst, let him come to me and drink. He who believes in me, as the scripture has said, 'Out of his heart shall flow rivers of living water.'" Dodd, on the other hand, punctuates differently with the following result:

> If anyone is thirsty, let him come to me;
> And let him drink who has faith in me.

Dodd feels that this is the better punctuation.

It gives parallelism, though in a chiastic form not common in this writer. . . . It also allows the αὐτοῦ of the quotation to refer to Christ as the source of living water. The difficulty of identifying the γραφή remains, but it is at any rate no greater than that of finding a *testimonium* for the statement that the individual believer is a source of living water, an idea of which there is elsewhere no trace in this gospel, or anywhere in the New Testament.[39]

Hoskyns, after mentioning the possibility of the double punctuation, goes on to say that both meanings are wholly Johannine. He points out that in the discourse with the Samaritan woman Jesus appears as the giver of the water of life, and, at the same time, the believer himself becomes a well of water springing up unto eternal life (4:14).

The explanation of the possibility of a double punctuation and of the consequent obscurity both of the grammar and of the application of the citation is that the subsidiary meaning presses upon the primary meaning in the author's mind and this jostling causes a disturbance in the construction of the Saying. Jesus is the Savior of the World, but the mission is entrusted to His faithful disciples (21:1-17; cf. 14:12; 15:18); consequently, words which apply primarily to Jesus may also be applied to His disciples. For example, the ignorance of the Jews concerning the origin and destiny of Jesus, *ye know not whence I come or whither I go* (8:14), reappears in the ignorance concerning the nature of all who are born of the Spirit (3:8). Similarly, the metaphor of the seed dying in order that it may bring forth fruit is applied first to the death of the Christ and then to the necessity of the suffering of the believers (12:23-26.)[40]

If what Hoskyns says is true, then both ideas conveyed by the double punctuation were in the mind of the fourth evangelist, and this fact accounts for the ambiguous rendering of the passage. There can be no doubt that he held that Jesus was the *primary* source of living water. The entire Gospel supports this, and the first part of the invitation in this passage makes it clear: "If any one is thirsty, let him come to me." But it is also true that the believer becomes the possessor of eternal life, and so himself shares in the same quality of life which is suggested by the metaphor "living water." Now is this life so contained within the believer that the "spring of water gushing

[39] *Op. cit.*, p. 349, n. 2.
[40] *Op. cit.*, II, 366-67. Used by permission.

up to eternal life" (4:14) is for his own personal satisfaction, having no outlet for redemptive contact with others? It seems that the whole weight of the Gospel is against it, especially those passages which have to do with the oneness of the believer with Christ. Particularly apt, in this connection, are two passages: (a) "Just as you sent me into the world, so I send them into the world" (17:18); and (b) " 'As the Father sent me, I, too, am sending you.' When he had said this, he breathed on them, and said to them, 'Receive the holy Spirit. If you forgive the sins of any, they are forgiven, and if you retain them, they are retained.' " (20:21-23.) The second passage is, in one of its phases, a repetition of the first, but goes beyond it. The meaning seems to be this: "The Father sent me, as the Spirit, into the world, and now in the same manner I am giving you the Holy Spirit and sending you into the world. Your ability to forgive and retain sins derives from your possession of the Spirit." If this is so, then functions which in the first instance belonged to Jesus, now become functions of the disciples, so that all possessors of the Spirit, Jesus himself or others, become creative centers of life. Is it too much to say that in the Fourth Gospel, as in Gnosticism, the believer is one with the Redeemer? [41]

The invitation set forth in 7:37-38 causes a certain kind of belief on the part of the people: Perhaps he is the prophet! Perhaps he is the Christ! But the possibility that Jesus is the Christ is rejected on the grounds that he is a Galilean, while the scriptures hold that Bethlehem is to be the place of the Messiah's origin (7:42). Neverthless, the people are divided.

At this point, the officers who had been dispatched by the chief priests and Pharisees to bring Jesus to them return empty-handed. The reason for the failure of their mission is that the words of Jesus are not the words of a man. The Pharisees reject this explanation, pointing out that official Judaism has rejected Jesus' messianic claims. On the other hand, nothing better is to be expected of the mob, the amme ha-arez, who, in

[41] Cf. Irenaeus *Against Heresies* I. xxi. 4.

their willingness to find hope in Jesus, are in reality under the curse of the law of which they are ignorant (7:47-49).

In vs. 50, Nicodemus is introduced as a protagonist of Jesus' cause, though strictly in legalistic terms. He raises the question of the legality of judgment before trial. For the Pharisees this places him in the same camp with Jesus: he must be from Galilee also (7:52). These "searchers of the scriptures" (cf. 6:39) are blind to their real meaning; the limit of their horizon is indicated by the injunction, "Search and discover that no prophet is to arise from Galilee" (7:52).

The similarity between the role of Nicodemus in the Fourth Gospel and that of Gamaliel in Acts is striking (Acts 5:33-39). In Acts, the apostles are brought before the Sanhedrin; members of the council want to put them to death. But Gamaliel, a Pharisee, points out that abortive messianic movements, like those instigated by Theudas and Judas, failed. If this movement is a false one, it will likewise fail. If, on the other hand, it is of God their efforts will be fruitless, and, moreover, they might even be found opposing God. It is a bare possibility that Nicodemus represents a composite of the rich young ruler (Mark 10:17-22), as suggested by the first Nicodemus scene in John 3:1-21, and Gamaliel, and that the present scene (John 7:45-52) is a throwback of a reconstructed incident of the apostolic age into the career of Jesus.

Ch. 8 continues the dialogue between Jesus and the Jews, with Jesus occupying a more prominent role as spokesman, and culminates in a devastating attack upon the Jews.

In vs. 12 Jesus is represented as speaking to the Jews again, as if he had been present at the Nicodemus episode. His words contain the second great proclamation of this section, "I am the light of the world. He who follows me shall not walk in the darkness, but shall have the light of life." Perhaps the reference to "light," like that to "water," is called forth by ritual acts associated with the feast of Tabernacles.

Jesus' claim to be the world's light stands in sharp contrast to his teaching in the Sermon on the Mount; there, he tells his disciples that they are the light of the world (Matt. 5:14). But such a statement would be out of place in the Fourth Gospel. In it, Jesus alone possesses this distinction; the disciples possess light only as they share in the light which emanates from him.

The legalistic orientation of the Pharisees again emerges in their response to Jesus' fantastic claim to be the light of the world. They believe him to be wrong, since his testimony is legally invalid. They base their judgment on the grounds that he is testifying on his own behalf, while the law requires the testimony of independent witnesses (8:13; cf. Deut. 19:15). Jesus grants that the law stipulates such a requirement (8:17), but advances two arguments: (a) his own testimony is sufficient, for he represents a special case, having come from God himself and is destined to return to him; and (b) he possesses the required number of witnesses, himself and God. This, of course, would hardly fulfill the demands of law as interpreted by the Jews, but for the Christian church Christ and God would constitute the most excellent of possible witnesses.

This legalistic turn of the dialogue introduces the problem of judgment (8:15-16). The Jews are accused of judging Jesus purely on external evidence, κατὰ τὴν σάρκα ("after the flesh"), knowing nothing of Jesus' divine origin or destiny; that is, they know nothing of the higher world of the Spirit in which he operates. The context of his life is the eternal world, not the world of flesh in terms of which they judge him. The Jews assume the role of judges, a role which Jesus disclaims. Yet, if he were to judge, his judgment would be just because he works in association with God (8:16). Hence, any judgment he might pronounce would be the verdict of God himself.

A transition occurs with vs. 18. Jesus' reference to his Father as a witness on his behalf prompts the Jews to ask, "Where is your Father?" This allusion to Jesus' Father provides the basis for the remaining argument. The two levels of fatherhood are in the background of the account: Jesus, son of Joseph, for the Jews, and Jesus, Son of God, for Jesus himself. But of the second level

139

the Jews are ignorant (8:19). This ignorance accounts for their inability to understand Jesus' words in vss. 21-30. Jesus speaks of "going away," by which he means return to the Father. But the Jews speculate that he may be contemplating suicide (8:22). Their ignorance is due to the fact that they belong to the fleshly world of darkness (τὰ κάτω), while Jesus dwells in the world of the Spirit (τὰ ἄνω). In their bewilderment the Jews ask, "Who are you?" (8:25). The only thing that will demonstrate to their minds who he is will be the Crucifixion (8:28).

The concept of fatherhood is given a new turn in vs. 38: "I speak of the things which I have seen with my Father, and you do the things which you have heard from your father." This transfers the discussion of fatherhood from Jesus to the Jews. Three propositions are made in this respect: (a) Abraham is their father (8:39); (b) God is their Father (8:41); (c) the devil is their father (8:44). The first two are claims of the Jews themselves; the last is an accusation on the part of Jesus.

The reference to Abraham begins in vs. 33, and is the response of the Jews "who had believed in Jesus" to his words about freedom: "If you abide in my message, you are truly my disciples, and you will know the truth, and the truth will set you free" (8:32). They insist that they have never known slavery, a most remarkable statement in the light of the facts of history. But Jesus goes on to show that he is talking about slavery and freedom in relation to sin (8:34). Using the analogy of the slave, Jesus points out that deliverance from bondage can be granted only by one, the son, who belongs permanently to the household. The point is that Jesus is the divine Son of the master of the household, God, and that he alone guarantees freedom from sin.

This passage is of special interest in that it illustrates John's method of treating that massive antilegalistic element in the Synoptic sources. But between Jesus and the fourth evangelist's position lies the interpretation of Paul. Pauline ideas are clearly indicated in this section. Especially relevant are passages in Romans and Galatians which also use the analogy of the slave (Rom. 6:15-23; 8:12-17; Gal. 4:1-7, 21-31). In the thought of Jesus the stress is on the religion of inwardness as contrasted with strict adherence to the letter of the law; but in Paul it becomes a matter of freedom from law by faith in Christ. Typical of Paul's thought is the Galatian assertion: "And because you are sons, God has sent the Spirit of his Son into our hearts, crying 'Abba! (Father).' So you are no longer a slave but a son, and if a son, then, through God, an heir" (Gal. 4:6-7).

For Paul, sin and the law have a causal connection. The Fourth Gospel is less pessimistic in its view of the law. If men had understood the law, they would have known Jesus to be the Christ. The trouble with the Jews lies not merely in their relation to the law; it is more basic than that. Their trouble is rooted in their nature, and this explains why they misread the law and why they reject the light. They belong to the lower world, a world ruled over by the devil himself as the father of the sons of darkness. The figure of "darkness" is used here because it seems most appropriate to the picture of the Jews' complete separation from God (the truth) in the succeeding verses. The Jews are not children of Abraham (8:39-40); they are not children of God (8:41-42); they are, instead, children of the devil (8:44); and since the devil is a murderer, a liar, and the father of the lie, they must act in terms of the nature which they inherit. This black picture is interposed dramatically between Jesus' proclamation "I am the light of the world" (8:12) and the account of Jesus as the giver of light, set forth in the story of the giving of sight to the blind man (9:1-41).

It is important to note that the words about freedom are addressed to Jews who had believed in Jesus (8:31). As the polemic increases in intensity they fade out as prospective disciples and become one with the Jews as a whole. This sifting of disciples continues through ch. 13, when it is completed, and Jesus is left alone with the faithful remnant.

Vs. 37 picks up the statement of the Jews made in vs. 33, "We are descendants of Abraham." This idea now becomes the foil against which Jesus proceeds to show that he is God's Son.

141

Abraham and God are rejected as possible fathers of the Jews (8:39-42). They have only one father and he is the devil (8:44). In devastating language Jesus affirms that their father, the devil, was both a murderer and a liar; these are the concrete expressions of his nature. The Jews, being children of the devil, and sharing in his nature, act in accordance with that nature. The gulf between those who are of God and those who are of the devil is wide and deep! [42]

Vs. 48 is a cross reference to 7:20, where Jesus was accused of being demon-possessed. The reference to the Samaritans in conjunction with the demon indicates the connotation of the name "Samaritan" for second-century Christians. It became associated in this period with all kinds of heresy, sorcery, and magic. But the reference to the Samaritans is not carried forward as is the reference to the demon. Jesus disclaims any association with demons, insisting that he honors God, and that God will be the judge (8:48-50). Jesus' words, which prompted the accusation that he is a Samaritan and demon-possessed, are the words of God; and if anyone keeps Jesus' words he will be immortal (8:52).

This introduces a new element into the account, and confirms the suspicion that he has a demon. The Jews point again to Abraham. Abraham died; is Jesus greater than Abraham? The argument concludes: "My claim is grounded in God himself. If I were to say that I did not know God, I should be placing myself in the liar's camp with you. But I can say no such thing. Abraham himself rejoiced at my coming into the

[42] This section of the Fourth Gospel brings to its strongest focus the element of polemic aganist the Jews which infuses its pages. One finds himself wishing it were possible to read this element out of a Gospel, which in other ways calls forth his deepest admiration. But it must be allowed to remain. This anti-Jewish polemic, however, should not be equated with modern anti-Semitism, for it belongs to that period of history when the church is precariously finding its way out of its Jewish rootage, and feels called upon to isolate those factors which distinguish it from Judaism and give it the right to the status of an independent religion. In doing so it takes on the characteristic of exclusivism, partly, at least, as a mechanism of defense. The Fourth Gospel, then, is to be viewed as one expression of the anti-Jewish polemic that characterized the church during the second century and is further illustrated by Justin's Dialogue with Trypho.

142

world." Such a fantastic claim can only call forth derision: a man not half a century old claiming acquaintance with Abraham! But Jesus' reply indicates that he has a timeless existence, while Abraham was born at a certain point in time: πρὶν 'Αβραὰμ γενέσθαι ἐγὼ εἰμί: "I existed before Abraham was born" (8:58). Humanly speaking, the claim of Jesus would be an example of intolerable arrogance. But in terms of the Fourth Gospel it is the statement of one who has an absolute existence, dipping into the stream of human history for a brief, though meaningful, career, only to return to the Father by way of the cross. But for the Jews it is a blasphemous claim which no man should make with impunity. So they attempt to stone him, but Jesus enjoys the divine protection which surrounds him until the appointed hour (8:59).

Note on the *Pericope Adulterae*
7:53–8:11

THE MEANINGFUL STORY OF JESUS' MEETING WITH THE ADULTERESS was not part of the original Gospel of John. Both internal and external evidence is against it. On the side of the external evidence, it is sufficient to note that the oldest manuscripts almost unanimously omit it; the early church fathers show no knowledge of it; while some later New Testament manuscripts place it after Luke 21:38.[43]

The internal evidence is also against its authenticity. A major difference in thought exists between this story and the Gospel in its concept of sin. Sin, for the fourth evangelist, is unbelief; sinners, in the moralistic sense, do not appear in his Gospel. The *pericope adulterae* simply is not at home there.

How, then, did it find its way into the text? One answer is that some scribe interpolated it in order to counteract the implication of 7:15 that Jesus was illiterate: the story makes it plain that Jesus could write (8:6, 8). But this suggestion has little

---

[43] See Macgregor, *op. cit.*, pp. 210-11, for a good statement regarding the external evidence.

force. It is more likely that the story came in by attraction to the legal emphasis of 7:45-52. The pericope reverses the roles of Jesus and the Pharisees. In the Gospel the Pharisees assume the role of judges; in the pericope Jesus is the judge, but justice is tempered with mercy. The Pharisees, says the Gospel, judge after the flesh, while Jesus judges with just judgment. The pericope adulterae is, for the copyist, an illustration of the kind of justice administered by Jesus.

Jesus as Light-Giver
9:1-41

IT IS TO BE NOTED THAT THERE IS NO REAL BREAK IN THOUGHT between chs. 9 and 10. For convenience, however, it seems best to make a break at the end of ch. 9. There is some literary justification for this procedure. Ch. 10, beginning with the double "amen," represents a change from dialogue to monologue. Nevertheless, the close relationship of one chapter to the other must be kept in mind.

The great proclamation, "I am the light of the world" (8:12), is now given concrete expression in this story which pictures Jesus as light-giver. The proclamation is repeated in slightly different form in 9:5: "While I am in the world, I am the light of the world." The point of the sign is succinctly stated in 9:39: "I came into this world to judge so that the people who do not see may see, and that those who see may become blind." Judgment and light are associated because judgment is inherent in light. This is made evident by a similar usage in 12:27-50: Jesus is the Light, and as the Light he is to be present with men for a "little longer." But soon the Light will be withdrawn and darkness will take its place. Men must believe in the Light while it is still present so that they may become sons of Light. But in spite of the manifestation of the Light they refuse to believe. This unbelief is in fulfillment of Isaiah's words, "He has blinded their eyes and hardened their heart, lest they should see with their eyes and perceive with their heart, and turn for me to heal them." The section (12:27-50) culminates in words of Jesus which are reminiscent of the present passage: "I have come as a light into the world, that whoever believes in me may not remain in darkness." The whole section has a judicial reference.

In view of this association of judgment with light in the Gospel, it is not surprising that ch. 9 concludes with what Dodd calls a trial scene.[44] The healing of the blind man is the one sign which specifically makes Jesus the light-giver, so that the function of light to separate the believer from the unbeliever must be made clear. This is accomplished in part by the trial scene, and is carried forward under other symbols in the monologue of ch. 10.

Having indicated the general import of the chapter, we are now in a position to consider it in detail.

The sources of this story seem to be the Synoptic series which represents Jesus as *restorer* of sight to the blind (Mark 8:22-26; 10:46-52; Matt. 20:29-34; Luke 18:35-43). Mark 8:22-26 seems to have special bearing on our passage since it contains the reference to the curative power of saliva (Mark 8:23). But other elements of the story are drawn from various stories: the man was a beggar (John 9:8; cf. Mark 10:46; Luke 18:35); the proper object of praise for the gift of sight is God (John 9: 24; cf. Luke 18:43); the word ἀναβλέπω, "to receive sight" (John 9:11), belongs to the whole series of Synoptic stories of the healing of the blind. It may mean "to see again," "to recover sight," "to look up." It is not altogether suitable to the Johannine story where the man is said to have been *born* blind. The influence of the Synoptic tradition is sufficient to explain its presence, although it may be as Hoskyns suggests, that the secondary meaning, "to look up," adapts it sufficiently to the Johannine story in that the blind man "looks up" and sees the Christ and believes in him.[45]

It is of significance that the man had been blind *from birth*

[44] *Op. cit.,* p. 354.
[45] *Op. cit.,* II, 409.

(9:1). This is reminiscent of the description of the lame man at the temple gate in Acts (Acts 3:2). This original and continued blindness is descriptive of the Gospel's teaching as a whole. Men do not come into the world with the faculty of sight; it is a gift which comes to them from the outside, from Jesus. Apart from his gift of light they remain in darkness. In terms of the evangelist's thought, the Pharisees of the story are similarly blind, and their eyes are never enlightened.

The affliction of blindness leads naturally to the problem of the relation between the man's condition and sin, the man's or his parents' (9:2). Jesus' reply does not help to determine either his view or that of the evangelist on the cause of suffering. It is made clear that the man's blindness is a special case, divinely planned, in order that Jesus might reveal the works of God (9:3-4). The Synoptic Gospels, on the whole, support the position that Jesus rejected the traditional view that sin is the cause of any calamity (Luke 13:1-5; compare the implication of the healing activity of Jesus in the Synoptics which, on traditional grounds, would represent a thwarting of divine punishment. But compare also Mark 2:1-12 which seems to support the orthodox view). In any case, the present passage throws no light on Jesus' attitude toward the cause of suffering.

Nor is the evangelist's position on the problem made clear by this passage. However, 5:14 assumes the correctness of the cause and effect relationship between suffering and sin. But then that passage shows other connections with Mark 2:1-12 (e.g., the injunction to the crippled man to take up his mat and walk). We must remember that the fourth evangelist views both physical suffering and sin (unbelief) as belonging to the lower order. His view of the relationship between them must be considered close. But his thought is not centered on a cause and effect relationship in the moral sense. His concern is for belief which will free men from the lower sphere, characterized by suffering and sin, and elevate them to the realm of the Spirit. Sin as unbelief is helplessness; it is blindness. Belief, on the other hand, creates health, i.e., gives illumination. In terms of the evangelist's concept of sin as unbelief, Jesus' command to the crippled man to go and sin no more (5:14) would be a warning against return to unbelief with its resultant impotency. In both instances the evangelist uses the ancient assumption that suffering presupposes sin and assimilates it to his own religious viewpoint, excluding the moralistic approach to the problem.

The act by which the cure is effected is true to the thought of the period which believed in the curative powers of saliva. The technique of cure, however, is one of the external features of the story; it leads naturally to the "washing" at the Pool of Siloam. The word "Siloam," carefully explained as meaning "sent," is the important point. The reader of the Gospel is aware by now of the reiterated characterization of Jesus as the One Sent to give eternal life to the world. Illumination comes from washing in the water of Siloam, that is, in him whom God has sent. "Water," which is the symbol of the Spirit, gives illumination to the blind.

The movement of the story is interesting. First, there is the controversy as to the man's identity. Is he really the blind man who used to sit and beg? (9:8-9). But the uncertainty is ended by an appeal to the man himself who leaves no doubt on the matter. He says quite simply, "I am he" (9:9). Similarly, beginning with vs. 18, the Jews are pictured as questioning whether or not the man had really been blind, only to have the fact confirmed by the man's parents (9:20).

The same pragmatic kind of evidence is presented with reference to how the healing was effected. In the first place, the neighbors ask the man who it was that healed him. Forthrightly, he replies that it was "the man called Jesus," but is unable to tell them where Jesus is (9:10-12). At this point the Pharisees enter the narrative (9:13). Not yet having seen Jesus, they condemn him as a Sabbath-breaker since he healed on the Sabbath (9:16). They question the man about Jesus and evoke from him the judgment that he is a prophet (9:17). Then follows the dialogue between the Jews and the man's parents. The parents identify their son as the one who had been blind,

147

but refuse to tell how the healing had been accomplished because of fear of excommunication (9:22). This calls for a second meeting with the man who had been blind (9:24-34). The Jews exhort the man to give God, not some sinner, the praise for his cure. He replies in words which are difficult to refute since they are based on personal experience, "I do not know if he is a sinner, but I know one thing, that I was blind and now I see" (9:25).

The strength of this personal testimony confounds the Jews. They are put on the defensive. Their argument runs as follows: "You are disciples of a man whose origin is unknown! We, on the other hand, are disciples of Moses to whom God revealed himself. It is ridiculous to suppose that God has revealed himself to this impostor!" Then follows the man's reply, "Now this is a marvel! You do not know his origin, yet he gave me sight—a fact which Moses never accomplished. This is proof that he came from God." But the Jews are unable to accept such pragmatic evidence and they excommunicate him for his presumption (9:34).

The role of Jesus in all this is remarkable. One feels his presence in the background, but he appears only to heal (9:1-7), and, finally, to seek out the excommunicated man and to complete his faith (9:35-39). The interim section (9:8-34), which contains the greater part of the narrative, is structured on the role of the man himself, his neighbors, and the Jews.

The normative meaning of the sign is contained in vs. 39: "I came into this world so that the people who do not see may see, and that those who see may become blind." This makes it clear that the incident of healing is concerned, not with the giving of physical sight, but with its spiritual counterpart.

Jesus the Good Shepherd

10:1-42

To grasp the import of ch. 10 one must first of all clarify the complex of figures employed. Two explicit claims are made:

Jesus is the door (10:7); and he is the good shepherd (10:14). The sheep are the people, first Jews and secondly Gentiles as is clearly indicated by vs. 16. Contrasted with the good shepherd are the robbers, strangers, and hired men. The sheep, at first belonging to two separate folds, are to be united in one flock under one shepherd (10:16).

The interpretation of this chapter must be made in the light of the incident of the healing of the blind man. The cross reference in 10:21 makes the connection certain. The Jews figure strongly in the story of the healing and continue to be present throughout ch. 10. This would naturally make the opponents of the good shepherd the false leaders of the Jews, who claim Torah as the way to life. Scholars have seen behind the passage the scathing denunciation of the false shepherds of Israel given by Ezekiel (Ezek. 34). There is also a striking similarity of language and idea between this passage and a section of Paul's speech to the Ephesian elders (Acts 20:28-29).

One of the important problems advanced by the chapter concerns the identity of the false shepherds. They are characterized as "strangers" (10:5), "thieves and robbers" (10:8), and "hired men" (10:12). As strangers they are unable to exercise leadership; the voice of the stranger is unknown to them, so they flee from him (10:5). They do not find in his voice the familiar sound with which they associate concern, protection, and good pasture. The "thieves and robbers" are all who came before Jesus. This is a very sweeping statement and exceedingly severe if the reference is to include the great men of Hebrew history such as Abraham, Moses, and the prophets. The objective of the thief is thievery, murder, and destruction (10:10). The "hired man" is one who has no real concern for the sheep, but is concerned for his own interests. Since this is so, when danger comes he thinks only of his own safety and runs, leaving the sheep to their fate.

Jesus, on the other hand, is the Good (true) Shepherd. As the Good Shepherd, his voice is recognized by the sheep, who are content to follow him (10:3-4). In contrast to the false shep-

149

herd, Jesus does not steal, kill, or destroy; instead he gives abundant life to the sheep (10:10). He gives them this life by laying down his own (10:11). Jesus differs from the hired man in that he truly belongs to the sheep and they to him, not superficially, but in the same way that he is related to God and God to him (10:14-15).

It is to be recognized that the figure of the shepherd is mixed with that of Christ as the Door (10:1-2, 7, 9). This is an example of how readily the author moves from one symbol to another. The only access to God is through Christ, the Door; all other doors lead to destruction. But the dominant theme of the section is that Jesus is the Good Shepherd.

The problem of identifying the false shepherds still remains. In the context, one would naturally think of the Good Shepherd passage as a part of the polemic against the Jews (Pharisees) of ch. 9, and those of 10:19 ff. But the discussion moves on a level which makes this identification doubtful. The title "Good Shepherd" is equivalent to "Christ," for it is precisely the messianic problem which the monologue on the Good Shepherd raises: "If you are the Christ, tell us openly" (10:24). The competitors of Jesus, therefore, are more probably individuals within the "fold" of Judaism who advance claims to a messianic function and so operate on a level comparable to that ascribed by Christians to Jesus himself.

It must always be remembered that the milieu of the evangelist is constituted by developments of the second century, and that problems confronted by Jesus in Palestine in relation to Jewish ecclesiastical leaders of his time are, in the final analysis, secondary. These earlier problems, to be sure, form the starting point of the evangelist's presentation, but he moves away from them to deal with pressing problems of his own day. For the Christian of the second century the claims of Judaism covered not only the generalized position of a religious movement but also specific claims of leadership as represented, for example, by the movements of a Judas or a Theudas (Acts 5:33-39), and perhaps even more significantly by the claims of Bar Kokhba (cf. John 5:43).

By the time the Fourth Gospel was written it was all too well known what killing and destruction such abortive messianic movements entailed. Political in their objective, they ran headlong into the military might of the Roman Empire, and hence to destruction. The movement of Jesus, on the other hand, had a religious purpose and offered its followers eternal life.

The difference between Jesus and the false shepherds is made clear in vs. 17, an allusion to Jesus' death and resurrection. Before this, in vss. 11 and 15, Jesus had compared himself to the hired man, who, in the presence of danger, leaves the sheep and flees. Jesus, as the Good Shepherd, differs from him in that he remains with the sheep and gives his life on their behalf. But his death is only half of the story. Death, apart from resurrection, would not distinguish him from many a leader who had gone before. So it is made clear that Jesus goes *voluntarily* to his death, knowing that he has the power to take up his life again. This idea is made explicit (10:17-18). It is to be noted, however, that vss. 11 and 15, which, superficially read, refer only to the death of Jesus, contain the ideas both of death and resurrection since crucifixion is at the same time glorification. To speak of Jesus' death *and* resurrection, is to be somewhat untrue to the author's viewpoint. It is more accurate to speak of it as glorification. Jesus lays down his life *that he may take it again*. A real effort is required for the reader of the Gospel, steeped in the Synoptic tradition, to divorce tragedy from the story of the cross. But this effort is an absolute necessity for an appreciation of its function. Put positively, the cross is the instrument of eternal life and death is foreign to it. In the thought of ch. 10 the cross becomes the unifying agent, gathering together into one the followers of Jesus both from the Jewish and Gentile folds (10:16).

Vss. 19-21 are of special interest in that they reintroduce the suggestion that Jesus is demon-possessed (cf. 8:48-49). This reference to demons may reflect Mark 3:21-27 where Jesus is

151

accused of being possessed by Beelzebul (cf. Matt. 11:18; Luke 7:33). References to demons stand out in bold relief in this Gospel, for it has suppressed the tradition that Jesus was an exorcist. The absence of this strain of tradition may be part of the evangelist's effort to dissociate Jesus from magic.[46] In the present passage, the accusation that Jesus has a demon is effectively refuted by the Jews themselves. The power of his words and deeds is evidence to the contrary: "These are not the words of one who is demon-possessed. Can a demon open the eyes of the blind?" (10:21). This treatment of the problem holds in suspension the impression that, whatever else may be said, Jesus' words and deeds are not those of the demon-possessed.

The next step is to make Jesus' identity clear once more (10:22-30). Jesus is pictured walking about in the temple, in the portico (stoa) of Solomon. The setting is an interesting one. Moffatt saw here a datum for chronology and rearranged the sequence to conform to a more intelligible chronological pattern. But this is unnecessary. The whole setting is intensely dramatic: The phrase "it was winter" (10:23) gives a touch of dramatic atmosphere; Jesus is surrounded by the cold, implacable hatred of the Jews. The Feast of Dedication, celebrating the reconsecration of the temple by Judas Maccabaeus after its profanation by Antiochus Epiphanes, reminds the reader of one greater than the temple, who is indeed the true Temple, consecrated and sent into the world by the Father (10:36). In the reference to Solomon's portico we may see an attempt to elevate Jesus in terms of wisdom, giving greater weight to his utterance, and affirming that one "greater than Solomon is here" (Matt. 12:42; cf. Acts 3:11; 5:12). It is in this place that the Jews encircle him, giving the impression that he is trapped, but later on, when they try to arrest him, he escapes from their hands (10:39).

The question which the Jews put to Jesus is strange if viewed as history: "How long will you keep us in suspense? If you are the Christ, tell us openly" (10:24). In reply, Jesus refers both

[46] E. C. Colwell, *John Defends the Gospel* (New York: Willett, Clark & Company, 1936), pp. 17-31.

to his words and his works. But these manifestations of his messianic character cannot be expected to produce belief on their part, for they "do not belong to his sheep" (10:26). His sheep respond to his voice, he gives them eternal life and continuing protection from seizure by others. The reason for this is that they are God's gift to him, and God's power is supreme (10:25-29). Then follows the important pronouncement, "I and the Father are one" (10:30).

This pronouncement belongs to a series of arresting statements which stand out in bold relief against the background of Gospel material. Examples may be cited:

My Father is working until now, and I am working also. (5:17.)

I am the life-giving bread. He who comes to me shall never be hungry, and he who believes in me shall never be thirsty. (6:35.)

You know me, and you know where I am from? And I have not come of my own accord, but he who sent me is true, whom you do not know. I know him, because I am from him, and he sent me. (7:28-29.)

If any one is thirsty, let him come to me; and let him drink who believes in me. As the scripture said, "Out of his belly shall flow streams of life-giving water." (7:37-38.)

I am the light of the world. He who follows me shall not walk about in the darkness, but shall have the light of life. (8:12.)

Amen, amen, I tell you, I existed before Abraham was born. (8:58.)

I am the Resurrection and the Life; he who believes in me, though he were dead, yet he shall live, and whoever is alive and believes in me shall never die. (11:25-26.)

He who has seen me has seen the Father. (14:9.)

Two passages (10:30 and 14:9) make explicit the oneness of Jesus with God. A question arises concerning the nature of this unity. Some commentators consider it to be ethical in character. A unity of will is intended rather than of essence and personality.[47] But this fails to take into account the clear distinction between those aspects of the Synoptic picture of Jesus

[47] Macgregor, op. cit., p. 241.

where moral struggle is evident, and the Johannine picture from which all such struggle is absent. In spite of the fact that we have come to view the Synoptics as closer to John than was formerly supposed, there is still a vast difference in this respect between John's Jesus and the Jesus of the Synoptics. In the former case there is no drag of the flesh on the divine Spirit resulting in the weighing of alternative courses of action, the steeling of the will to the accomplishment of high purpose in the presence of danger. Jesus speaks, and acts, and is, because he has come forth from God as the divine Spirit, one in essence with the Father, though maintaining a separate existence. One can put it thus: Jesus is not God (in the sense of *the* God, i.e., in the sense that the Father is God), but he came from God (ἀπὸ τοῦ θεοῦ), where ἀπὸ denotes departure from God, and is of God (ἐκ τοῦ θεοῦ) where ἐκ signifies origin. "He had His origin in the being of the Father." [48]

If, on the other hand, the problem of Jesus' unity is correlated with the Gospel's view of the descent of the Spirit, the nature of this unity becomes clear. God's Spirit is sent out by and from God, and while it does not exhaust the being of God, it is nonetheless a projection of his being. It is subordinate to God since its function is revelatory only, though revelation itself, when appropriated by faith (a kind of vision) produces the same quality of life enjoyed by the Spirit. It is this oneness of essential life which is expressed by the statement, "I and the Father are one." Similarly, the followers of Jesus, on whom the Spirit is to be bestowed after Jesus' death, participate in the divine Spirit and are, by virtue of the fact, lifted out of the lower to the higher world to be in union with Christ and God. This explains the interlacing of God, Jesus, and the disciples which is the outstanding characteristic of ch. 17, a chapter which may be described as a treatise on the nature of Christian unity.

In the progress of the story, 10:30 has a transitional function, inviting controversy. It is therefore seized upon by the Jews as constituting a blasphemous claim: Jesus, a man, makes himself

[48] Dodd, *op. cit.*, p. 259.

a god (10:33). Since he has committed the crime of blasphemy he deserves to die by stoning (10:31-33). The informal nature of the intended stoning suggests that the evangelist's knowledge of (or perhaps interest in) the formal and legal aspects of the Jewish punitive system was no greater than that of the writer of Luke-Acts (Acts 7:57-58).

Jesus' reply to the charge of blasphemy is an example of a method of exegesis common in the period. It is often termed the "rabbinical method," but its usage extended far beyond rabbinical circles, and was used extensively by the Christian apologists. In the present connection, the method has the advantage of putting the Jews on the defensive by appeal to their own authoritative writings. The argument may be summed up as follows: "In your law [the term is used in its broader reference to include the whole body of scripture] there is a particular passage which calls men gods, and scripture cannot be controverted. Why then do you accuse me of blasphemy, one whom God himself has consecrated and sent into the world? My claim to be the Son of God is demonstrated by the works which I perform. If you cannot believe me, believe them, for they are revelations of the Father."

Of course the Jews could hardly be expected to accept the premise that Jesus had been consecrated by the Father. The argument might be convincing to Christians, but certainly not to Jews. The argument is from the lesser to the greater, from men to the Son of God. If men are called gods in the sacred writings, how much more valid is the term when applied to him who is God-sent.

Vss. 40-41 introduce the final reference to John the Baptist. Jesus retires to the place across the Jordan where John used to baptize. Even when John himself is off stage, he is utilized indirectly to suggest the greater mission and success of Jesus. John is now completely eclipsed by Jesus. The people recall how John had performed no signs, but that his testimony about Jesus was unmistakably true. This belief in Jesus as the Son of God counterbalances the unbelief and antagonism of the Jews. The

Gospel writer is too loyal a Christian, and his concept of Jesus too lofty, for him to leave the impression at the close of this important episode that the best Jesus could do was to create unbelief.

Jesus as Life-Giver

11:1-44

THE STORY OF THE RAISING OF LAZARUS IS GENERALLY RECOGNIZED as of prime importance both as a self-contained unit setting forth a fundamental aspect of the Gospel's teaching, and as a functional element designed to assist its structural development. Its primary emphasis as a story is on Jesus as the giver of eternal life, while in relation to the Gospel as a whole it climaxes the series of signs and becomes the incident which leads to Jesus' death on the cross.

In the Synoptic Gospels the "inciting incident" is Jesus' radical action in the temple, commonly called the Cleansing of the Temple (Mark 11:15-17; Matt. 21:12-13; Luke 19:45-46). But, as we have seen, the fourth evangelist has transposed this event to the opening phase of Jesus' ministry and adapted it to his own purposes.[49] But why, we may ask, did the evangelist choose to substitute this particular story for that of the Cleansing? It may be observed that the meaning which he gives the Cleansing episode has much in common with the story of the Raising of Lazarus. He had made it clear in that episode that the ultimate sign of Jesus' messianic authority is his death and resurrection. Now both death and resurrection are present in the Lazarus narrative also. The great difference is that in the Cleansing story Jesus' death and resurrection constitute the major theme, while the Lazarus story has to do with the death and resurrection of another. But this does not mean that attention in the latter story is centered on Lazarus; the point is that Jesus gives life to the dead man. In other words, the inciting factor is not merely Jesus' claim to messianic status, even though under-

[49] Supra, pp. 89-91.

scored by reference to his ability to die and rise again; it is that Jesus demonstrates his ability *to give life to others*, and that he does for men what Judaism is powerless to accomplish. The death-resurrection of Jesus by itself would mean little. But death-resurrection of other men based on the death-resurrection of Jesus, that is to say, on the power which makes it possible, has social consequences.

The story of the Raising of Lazarus, then, becomes a dramatic illustration of the power of Christianity to give life, whereas (as the church would claim) Judaism was impotent. The fourth evangelist has lifted the "religion of legalism—religion of the spirit" antithesis, which is at home in the Synoptics, to a new level. As Loisy has put it:

The essence of the matter lies, not in the miracle as such, but in the truth it offers to belief, truth which the miracle is intended to drive home and make good. Nothing else really counts. The work of raising a dead body to life is but the guarantee of a work with importance of another and higher kind, the universal and final work of raising humanity to life in the Spirit.[50]

When viewed against this background, the hostile action of the Jews, citizens of the lower world, becomes understandable. Two kingdoms stand in opposition, one of light, the other of darkness or, to change the figure, the army of Satan is in the act of invading the kingdom of light. This invasion results in the apparent downfall of that kingdom, and with its destruction its power is likewise destroyed. But the kingdom of light is eternal, and the efforts of men to destroy it prove to be futile; indeed they become an instrument in the furthering of its expansion. The source of life must be destroyed, and finally, to their own satisfaction, they accomplish their aim.

The story seems to have its literary base primarily in Luke. Luke has the story of Mary and Martha (Luke 10:38-42), where Martha is pictured as an activist, while Mary sits at the feet of

[50] *Op. cit.*, p. 214.

157

Jesus. These characteristics are retained by John (11:20). Luke locates the sisters in "a village." Our author identifies this village with Bethany, probably on the basis of Mark 14:3 or Matt. 26:6 since he later equates the woman of the anointing story with Mary of the Lazarus episode (12:1-3).

With these Synoptic elements the evangelist combines others taken from the parable of the Rich Man and Lazarus (Luke 16:19-31). Chief among these is Lazarus. In the parable he is characterized as a poor man who had died and gone to Abraham's bosom. The rich man, who at his death had gone to Hades, pleads with "father Abraham" to send Lazarus to earth to warn his "five brothers" of the torments of Hades. But this request is rejected on the grounds that if they do not hear Moses and the prophets neither will they be persuaded if someone should rise from the dead (Luke 16:31). The story is an open invitation to a creative mind to accept the suggestion: to have Lazarus actually rise from the dead, and to demonstrate the terrible consequences of rejection.

It has already been noted that the evangelist does two important things with the Lucan suggestion: (a) he makes the story a demonstration of Jesus as the resurrection and the life (11:25); and (b) he makes the resurrection of Lazarus the basis of Jewish opposition leading to Jesus' death. The first idea is not inherent in the Lucan account, although the church may have used the story as anti-Jewish polemic. But given the concept of Jesus as the life which the Gospel has repeatedly asserted, an adaptation of the Lucan story in this regard would not be difficult.

It may be objected that Johannine dependence on the Lucan parable breaks down since 11:45 asserts that many of the Jews believed in Jesus as a result of the miracle. But belief of this sort is not to be taken too seriously. It will scarcely stand the test of "abiding belief" which the evangelist makes normative (8:31). More weighty still is the evidence for unbelief and rejection set forth clearly in the reference to the peoples' blind eyes and hard hearts (12:40). The most that can be said about the element of belief contingent on the resurrection of Lazarus is that it is part of a persistent strain of temporary, and consequently not real, belief. At any rate, this "belief" is a minor factor when compared with the vast weight of unbelief which inexorably leads to the cross. It is the fact of the cross, not the element of untested belief, which the story envisages. The argument against John's use of the Lucan story is therefore unconvincing.

Other features of the story may be drawn from the Synoptic accounts of the raising of Jairus' daughter (Mark 5:22-24, 35-43) and the young man at Nain (Luke 7:11-17).

As the story goes, a man named Lazarus of Bethany is ill. Bethany is described as the home of the sisters, Martha and Mary; the sick man is their brother. Mary is identified by a cross reference as the one who anointed Jesus' feet with ointment (11:2), an incident which has not yet taken place in our Gospel but is nonetheless brought into close relation with the story of the Raising of Lazarus (12:1-8, note especially vss. 1-2). It could be argued that the story of the anointing has been misplaced, but this seems unnecessary. It is more probable that the evangelist, when writing the Lazarus story, had the story of the anointing in mind with the intention of using it at a later point in his Gospel. It is to the tradition, held in abeyance in the author's mind, that the reference applies.

The sisters send word to Jesus of Lazarus' illness. Jesus' response parallels that made in 9:3, where the blind man's affliction is said to exist so that "God's work might be made evident." Here, Lazarus' illness (and subsequent death) is for the purpose of glorifying the Son of God (11:4). There is therefore no hint of sorrow on the part of Jesus when he receives the message. This lack of interest in Lazarus' misfortune is heightened by the characterization of Lazarus as the one whom Jesus loves (11:3). In this may be seen a striking feature of the Johannine sign. Where, normally, we should expect concern on Jesus' part for grief-stricken people and for the misfortune of a friend, attention is centered, not on them, but

159

on Jesus, and even then not on his concern, pity, or compassion, but on his nature, more fundamental than any of its attributes. This feature is a constant in the Fourth Gospel. Never does the evangelist allow ethical aspects of the person of Jesus, no matter how important, to swerve him from his concern with the basic issue of Jesus as revealer of God: the glory which Jesus reveals is God's glory and is revealed in terms of Life.

Nevertheless, we are not permitted to lose sight of the fact that Jesus loves the three members of this Bethany family (11:3, 5). Two purposes are served by this reminder: (a) it highlights the deliberateness with which Jesus responds to the implied request that he go to Lazarus' side (11:6, 17, 30); and (b) it gives credence to the Jews' belief that Jesus' tears (11:36) were due to his love for Lazarus.

The first of these functions is of particular interest and illustrates John's superb literary skill as well as his religious insight. The point is this: What need is there for feverish haste, when in the midst of all this confusion, bewilderment, and sorrow, walks the Giver of Life himself? One would normally expect that Jesus, the friend of this unhappy family, would, on receipt of the message, rush immediately to his side. But instead we read, "When he heard that he was sick, he remained two days in the place where he was" (11:6). Jesus is far removed from the panic and disruption which sickness and death produce. But, certainly, there is no intention to suggest that God has no regard for those in desperate straits. The teaching is entirely in the opposite direction. Men of genuine faith in the ultimate preservation of spiritual values, in the underlying goodness of God, display a kind of detachment from the disrupting aspects of human experience. The Fourth Gospel, with its emphasis on the higher order of reality, the realm of eternal life, thinks of that order and that realm as lifting men above the temporal to the eternal order with a corresponding serenity of soul; they have overcome the world. At such a point, and in such

160

a manner, the Fourth Gospel makes contact with human experience.

In vs. 7 Jesus announces to his disciples his intention to return to Judea. The disciples protest in view of the recent attempt on his life (10:31-33). This prompts the enigmatic statement, "Are there not twelve hours in the day? If any one walks about in the day, he does not stumble, because he sees the light of this world. But if one walks about in the night he stumbles, because he has no light" (11:10-11). Jesus' hour has not yet arrived, and so both he and his disciples can go safely into Judea. The argument is that the disciples have no need for fear while Jesus is with them, for there is an appointed hour for his death. But at the end of the "twelve hours" of the day, the period reserved for Jesus' work, the light will be withdrawn (cf. 8:12; 9:4b-5; 12:35-36; 12:46).

In the sequence of the narrative, Jesus now announces to his disciples that Lazarus has "fallen asleep," and that he is going to "awaken" him (11:11). This is the sort of play on words in which the evangelist delights.[51] In Greek, as in English, "to fall asleep" has a double meaning; literally, "to take natural rest in sleep," and secondly, "to die." Biblical passages which support this are Matt. 27:52, Acts 7:60, I Thess. 4:13, and I Cor. 15:6. But the evangelist makes it plain that Jesus was referring to Lazarus' death (11:13). And as a follow-up on vs. 4, Jesus explains that he is glad he was not with Lazarus (the implication being that had he been there Lazarus would not have died; the presence of the Life would have prevented it), for the death of Lazarus will lead to their belief (11:15).

The introduction of Thomas in vs. 16 with his courageous exhortation, "Let us go also, that we may die with him," emphasizes the element of danger first introduced in vs. 8. The attentive reader of the Gospel knows that Thomas is right on one score and wrong on another. He is right in expecting danger in Judea, not only on the basis of past events but even more

---

[51] The Greek word κεκοίμηται, translated "has fallen asleep," also provides the derivation of the word "cemetery."

on the basis of the raising of Lazarus which is to take place. But Thomas is wrong in thinking that the disciples can be in danger so long as Jesus is with them. They cannot "die with him," for they are under divine protection (11:9; 17:12; 18:8-9).

The evangelist leaves no doubt as to the miraculous character of the deed which Jesus is about to perform. On his arrival at Bethany, Jesus finds that Lazarus has been in the tomb four days (11:17). Any doubt as to the authenticity of the miracle, such as that attaching to the story of the raising of Jairus' daughter (Mark 5:39), is completely removed. Lazarus is dead beyond the shadow of a doubt!

The remainder of the story is in three episodes: (a) the meeting of Jesus with Martha (11:20-27); (b) the meeting of Jesus with Mary and the mourning Jews (11:28-37); (c) the scene at the tomb: the raising of Lazarus (11:38-44).

In connection with the first of these, Martha (true to her character in the Synoptics) goes out to meet Jesus. It is interesting that here Martha plays a more prominent role than Mary, the reverse of the Lucan story. Her more aggressive disposition serves the evangelist in good stead, for he has her take the lead in hastening to Jesus with her despairing words (11:20-21). But the winsome character of Mary is not to be totally neglected. Her role as a prominent character is reserved, however, for the story of the anointing (12:1-8).

Martha greets Jesus with the words, "Lord, if you had been here, my brother would not have died, and now I know that whatever you ask of God, he will give you" (11:21-22). Jesus' reply sounds thoroughly conventional, but it is another of those characteristic statements which is capable of conveying a radically different meaning. Martha, playing the part of the representative of orthodox Judaism, declares her belief in the resurrection of her brother at the last day (11:24). So Jesus clarifies his statement in words which indicate clearly the revolutionary reconstruction of eschatology advanced by the evangelist: "I am the Resurrection and the Life; he who believes in me, though he were dead, yet shall he live, and whoever is alive and believes

162

in me shall never die" (11:25). This affirmation is the main burden, not only of this particular story, but of the Gospel generally (cf. 20:30-31). In vs. 27 Martha professes belief.

The second episode (11:28-37) is introduced by the words of Martha to Mary: "The Teacher is here, and is calling for you" (11:28). The word "teacher" seems strange in view of the fact that Martha has just acknowledged Jesus as Christ and Son of God, but probably the title is used to suggest the authority of Jesus[52] and does not imply reversion to a lower level of faith. The reference to Jesus as having asked for Mary implies unexpressed action which has taken place off stage. It serves as the connecting link between the first episode and the second, now being considered.

This second episode is of interest in that Mary, whom we would expect to play a role parallel to that of Martha, fades into the background. Mary finds Jesus in the same place where Martha had met him (his speed is provokingly slow), and addresses him with the identical words used by her sister in the first instance (11:32; cf. 11:21). These are the only words spoken by Mary in the entire story. Her function is served, not by a conversation with Jesus, but (a) by her tears (11:33), and (b) by the association with her of the mourning Jews (11:31, 33-37).

The Jews enter in vs. 31. They are in the house with Mary, consoling her. Their attention being centered on the loss of a brother and a friend, they think that Mary's exit means she is going to the tomb to weep there. They follow her to her meeting place with Jesus. Then follows a scene in which the emotion of grief is paramount. In vss. 33-35 it is made to appear that Jesus himself has joined in the general expression of grief over Lazarus' death. But the reader of the Gospel knows better (or should know better by now!), for it has been made plain repeatedly, under one symbol or another, that Jesus is life and that death cannot stand in his presence. At the very beginning of the story

[52] R. H. Strachan, The Fourth Gospel (3rd ed. rev.; New York: The Macmillan Co., 1942), pp. 236-37.

we were told that Lazarus' illness was not to result in death, but in the glorification of the Son of God (11:4).

It is evident, therefore, that the violent emotion of Jesus is due to something other than the loss of a friend. It should be observed that Jesus is deeply moved in the Spirit *when he sees the tears of Mary and the Jews* (11:33), that is to say, where he has been unmoved by the knowledge of Lazarus' death, he is now deeply moved when he sees the expression of grief on the part of the people. The point is that their grief reveals their belief in the finality of death: grief and unbelief belong together. The Jews' explanation of Jesus' tears, while reasonable from the point of view of human life unrelieved by hope of immortality, is inadequate from the standpoint of the Gospel, whose whole emphasis is on the gift of eternal life through Jesus. Jesus' tears are the tears of God in the presence of the great evil, unbelief, while the very Life himself abides in their midst. The contrast is great: on the one side there is sickness, death, grief, tears, the tomb, a putrefying corpse, and unbelief; and on the other side, the calm, deliberate, reassuring, and life-giving presence and power of the Son of God.

The third of our episodes, the scene at the tomb (11:38-44), contains the story of the actual raising of Lazarus. The story of the resurrection proper is brief. There is a contrast between natural repugnance at the prospect of seeing a corrupt human body, and the promise of beholding the glory of God (11:39-40); there is the prayer of Jesus for the sake of the onlookers (11:41-42); and then comes the miracle itself (11:43-44).

The form of the story, as a whole, is interesting. There is no discourse based upon the miracle. Dodd points out that we are to see in this *pericope* a "special variation upon the regular Johannine pattern of sign + discourse." [53] The closest approximation to the usual discourse based on miracle is found in the dialogue with the disciples (11:7-16), and especially in the dialogue with Martha (11:21-27) in which occurs the central teaching on the Resurrection and the Life (11:25). It seems

[53] *Op. cit.*, p. 363.

164

that the placing of the central thought of the story *prior* to the miracle is artistic. The declaration of Jesus as the Life comes first, confirmation second; the miracle will follow as naturally as the day follows the night. The sequel, declaration-confirmation, belongs to the same subtle artistic pattern as the deliberate motion of Jesus toward the tomb; it serves to heighten the impression of Jesus as irresistible Life, moving confidently to the confirmation of an announced fact, the certainty of which is a foregone conclusion.

Caiaphas Speaks Ex Cathedra
11:45-57

THE DESIGNATION "INCITING INCIDENT" IS, IN A SENSE, FAIR enough as applied to the Raising of Lazarus. But its sequel introduces a response other than that of antagonism. The reference is to the ex-cathedra utterance of the high priest, Caiaphas (11:50). Vs. 53, "So from that day they planned to kill Jesus," should be read as the logical result of Caiaphas' inspired words. The death of Jesus is a necessity if the Jewish nation and people, both at home and abroad, are to be preserved. Exactly how important a part this motivation plays in the passion narrative as a whole is a question, but that the evangelist had it in mind when he wrote the trial scene is demonstrated by 18:14: "It was Caiaphas who counseled with the Jews that it was to their advantage for one man to die for the people." Probably the author intended a mixed motivation, for enmity has been present far earlier in the account than Caiaphas' announcement. However, even in their general animosity toward Jesus, the Jews are unconsciously furthering the purposes of God. Ultimately, the actions of the Jews are controlled from the outside in such a manner that Jesus is preserved from being the mere victim of misguided or evil men.

The utterance of Caiaphas is oracular rather than the reasoned statement of an individual Jew, and, doubtless, is meant to be as mystifying to him as to his fellow Jews. From their point of view, the oracular announcement would mean the preservation of the Jewish nation (cf. 11:48) and of Diaspora Jews. But a deeper meaning lies embedded in the words than the preservation of Jews from military disaster at the hands of Rome. The Christian would see here a reference to ch. 10 where a distinction is made between the sheep of the fold of Judaism and the sheep of another fold, the two to be united as one flock under one shepherd (10:16). In other words, the oracle of Caiaphas predicts the redemptive function of the cross.[54]

Vss. 45-57 are unified by the pervasive element of opposition. There are three divisions: 11:45-53; 11:54; and 11:55-57. They must be considered as the prelude to the Crucifixion, but also flow naturally from the story of the Raising of Lazarus. The first, the Caiaphas incident, provides an additional motivation for opposition, while the second results from it: Jesus withdraws to the country near the desert, to a place called Ephraim (11:54). Macgregor holds that "this sojourn in the desert compensates for the omission from our Gospel of the 'Temptation,'" and asks, "Would not Jesus be facing precisely the same problems?" Macgregor's question is rhetorical, and anticipates the answer "Yes." But an affirmative answer is scarcely justified in the light of the Gospel's picture of Jesus. To put another rhetorical question, Where in the Fourth Gospel is Jesus ever put to the test? It is more likely that Jesus' withdrawal to the region near the desert, to the town of Ephraim, is a phase of the divine protective plan, designed to keep Jesus safe until his hour has come—that, and nothing more.

Vss. 55-57 continue the element of Jewish opposition. It is near the time of the Passover, and people from the country are

---

[54] The representation of Caiaphas as "high priest that year" (11:49, 51; 18:13) is often taken to be an indication of the evangelist's gross ignorance of the Jewish system in which the office of high priest was for life, not an annual appointment. Perhaps the explanation of Hoskyns is best: what the evangelist "wishes to emphasize is that the office of Caiaphas coincided with the year of the salvation of the world, and that this coincidence evoked a prophetic utterance from the High Priest of that year under the constraining power of God himself." Hoskyns, op. cit., II, 480-81. See infra, pp. 212-14.

flocking to Jerusalem. But their real concern is whether or not Jesus will come to the Passover feast (11:55-56). Vs. 57 makes it clear that if Jesus is seen by anyone he must be reported to the authorities. This directive is of special interest since it refers to the actual Passover when Jesus is to die. The orders of the authorities are ultimately carried out by Judas who leads the soldiers to the garden (18:1-3). But this action is delayed; first, by the significant events of ch. 12, and secondly, by Jesus' meeting with hs own (chs. 13–17).

The Anointing
12:1-11

THIS INCIDENT AND THAT OF THE ENTRY INTO JERUSALEM ARE related to the Raising of Lazarus by cross references (12:9, 17). Coming as they do after the great hostility-producing sign, and preceding the coming of the Greeks (12:20-21) with the consequent announcement that the hour of glorification has arrived (12:23), these events must be conceived as standing in vital relation to the Cross. Ch. 12 serves as a meaningful interlude between the two great divisions of the book; the one dealing with Jesus as the Spirit which gives light and life; the other, under the immediate glory of the Cross, setting forth his continuing, intimate, and creative fellowship with his own. The story of the anointing, in delicate and solemn manner, anticipates his burial (death), while the entry into Jerusalem interprets his final visit in terms of victory. So understood, the latter complements the former.

The setting of the anointing is Bethany, the natural inference being that the dinner took place at the home of Jesus' three friends: Martha, Mary, and Lazarus. The time is six days before the Passover, that is, six days before Jesus is to die. Jesus is indeed invading dangerous territory, not only because of the nearness of Bethany to Jerusalem, but also because Lazarus is present, and he is evidence of Jesus' life-giving power. This is pointed out forcibly in vss. 9-11. Jesus' enemies intend to destroy both the giver of life and evidence of the fact.

The Johannine story of the anointing is a composite of the Synoptic accounts (Mark 14:3-9; Matt. 26:6-13; Luke 7:37-38, plus Luke 10:38-42). The location at Bethany is drawn from Mark-Matthew; the two women come from the Lucan story of Mary and Martha (Luke 10:38-42, note especially vss. 39-40); the ointment is common to the three Synoptic accounts, although the dependence seems to be on Mark-Matthew for the particular form (John 12:3; cf. Mark 14:3; Matt. 26:7); the protest at the waste of expensive ointment is drawn from Mark-Matthew, although the specific reference to three hundred denarii suggests its Marcan origin (John 12:5; cf. Mark 14:5); the anointing of the feet (rather than the head) is taken from Luke (John 12:3; cf. Luke 7:38); the reference to the poor (John 12:8) is more clearly akin to Matthew than to Mark (Matt. 26:11).

The additions and changes introduced are as follows: a change in time reference (John 12:1; cf. Mark 14:1); identification of the unnamed woman of the Synoptics with the Mary of the Lazarus episode (John 11:1-44), itself dependent, in this connection, on Luke 10:38-42; the presence of Lazarus (12:1-2); identification of Judas as the one who protests about the waste of expensive ointment and his characterization as a thief (John 12:4; cf. Mark 14:4; Matt. 26:8); inclusion of the phrase, "And the house was filled with the fragrance of the ointment" (John 12:3).

The story represents an amazingly complex, yet artistic, blending of materials from the earlier stories with new and apparently original additions. These are combined to form a story completely at home in its new setting. It may be noted, however, that the story in any of its Synoptic forms is readily adaptable to Johannine usage, since it centers attention on Jesus as the object of love and devotion.

The account of the anointing falls into two parts: (a) the anointing proper (12:1-3); and (b) Judas' protest and Jesus' response (12:4-7). The stress, in the first instance, falls on 12:3b:

"And the house was filled with the fragrance of the ointment." This is undoubtedly symbolic, and we may assume that it takes the place of the Synoptic statement which makes the anointing a universal memorial to the woman's devotion (Mark 14:9; Matt. 26:13). But John removes the reference from the woman's act of devotion and uses it, instead, to symbolize the universalizing of the Spirit of Jesus.[55]

In the second division (12:4-8), the stress falls on vss. 7-8, especially on vs. 7, while vs. 8 reinforces the importance of devotion to Jesus while he is with them, an idea which appears in vss. 35-36. The translation of vs. 7 is difficult. It may be translated, "Let her alone, so that she may keep it for the day of my burial," "Permit her to keep it for the day of my burial," "Let her alone. Let her keep it for the day of my burial," or, if the reading of the received text is accepted, "Let her alone. She has kept it for the day of my burial." It is probable that the wording is intentionally obscure in line with the cryptic symbolism employed. The anointing is a symbolic preparation of the body of Jesus for burial. Hoskyns, following Lagrange, thinks that the *Textus Receptus* has adequately preserved the original meaning of the passage by removing its grammatical obscurities.[56] There is no reason to draw the conclusion that the phrase, "Let her keep it for the day of my burial," refers to an unused portion of the ointment. The ointment has already been used; hence the protest of Judas.

We may see in this story another example of the sign. It has the usual characteristics of the sign: the external act, the inner meaning, focus of attention upon Jesus, and misunderstanding on the part of an individual who is concerned merely with externals. In one important detail, however, it differs from all the rest. In the other signs it is Jesus who carries on the action: changes water into wine, cleanses the temple, heals the sick,

---

[55] For ointment as a symbol of the universalizing process, see Walter Bauer, *Das Johannesevangelium* (Tübingen: J. C. B. Mohr, 1912), p. 118; Hoskyns, op. cit., II, 484-85; Strachan, op. cit., p. 248.

[56] *Op. cit.*, II, 486-87.

multiplies the loaves, walks on the water, gives sight to the blind, raises the dead, and washes the disciples' feet. In this case, on the contrary, the action is carried on by a second party. But the difference can be easily overstressed. It is to be noted that Jesus, not Mary, explains the meaning of the act, and that attention is not concentrated on the loving act of devotion, but on the death of Jesus, and its universalizing function. This is thoroughly consonant with the Johannine sign.

It may be said that ch. 12 presents a symbolic enactment of the death, the victory over death, and the result which accrues from these, as indicated by the anointing, the entry into Jerusalem, and the coming of the Greeks, respectively. This chapter, therefore, anticipates the great drama of salvation. The anointing, standing as it does in strategic relation to this drama, plays a part very similar to the Changing of the Water into Wine. As in the earlier story, there is an anticipation of the cross with its new religious consequences, and in each instance a series of events is inaugurated. But the anointing expresses a mood much more in keeping with the imminence of the climactic event.

The Victorious King
12:12-19

THE DRAMATIC ACCOUNT OF THE ENTRY INTO JERUSALEM EMphasizes (a) the kingship of Jesus (12:13-15); and (b) that Jesus irresistibly draws all men to himself (12:19).

It may also be observed that just as the anointing parallels the Changing of the Water into Wine (2:1-11),[57] so the Triumphal Entry parallels the Cleansing of the Temple (2:13-22), the latter anticipating Jesus' death and resurrection. However, the parallels are not exact on every score. The anointing centers attention both on Jesus' death and on the diffusion of the Spirit, while the Changing of the Water into Wine stresses the idea of the Spirit which Jesus' death will make available. Simi-

[57] *Supra*, p. 170.

larly, the Triumphal Entry interprets the Jerusalem events of the last days as victorious, while the Cleansing of the Temple is content to prefigure death and resurrection without any qualitative remark.

It is not clear whether the evangelist intended the crowd's acclamation to be with true discernment or to have a superficial, political meaning which would place Jesus in the category of a messianic aspirant to the throne. It is to be observed that the people who hail him king are not Jerusalemites, but pilgrims who have come up to the feast (12:12). This might add weight to the correctness of the former alternative, since Jerusalemite Jews are more likely to be considered hostile. It is more likely, however, that the evangelist intended the people's zeal to be an expression of popular messianic expectations, and that Jesus' voluntary acceptance of the role is an example of giving a higher meaning to a political category. This is exactly what is done later. When Pilate questions Jesus regarding his kingly claims (18:33-38), the former assumes political ambition on Jesus' part. But Jesus, while not denying the aptness of the title "king," insists that his kingship is not of this world; he is king of the realm of Truth (18:36-38). We may believe, therefore, that King Jesus of the Triumphal Entry has accepted kingship in a sense higher than the crowd could discern, and only understood by the disciples themselves after his triumph had become an accomplished fact (12:16).

The scene is one of acclamation of a victorious king of Israel. The people's cry (12:13) is from Ps. 118:25-26, to which has been added the Lucan element of kingship (Luke 19:38). The palm branches underscore the note of victory (Rev. 7:9; I Macc. 13:51; II Macc. 10:7) and appear only in the Johannine version of the story. The appearance of Jesus riding on the ass (he does not send for the animal, but simply "finds" it conveniently at hand; cf. Mark 11:2-7; Matt. 21:1-7; Luke 19:29-35) is an open fulfillment (in Johannine terms) of Zechariah's prophecy (Zech. 9:9). But the evangelist, in contrast to Matt. 21:5, omits any reference to humility on Jesus' part. Strachan has rightly pointed

171

out that the picture of Jesus riding into the city on a young ass is not a suggestion of humility, but of kingship, specifically of messianic kingship.[58] The two crowds, one acclaiming him king (12:12-13) and the other bearing witness to the event, represent approaches to the meaning of Jesus. For one group he is a political Messiah, while for the other he is Life-giver. The second crowd had been present when he raised Lazarus from the dead (12:17). But this is only to say that the messiahship of Jesus is not in terms of the traditional expectation represented by crowd number one, but in terms of Life, as witnessed by crowd number two. The reader of the Gospel, knowing of the persistent and consistent misunderstanding of the real meaning of events, is aware that the only one on the scene who knows the full import of the action is Jesus himself. Even the disciples are not to understand until Jesus' glorification takes place (12:16).

The action of the crowd provokes the Pharisees to exclaim in despair, "See, you gain nothing; look, the world has gone out after him" (12:19). Their words carry meaning far beyond their original intent, for the entry into Jerusalem of the victorious King, symbolic of the victory of life over death, brings the whole world to Jesus' feet. This is symbolized in the sequel by the coming of the Greeks (12:20) and made explicit in an expression of the magnetic power of the Cross: "And when I am lifted up from the earth, I will draw all men to myself" (12:32).

The Coming of the Greeks

12: 20-36a

THE BRIEF REFERENCE TO THE COMING OF THE GREEKS MARKS an important step in the development of the narrative. It represents the parting of the ways between Jews and non-Jews, and parallels the development of Christianity itself in its movement

[58] *Op. cit.*, p. 251.

172

away from its Jewish matrix. Placed as it is in the midst of the momentous events of ch. 12, at the end of the Book of Signs (Dodd's term), and just before Jesus turns to his own (13:1), it marks the great watershed in the drama. Since the Gospel was written after the break between Judaism and Christianity, we may suppose that the coming of the Greeks is an example of later developments being read back into the lifetime of Jesus, and that it symbolizes the universalizing process attendant on the death and resurrection of Jesus.

This "watershed" is dramatically stated in Acts (13:46-48) where Paul and Barnabas are represented as addressing the Jews of Pisidian Antioch:

The word of God had to be spoken to you first, but since you reject it, and judge yourselves unworthy of eternal life, see, we turn to the Gentiles. For thus the Lord commanded us, "I have made you for a light to the Gentiles, that you may be the means of salvation to the ends of the earth."

What the author of Acts does by the narration of events the fourth evangelist accomplishes symbolically, and relates the break closely to the Crucifixion and Resurrection. This symbolic method permits the Greeks to fade from the picture as quickly as they appear. Their further presence is not required since the *implications* of their arrival become the content of the discourse in vss. 22-36.

Jesus learns of the arrival of the Greeks by a circuitous route: the Greeks to Philip; Philip to Andrew; Andrew and Philip to Jesus (12:21-22). The language and form are reminiscent of the call of the disciples in 1:43-45. Perhaps this is intended to suggest the "call" of new Gentile disciples, though it would be more appropriate to speak of it as an attraction than as a call. Appropriately enough, the disciples involved in mediating to Jesus the information of the Greeks' revival are Philip and Andrew, the only disciples of Jesus to have Greek names. Philip, the more prominent of the two, is probably confused (perhap'

173

intentionally) with the evangelist of the same name in Acts. There, he is pictured as prominent in the Gentile mission (Acts 8:5 ff.).

The Greeks' request, "Sir, we wish to see Jesus," is directly joined with Jesus' announcement that the hour of his glorification has arrived (12:21-23). A deeper meaning than a mere desire to visit Jesus is contained in the words; the Greeks wish to see Jesus in reality, a "seeing" which is given them through the glorification which is now announced. Thus, while in terms of the story there is no account of their meeting Jesus, the announcement of his exaltation on the cross is a far deeper answer to their request, for Jesus will become available to them without limitations of incarnation, in the full burst of eternal life (12:24-25).

A reflection of the Synoptic Gethsemane scene begins with vs. 27. But it is a faint reflection. In the Synoptics, Jesus prays that, if possible, the cup might be removed (Mark 14:36; Matt. 26:39; Luke 22:42). In the Fourth Gospel he questions, in effect, the appropriateness of that prayer and rejects it since his death is the fulfillment of the divine purpose (12:27). There is a prayer here, to be sure, but it is that God's name might be glorified (12:28). There is also a lofty detachment from the impending events: God's voice is heard, not for Jesus' sake but for the crowd's (12:30).

Yet the section begins with the words "Now my soul is troubled" (12:27). Is this the same thing as the conflict in Gethsemane? It should be observed that it is the soul ($\psi\nu\chi\acute{\eta}$) that is troubled, and that it is due to the fact that he has now entered the period when he will lose his life ($\psi\nu\chi\acute{\eta}$). This disturbance differs from that mentioned in the Lazarus story (11:36, 38), in that the latter relates to his Spirit ($\pi\nu\epsilon\tilde{\nu}\mu\alpha$). But here the Spirit is not disturbed. In the Lazarus story the disturbance of the Spirit is due to the unbelief of the people, but in the later story where $\psi\nu\chi\acute{\eta}$ is involved, distress is due to the impending hour: $\pi\nu\epsilon\tilde{\nu}\mu\alpha$ cannot be destroyed, but $\psi\nu\chi\acute{\eta}$ is subject to death (12:24-

174

25). One must find here a reflection, however weak, of the Gethsemane incident.

The reference to the cross is made plain in vs. 32. The verb ὑψόω contains a double meaning: (a) "to lift up," as from the ground, and so applies to the lifting up of Jesus on the cross; and (b) "to exalt," and so becomes descriptive of the glorification of the Son of Man. It is important to grasp the full implication of this interpretation of the cross. In the Fourth Gospel the cross is in no sense a tragedy for Jesus or for those who believe in him. It is tragedy only for those who reject him, and these people stand in the background ready to bring rejection to its conclusion by demanding his death.

Isaiah's Prophecy Fulfilled
12:36b-50

THIS SECTION PRESENTS US WITH THE BEST ILLUSTRATION OF THE element of predestination in the Fourth Gospel. The evangelist represents Isaiah as having had Jesus in mind when he uttered his words regarding the unbelief of the people (12:38-41). The Old Testament passages are drawn from the famous servant passage (Isa. 53:1) and Isaiah's temple vision (Isa. 6:9-10) in their Septuagint form. Their position at the end of the first great division of the Gospel makes them most effective as the clinching argument as to why the Jews reject the revelation in Jesus. In spite of all the signs that Jesus performed, they had failed to believe in him. In this unbelief the evangelist finds the precise fulfillment of prophecy.

The element of predestination raises the whole question of freedom of the will. Attempts have been made to relieve John of any iron-clad doctrine. Macgregor has pointed out that "John expresses himself as if it were not the coming event which prompted the prediction but the prediction which determined the event." [59]

[59] Op. cit., p. 271.

175

The meaning of the prophecy is then that the Christ revealed to the prophet that God would blind the eyes of the Jews lest they should perceive the significance of His miracles, and He (the Christ) would then of necessity heal them, and consequently obscure the judgement of God upon unbelief.[60]

Hoskyns realizes that this appears like "a naked doctrine of predestination," but he does not think that this is the evangelist's intention. Johannine language prompts a controversy on predestination, not the reverse:

Throughout his gospel the author insists that, though the life and death of Jesus was for the salvation of the world, this very fact involved the ultimate judgment of God upon those who rejected Him. It is the clear recognition of the alternative of judgment or salvation that provides the acute tension which runs throughout his narrative from beginning to end. The Jews did reject Jesus, and consequently they remain dead in their sins (8:21, 24) and under the judgment of God (v. 48). The Jews are manifestly culpable, since the Evangelist has recorded the mission of Jesus in such a manner as to exclude the thought that it was impossible for them to recognize Him as the Son of God. The purpose of his final summary of the public ministry of Jesus is not to deny the whole tenor of his narrative, but to point out that the rejection of the Messiah by His own people ought not to surprise those familiar with the Old Testament Scriptures. He therefore sees in the foresight of the prophet Isaiah the foresight of God Himself; and, in accordance with the natural instinct of those who are filled with the sense of the power of God (6:44), teaching concerning divine foresight passes over into the expression of the inevitability of that which is foreseen. Hence he ends his summary with a glaring paradox: *For this cause they could not believe. . . . Nevertheless even of the rulers many believed on him. . . .* And this is no naked doctrine of predestination.[61]

Hoskyns' statement is a good attempt to preserve freedom of choice for the Jews of our Gospel. And it must be admitted

[60] Hoskyns, *op. cit.*, II, 502.
[61] *Ibid.*, II, 502-3.

that the persistent reference to judgment is strange unless freedom of choice is allowed. But it seems that the fourth evangelist cannot be relieved of the paradox by attributing his concept of Jewish unbelief to the foresight of God himself. The evangelist makes it clear that it is *impossible* for the Jews to believe since they are sons of the devil and so belong to an order of existence which has no point of contact with the higher order of reality.

It is better to explain the contradiction as a reflection of the confused position of the church itself relative to the problem of the Jewish rejection. On the one hand, the Jews stood condemned for their failure to recognize Jesus as the Christ, and, on the other hand, they were instrumental in bringing the divine drama of salvation to its conclusion. It was, of course, precisely at the point of the Cross that the problem became most acute. The Christian church was hard pressed to explain the relation of the Cross to the messianic claim from any point of view. Perhaps one of the earliest (and kindest) explanations is given in Acts where Peter tells the Jews that they acted in ignorance (Acts 3:17). For Paul, too, the problem was acute, and he struggled with it in any agony of spirit. His answer contains an element of hope: the Jews will finally be saved (Rom. 9-11). It is noteworthy that Paul quotes the Old Testament, notably Isaiah, in his effort to explain the rejection, Rom. 11:7-8 having much in common with the Johannine passage under discussion. By the time the Synoptics were written, the Isaiah passage (Isa. 6:9-10) had become a standard item of Christian apologetic. The Fourth Gospel merely carries forward a practice already established in the church. So conceived, the determinism of the Fourth Gospel is a phase of the wide practice of the church in finding all developments relating to Jesus' career in the Old Testament.

But along with the proof-texting of Jewish unbelief went the psychological antagonism of a group remembering the painful events which took place at the first, together with the animosities of competing religious movements having peculiar relationships one to the other. This spirit is given extreme expression in the language of ch. 8 of our Gospel. This means that the determinism of the Fourth Gospel is not a reasoned, well-calculated, interpretation of Jewish unbelief in terms of the omniscience of God, but, at least in part, an emotional reaction on the part of a man who felt keenly the impact of adverse historical circumstances on the Person and Fellowship to which he had given his allegiance.

This is but to say that the evangelist *starts* with the problem of the Jewish rejection; then he reacts to it, explaining it in terms of scriptural prediction on the one hand, and on the other forthrightly condemning it as the great evil. It is doubtful if he went so far as to attempt a reasoned, not to say philosophical, reconciliation of the two positions. But if he did, Hoskyns' position seems to be the most probable solution.

In part, our author's problem grows out of his estimate of the person of Jesus. Jesus comes before us in these pages as the Light of the World, resplendent in his glory. The evangelist thinks of him as a divine being possessing an almost irresistible attraction. This causes him to inject into his narrative an element of belief on the part of the Jews—even Jewish authorities (12:42), though one is never sure that this belief is permanent (12:43). But it is to this level of their ability to believe that judgment on the Jews properly belongs.

In the over-all picture, the main emphasis of the Gospel is on the judgment which results from rejection. This element of judgment brings ch. 12, and, indeed, the first great section of the Gospel, to its conclusion (12:44-50). The judgment, which is the result of unbelief, is introduced by the phrase, "But Jesus cried out," not merely by the conventional "Jesus said," as if to make it a most important proclamation (12:44; cf. 7:37). The main points are as follows: (a) belief in Jesus is belief in God (12:44); (b) seeing Jesus is the same as seeing God (12:45); (c) Jesus has come into the world as a light; the relief of the darkness takes place by belief in Jesus (12:46);

178

(d) the function of Jesus is not to judge the world but to save it (12:47); (e) men who reject Jesus will be judged on the last day by the message which he has spoken, for his message comes from God himself (12:48-49); (f) belief in the message of Jesus, the character of which has been ordered by God, results in eternal life (12:50).

These verses add nothing new. But their concentration at this particular juncture in the story lends them weight which, singly, they do not possess. The reader knows that this is the last solemn warning to an unbelieving world before the final act of unbelief, the act of crucifying the Son of God.

The Acid Test of Discipleship
13:1-38

WITH CH. 13 WE PASS FROM THE CONFLICT AREA OF THE GOSPEL to the farewell discourses of Jesus to his own disciples, with a corresponding change of mood. As James Drummond put it:

We pass now into the quiet retreats of private and sacred fellowship. . . . From the symbolic act of humility and love to the sublime prayer of consecration, we are in a region of holy peace and lofty communion, in which we have transcended the limits of the world and time, and have entered that eternal life which flows for ever from the Father upon those who apprehend in faith the spirit of the Son.[62]

Any breakdown of the Discourses is in a sense artificial. They all seem to flow from the act which stands at the beginning, namely, the Washing of the Disciples' Feet. After this, the discourse is broken by dialogue only at 14:5-9, 14:22-23, 16: 17-19, and 16:29-31. Yet each chapter could stand by itself, with the major themes being stated at the beginning: "Let not your hearts be troubled" (14:1), "I am the true vine and my Father

[62] An Inquiry into the Character and Authorship of the Fourth Gospel (London: Williams & Norgate, 1903), pp. 5-6.

is the vinedresser" (15:1), "I have said all these things to keep you from falling away" (16:1), "when Jesus had spoken these words, he lifted up his eyes to heaven and said . . ." (17:1). One gains the impression from reading them that they might well have been composed separately and that their present arrangement is highly artificial. Various hypotheses have been formulated to account for this impression, such as the work of a redactor or the accidental displacement of pages. The highly repetitious character of much of the material would perhaps support some such hypothesis. If we were dealing with an ordinary book, these literary phenomena would naturally lead to a redactional or displacement hypothesis. But the Fourth Gospel is no ordinary book! We are dealing with an author who cares little for logical or chronological arrangement, though that does not mean that he has no concept of literary arrangement. It merely means that his idea of development is not ours.

C. H. Dodd points out that "the thought of the Farewell Discourses has taken shape in a form which reproduces broadly a standard Johannine pattern, though here it is elaborated on an unparalleled scale." [63] That pattern is action, dialogue, monologue, appendix; it is evident in the "signs" section, and is paralleled here by the feet washing (13:1-30), dialogue on Christ's departure and return (13:31–14:31), discourse on Christ and his church (chs. 15–16), and the prayer of Christ (ch. 17).

Dodd resolves the thorny problem (which he recognizes as such) of 14:31, "Rise, let us go hence," by explaining it as "a movement of the Spirit, an interior act of will," and it is paralleled in 16:33 with an announcement of victory: "the attack and the victory are both upon the inward, spiritual plan." [64] Dodd's argument regarding the structure of the Discourses seems generally sound, but his explanation of 14:31 as a movement of the spirit is not convincing. Ch. 14 is the one section of the Gospel which provides strong grounds for the theory of displace-

[63] Op. cit., p. 400.
[64] Ibid., pp. 409-16. Dodd's whole discussion of the Farewell Discourses (pp. 390-423) is most helpful.

ment. Perhaps no reconstruction of sequence is now possible, but the summons to his disciples, "Rise, let us go hence," would be a very natural prelude to the events of 18:1 ff. Further-more, features of ch. 15 relate it closely to the symbolic cleansing of ch. 13 as will be seen. A tentative reconstruction might be suggested as follows: ch. 13 to be followed by chs. 15, 16, 17, 14, and 18. Dodd feels that "to place anything at all after xvii. 26 would be to create an intolerable anticlimax." [65] But is this necessarily the case? Ch. 14, with its strong element of encouragement—"Let not your hearts be troubled," "Peace I leave with you," etc.—would not at all be out of place immediately preceding the arrest. Moreover, vss. 30-31 (in spite of Dodd's insistence to the contrary) suggest the imminence of Jesus' meeting with the "ruler of this world": "I will not talk with you much more, for the ruler of this world is coming. He has no control over me; but that the world may know that I love the Father, and that I do what he commanded, rise, let us go hence." Ch. 18 is the fitting complement of this movement of Jesus. This concept of the imminence of his arrest would have little weight in a Gospel where the end is frequently proleptically conceived, were it not for the injunction, "Rise, let us go hence," which gives more precise meaning to vs. 30: "I will no longer talk much with you, for the ruler of this world is coming." This is the final action (the hour) which the whole Gospel account has been anticipating. As the ruler of this world advances, the Ruler of the realm of truth goes forth to meet him.

The story of Jesus washing the disciples' feet presents a baffling episode in John's interpretation of Jesus. For one thing, it appears out of character for the divine being of the Fourth Gospel to assume the role of a slave. And there is the further question as to why the evangelist would substitute this kind of story for the sacrament of the Lord's Supper.

Macgregor summarizes his position on the incident as follows:

[65] *Ibid.*, p. 407.

181

The incident of the washing of the disciples' feet takes in our Gospel the place occupied in the Synoptics by the institution of the Lord's Supper. . . . It is held by some that the Evangelist is a mystic who puts no value on Sacraments (cf. 4:2), surely a strange misreading of the mind of the man who could write 3:5 ["Unless one is born of water and the Spirit, he cannot enter the Kingdom of God"] and 6:52-58 [containing Jesus' words, "Unless you eat the flesh of the Son of Man and drink his blood, you have no life in you"]. Rather may we explain the omission by John's desire to detach his sacramental teaching from any historical occasion and attach it to the eternal realities of the Spirit. In particular John wishes to connect the Sacrament less with Christ's death and more with his life-giving power. Hence, in chapter 6 the institution is associated with the life-giving miracle of the feeding of the multitude, while the place held in the Synoptics by the institution is here filled by the feet-washing, which symbolizes not Christ's death but his spirit of lowly service. This suggests that once again John wishes to counteract superstitious sacramentalism: just as in 6:63 he insists that "what gives life is the Spirit," so in 13:8, 15 does he insist that the Sacraments can be effective only when the Spirit of the Master possesses the disciples. The bequest which Jesus left his disciples in the Sacrament was not a ritual ordinance but a spirit of love and service which would unite them in fellowship one with another and with himself and would be the badge of their discipleship (13:34 f.). John here emphasizes the ethical aspect of the Lord's Supper, the neglect of which renders impossible the appropriation of that undying love of Jesus which in the Sacraments we symbolize: "Unless I wash you," says Jesus, "you will not share my lot." [66]

There are several weaknesses in Macgregor's argument. The major weakness lies in his insistence on Johannine sacramentalism. It has been argued elsewhere[67] that the absence of the Lord's Supper may itself be a part of the evangelist's rebuttal of the sacramental position. If one views the discourse on the Bread of Life as a unit it becomes another item in the non-sacramental point of view. Emphasis on the flesh and blood

[66] Op. cit., pp. 272-73.
[67] Colwell and Titus, op. cit., p. 51.

passage (6:53) is due to an erroneous verse-by-verse interpretation of the Gospel. The final, and representative, position of the evangelist comes at the end of the discourse and its emphasis is on the Spirit—flesh profits nothing (6:63). Macgregor also fails to mention that water baptism, minimized as John's baptism, will yield to baptism in the Holy Spirit (1:33). Finally, no sacramentalist could say that the Spirit, like the wind, is unpredictable in its action. The sacramentalist knows precisely where and when the Spirit operates; namely, in the sacrament itself.

A second weakness in Macgregor's position is found in his assertion that the Lord's Supper is omitted from the Fourth Gospel because John wished to connect the Sacrament "less with Christ's death and more with his life-giving power"; hence, its removal to the earlier position in ch. 6. This position fails to take into account the nature and function of the cross in our Gospel. Crucifixion for the fourth evangelist is not tragedy but glorification. *The nearer one comes to the cross the nearer he is to life, not death.* The cross does not militate against the life-giving power of Jesus; rather, it is the instrument which releases that power into the world.

It appears that we need to look at the story from a different perspective. The major fallacy in many interpretations grows out of the symbol "water" which is employed. The tendency is to leap to the conclusion that this means baptism. C. H. Dodd says (in relation to ch. 13) that the "attentive reader of the Book of Signs will be aware that 'water' is the instrument of regeneration." [68] He bases this on one passage (3:5), "Unless one is born of water and the Spirit, he cannot see the kingdom of God," not taking into account that in the subsequent verses no reference is made to water but that the entire concern of the writer is with the Spirit.

We may perhaps start with the assumption that the washing of the disciples' feet is a "sign" in the Johannine sense that the bodily event carries an inner and spiritual meaning. This sign

[68] *Op. cit.*, p. 402.

differs from those in what Dodd calls the Book of Signs (chs. 2–12) in that, while they were performed in the presence of outsiders, this one is enacted in the presence of the disciples and on their behalf. This fact would tend to veer the teaching in a direction relative to the concerns of the church. And inasmuch as in the narrative of John, from ch. 13 on, the cross looms as central, it is evident that this sign is related to the church's concern with the meaning of the cross.

As one reads the account, one fact stands out clearly: Jesus voluntarily takes upon himself the role of a slave. It is true that Jesus is still aware that he is the disciples' Teacher and Lord (13:13)—the evangelist would not let his readers lose sight of that fact—but that is just the point! It was Jesus their Lord who had served when he might have ruled. Now behind this picture of Jesus one may discern the problem of the Cross for the early Christian church. Paul speaks of the Crucifixion as a stumbling-block to Jews and as folly to non-Jews. But to believers it is both "the power of God and the wisdom of God" (I Cor. 1:23, 24). Most of all, however, we are reminded of the famous Philippians passage (2:1-11) in which the divine pre-existent being, who might have grasped equality with God, chose rather to humble himself by assuming human form and submitting to death by crucifixion, the result being exaltation to the status of Lord.

There are two terms, both Johannine, which have special significance when brought in relation to ch. 13. These are καταβαίνω ("to go down") and ἀναβαίνω ("to go up"). The descent of the Spirit is clearly a κατάβασις ("a descent"), while exaltation on the cross is an ἀνάβασις ("an ascent"). In the Philippians passage, mentioned above, Paul seems to view Jesus' death by crucifixion as the lowest stage in the κατάβασις. Jesus' exaltation was an act of God based on his willingness to die so ignominious a death. But it is different in John. The κατάβασις seems to consist merely in the descent, the incarnation. There is, however, a sense in which it continues through the period of his involvement with the men of this world, that is, through the Signs-section of the Gospel. But when Jesus turns to his own followers, the section introduced by ch. 13, it is different. Now, the cross is anticipated; and not as a continuation of his κατάβασις but as the beginning of his ἀνάβασις—his return to the Father. The ascent has already begun!

The problem, so far as the early Christians were concerned, was due to the nature of crucifixion itself. How could they possibly vest this with religious meaning? It was the greatest possible distance removed from an act signifying deity. A slave might be crucified but not a god!

The author of the Fourth Gospel addresses himself to this problem. He well knew the historical connotations of crucifixion. He also knew the problem of the first disciples and of the church in this respect. In his presentation he reverses the ordinary estimate of Jesus' crucifixion. This is the way God operates! And this, too, is the way the disciples must operate if they are to remain his followers. Not that there is anything inherently God-like in crucifixion as such. But in Jesus' case the love of God was behind it. What men conceived as a shameful death was in reality the supreme demonstration of God's love for the world. Henceforth, then, the signature of discipleship must be that men love one another as Jesus loved them. Servanthood is elevated to the level of divinity.

But in the early stages of the story the disciples do not see this. This failure to understand accounts for Peter's protest, "You shall never wash my feet!" (13:8). So far, however, there emerges one important element: the divine servanthood of Jesus, symbolized by the washing of the feet, and made dramatically real by the Christian remembrance that he had died.

But this symbol is carried still further in vss. 12-17. Here it is explicitly stated that Jesus has set an example for his disciples to follow. Going behind the externals of the story, this means that they, too, are to give themselves in service. We are reminded of Paul's words, "Have this mind among yourselves, which you have in Christ Jesus" (Phil. 2:5). So a second

185

aspect of the story emerges: Jesus' followers must be servants also.

Now it was precisely this lesson that the church found difficult to learn. Men would rather be masters than servants; an attitude reflected by the Synoptic tradition in Peter's rebuke to Jesus on his announcement of his coming death, "God forbid, Lord! This shall never happen to you" (Matt. 16:22), and in the wistful reflection of the men of the Emmaus road, "We had hoped that he was the one to redeem Israel" (Luke 24:21).

But the problem became acute at the point of human relations within the fellowship itself. One might speculate about the meaning of the cross, and even find in it a demonstration of divine love. But to put the principle into operation in one's own relationships, and, at the same time, to see in it an expression of the divine life is infinitely more difficult. It is easy to view the Cross (literally or symbolically conceived) in purely mundane terms. The Jews of the Fourth Gospel did this, and, according to the evangelist, missed its divine glory. The disciples were in danger of doing the same thing. Ability to understand the principle of divine servanthood is the acid test of discipleship.

Several Synoptic passages may be in the background of the evangelist's thinking at this point. Mark relates how James and John came to Jesus asking for places at his right and at his left in his glory. Jesus then called the disciples to him and admonished them with these words:

You know that those who are supposed to rule the Gentiles lord it over them, and their great men exercise authority over them. But it is not that way with you; but whoever would be great among you shall be your servant, and whoever would be first among you must be a slave of all. (Mark 10:42-44.)

Probably the most pertinent passage is the Lucan parallel to Mark 10:42-45. It is placed in Luke in relation to the Last Supper:

186

Now a dispute occurred among them as to which one of them was regarded as greatest. But he said to them, "The kings of the Gentiles lord it over them, and their authorities are called benefactors. But it is not that way with you. Rather, let the greatest among you be as the youngest, and the ruler as the servant. For who is greater, the one who reclines at table or the one who serves? Is it not the one who reclines at table? *But I am among you as the one who serves.*" (Luke 22:24-27.)

The cleansing effect of Jesus' words is indicated in the Johannine story by the encounter of Jesus with Peter in 13:6 ff. Peter is near the borderline of exclusion from the group. Perhaps the Gospel writer is influenced here by Peter's protest at the idea that the Son of Man must suffer as reflected in Mark 8:32 and parallels, but probably more particularly by the denial of Peter at the time of the Crucifixion. An allusion to the denial is made explicitly in 13:38.

The cleansing effect of the call to service may also account for the fact that Judas goes out from the circle of believers at this time. It is true that the Fourth Gospel does not have Judas betray Jesus for thirty pieces of silver. But it is also true that Judas is characterized in this Gospel, and in this Gospel only, as the one who protested at the seeming waste of the precious ointment at the time of the anointing. In that story Judas is mentioned as a thief who stole money from the common treasury (12:1-8). On the one hand, Judas is predestined to "betray" Jesus as an act of divine Providence; and, on the other hand, Judas is unfit for the fellowship. It is in terms of the latter that Judas is purged, or, rather, purges himself from the group.

It may be, too, that the appearance of "the disciple whom Jesus loved" at this point in the account is related to the same theme of cleansing. If it is true, as Bultmann holds, that he is a symbol of Gentile Christianity, this possibility is strengthened; the whole church is symbolically present at this most solemn occasion.[69]

---

[69] *Infra*, pp. 237-38.

We have called the washing of the disciples' feet a symbolic act, signifying the cleansing power of servanthood. But it should be pointed out that it is servanthood expressed in terms of love. The context strongly underscores this: "By this all men will know that you are my disciples, if you have love for one another" (13:35). It may even lead to the giving of one's life even as Jesus gave his: "Greater love has no man than this, that a man lay down his life for his friends" (15:13). We are again confronted with the cross as the supreme demonstration of divine love.

A similar idea of the cleansing of the group of unworthy members is propounded in ch. 15; there, however, by the use of allegory. God is the vinedresser, Jesus is the vine, and the disciples are the branches. Fruitless branches are cut off. Fruit-bearing branches are cleansed that they might be still more fruitful. It is noteworthy that the word translated "cleansed" (15:2b) is καθαίρω. The word is then used in the next verse and related by a cross reference to ch. 13: "You are already made clean [καθαροί] by the word which I have spoken to you." The cross reference is a natural one in view of the fact that the Gospel writer interjects the word καθαρός ("clean") into the context of the pruning of the branches—a place where it ordinarily would not be used— indicating once more his interest in the symbol. Both ch. 13 and ch. 15 have to do with the cleansing process by which the true church is defined. The differences between them lie in the tests of discipleship which are employed and in the literary techniques. Just as love for the brotherhood is the test in ch. 13, so in the later chapter it is religious fruitfulness. And whereas in ch. 13 the literary technique is the "sign," in ch. 15 it is allegory. But the association between the two chapters is close and it may be that they belong together and that ch. 14 has been misplaced.[70]

One implication of this interpretation is that the Fourth Gospel, at least at this point, is not so far from the Synoptics in its thought of Jesus as we have sometimes held. This is true

[70] *Supra*, pp. 180-81.

188

only as one penetrates to the inner meaning, but it is there that the evangelist's view of Jesus is to be found in any case.

If what has been said of the meaning of this story is true, then it follows that the fourth evangelist wrote it with the historical Jesus in mind. That is to say, he knew full well that Jesus had given himself in death and that his death had been interpreted in terms of shame and disgrace; he knew also that the disciples had tended to shrink from association with one who had so died. It then becomes his task to interpret this death in other terms. What he does is to exalt the self-givingness of Jesus to the level of the divine. He, too, could have said that the man who humbles himself shall be exalted, and the man who exalts himself shall be abased. To give oneself in service is, humanly speaking, abasement, but to the mind of Jesus and God it is exaltation. The great power of the Fourth Gospel, in large part, lies in this, that ordinary human judgments are reversed so that the shame and degradation of the cross are seen as the glory of the divine.

Words of Promise and Reassurance

14:1-31

CH. 14 IS CONCERNED WITH THE THEME OF JESUS' DEPARTURE— his "going away." The inner disturbance which coming events will bring about is anticipated (14:1, 18, 27), and words of assurance are given the disciples. The historical facts surrounding the Crucifixion are in the background of this material—the grim fact of crucifixion itself, the fear of the disciples, and their flight (Mark 14:50). John now makes it plain that the meaning of these events is clear to the mind of Jesus, and that the Resurrection will not only make their meaning plain to the disciples (14:26) but will also illuminate the words of Jesus so as to show that he was no victim of circumstances (14:25-29).

In view of Jesus' imminent departure, reassurance is given the disciples in the following terms: (a) Jesus' departure will eventuate in their abiding relationship with Jesus in their Father's house (14:1-3); (b) Jesus is the Way to the Father (14:4-7);

(c) Jesus is the revelation of the Father (14:8-11); (d) Jesus' departure will mean greater power for the disciples (14:12-14); (e) Jesus' departure will mean the coming of the Helper who will take the place of his visible presence (14:16-29).

Paradoxically, the separation of Jesus from his followers means an eternal fellowship: he goes to prepare a place for them so that they may dwell with him forever. There is therefore no reason for their hearts to be disturbed; indeed, his departure should be an occasion for rejoicing (14:1, 28). The "abiding-places" (vs. 2) are to be interpreted in the light of the Gospel's teaching on the mystical relationship between the disciples and the risen Christ (or, more properly, the Spirit), which can become a reality only through the Cross. The disciples will dwell in him, and he in them, a relationship which constitutes eternal life.

The characterization of Jesus as the Way is initiated by a transition verse (14:4): "And you know the way where I am going." The incredulity of the disciples now takes the place of the unbelief of the Jews. Thomas, no less than the Jews who had formerly thought of his references to "going away" as either a journey to the Diaspora (7:33-35) or as suicide (8:21-22), is ignorant of his intention: "Lord, we do not know where you are going; how do we know the way?" (14:5). One is reminded of the description of Christianity as "the Way" in Acts (9:2; 19:9, 23; 22:4; 24:22); but the evangelist makes Chirst himself, not the institution, the way to God. Bauer thinks that the language and ideas used here have come into the Fourth Gospel from Hellenistic syncretism and oriental mythology.[71] Hoskyns, on the other hand, feels that the Christian background is itself sufficient to explain the language, citing Rom. 5:2; Eph. 2:13, 18; 3:15; I Pet. 2:2; 3:18; Heb. 7:25; 10:19-21, as well as Acts.[72] Perhaps it is better to assume that our author drew mainly from Christian tradition as Hoskyns suggests, but the popular concept of the journey of the soul would certainly rein-

[71] Op. cit., p. 135.
[72] Op. cit., II, 536-37.

force it, and make it more attractive to the Hellenistic world. The religious exclusivism of the Fourth Gospel is indicated by vs. 6: "No one comes to the Father except through me." The verse raises the whole question of the evangelist's thought relative to the knowableness of God before the coming of Jesus. Is there a doctrine here of the θεὸς ἄγνωστος ("unknown God"), which was a feature of gnosticism? The question cannot be dismissed lightly. Dodd refuses to grant the possibility on the grounds that "it is implied that God (through the Logos) is present in the world." [73] But this is an illustration of the danger of reading the Logos idea into the thought of the Gospel as a whole. In any case, it is a highly questionable interpretation of the Prologue. It seems impossible to find an example of knowledge of God in our Gospel which is not dependent on Jesus; the whole emphasis is on the fact that, apart from Jesus, God remains unknown. If this raises a problem with respect to the efficacy of Hebrew life and thought as represented in the Old Testament, we must remember that, for our author, the Old Testament *speaks about* Jesus; it does not carry God's revelation of himself (5:46). There is no weakening of the dualism of light and darkness by the assertion that a pervasive Reason or Word is available to men apart from Jesus. Light and darkness lie at opposite poles and may be bridged only by the redeeming activity of the Son of God. That such redemption has taken place is made evident by vs. 7: "From now on you know him, and you have seen him," an assertion which is reminiscent of 1:18: "No one has ever seen God; the only Son who is in the Father's bosom has made him known."

Thus, Jesus as the Way leads inevitably to the concept of Jesus as the Revelation. The ignorance of Philip parallels that of Thomas (14:8; cf. vs. 5). In spite of the fact that the disciples have been living with the Revelation, they have not been able to apprehend it. It is not necessary to assume that the question of Jesus, "Have I been with you so long, and yet you do

[73] *Op. cit.*, p. 156.

191

not know me, Philip?" is rhetorical, and requires the answer, "of course not," as Dodd suggests.[74] The point is that the disciples are not yet in the full light of the resurrection faith and their understanding of the meaning of their Lord is partial and fragmentary; they still retain some of the characteristics of the sons of darkness (1:49-50; 2:22; 6:5-6; 12:16; 13:6-10, 29-30; 14: 22; 16:4, 5, 6, 17-18, 29-32; 18:15-18, 25-27). The point which the evangelist makes is that the mighty events—career, crucifixion, resurrection, the giving of the Spirit—will, in the light of the subsequent illumination of their minds, be evident to them as a theophany. But, for the present, Jesus' visible presence is no guarantee of automatic recognition of his divine revelatory nature. The disciples are living in the half-light which precedes the brilliant dawn of the resurrection faith.

Part of their problem is identical with that of the unbelieving Jews: they see Jesus, the man, but they cannot see Jesus, the Christ. Thus "seeing" is much more than sensory experience; it is vision of the soul, apprehending the inner core of ultimate meaning which is the real Jesus. From the Gospel writer's perspective, it was entirely possible for men to have seen the historical Jesus and still remain ignorant of God. On the other hand, it was possible for men who had never seen Jesus in the flesh to see Jesus more profoundly than physical sight would allow, and so to experience the vision of God (cf. 20:24-29).

The departure of Jesus to the Father has the further consequence of empowering the church. Here, an amazing and daring statement is made, "Amen, amen, I tell you, he who believes in me will do the works that I am doing, and he will do greater works than these, because I am going to the Father" (14:12). The evangelist dares to believe that the era of divine power was not terminated with Jesus' death; indeed it had just begun! Moreover, the works of the disciples would be no weak imitation of those of their Lord; they would operate with greater power than Jesus. Not that Jesus was inferior in power, but

[74] *Op. cit.*, p. 164, n. 2.

because his voluntary death placed new forces at their disposal; they would go forth in the full power of the Spirit. Of course this view was no mere wistful hope. It had already been demonstrated both by the spread of Christianity westward (to "the Greeks," 12:20-31), and by the mighty deeds of the followers of Jesus to which the author of the Acts section of Luke-Acts had given eloquent testimonial. It might be well to point out, therefore, that the fourth evangelist's hope for the future is not centered in a single event, the coming of the Lord at the end of the age, but in a continuing ministry in which the divine, creative energy is powerfully manifest. This makes the Fourth Gospel contemporary, for the power of which it speaks is as much the property of the twentieth century as of the second. It is of great interest, and importance, that the evangelist, for all his attention to the person of Jesus, does not leave us with a "Jesusolatry," but passes freely to the universal stream of life which has its source in God himself.

Ch. 14 also introduces us to that element of the Gospel which relates to the promise of the Spirit.[75] The Spirit is first mentioned as the "other Helper" (14:16); it is described as "the Spirit of truth" (14:17); it is identified with "the Holy Spirit" (14:26); and with Jesus himself (14:17-23). The Spirit is also God's Spirit as is shown by the plural "we" in vs. 23.

It is important to see that these references to the Spirit are central, not peripheral. They represent the main line of the argument as to the meaning and function of Jesus in our Gospel. The Spirit which was "poured out" by the Father and entered into Jesus of Nazareth (1:29-34), manifested symbolically by "wine," "spring water," "bread," "light," etc., its vital nature indicated by acts of healing and of resurrection, is now given more attention at precisely the point were we should expect it, namely, when Jesus enters into that phase of his career which liberates the Spirit (20:22).

The major ideas regarding the Spirit presented by this chap-

[75] *Supra*, pp. 60-62.

ter are the following: (a) that the Spirit will be given only to the disciples (i.e., the church), not to the world (14:17, 22-24); (b) that the Spirit will be to the disciples as a teacher, and as a reminder of the words of Jesus while he was with them (14:26); (c) that Jesus will bequeath his "peace" to his disciples (14:27).

The Spirit is to be the exclusive possession of the church. In spite of the fact that the Fourth Gospel nowhere uses the term "church," it is highly ecclesiastical. But that does not mean that its concept of the church is conventional, or that it presents an institutional exclusivism. The church as an organization is not to receive the Spirit merely because it bears the name "Christian"; it is, rather, that the Spirit is organically related to individuals who draw their life from Christ. In other words, the giving of the Spirit is not an arbitrary act; it is instead conditioned by the relationship of the individual or group to the Giver. The gift of the Spirit, therefore, can of necessity be the possession only of the church, but it is the church as a fellowship of believers, of see-ers, of gnostics (in the Johannine sense). This position (which the evangelist develops more fully in chs. 15 and 17) rules out the institution per se as the natural habitat of the abiding Spirit.

It is this concept that lies back of Jesus' answer to the Judas mentioned in vs. 22. The answer is given in terms of love for Jesus, and of the keeping of his commandments (14:23-24). The two elements, love for Jesus and the keeping of his commandments, must be thought of in terms of the believer's relationship to Jesus on the one hand, and to his fellow believers on the other. The "new commandment" had already been formulated in 13:34: "Love one another, even as I have loved you." The life of love is therefore the life of the Spirit as it finds expression both in devotion to Jesus and to members of the fellowship. Conversely, the absence of this loving spirit excludes the Spirit's presence (14:17, 24).

The Spirit's function, as defined in these verses, is to serve as teacher and reminder in the period following Jesus' departure (14:26). But these two functions should not be considered

194

mutually exclusive. The point seems to be that in the future, with Jesus' glorification, the meaning of his words will be made clear, and that as new situations arise they will be met in the light of the truth which he has revealed. That truth is neither partial nor fragmentary, but as the church confronts the world in new and different circumstances it must make decisions, assume attitudes, etc., and on these matters Jesus gave no direct verbal counsel for they were not present in the Palestinian milieu of his historical career. But the Spirit will continue the instruction which Jesus had begun; there is no break in its continuity.

Perhaps we have tended to underemphasize the importance of the vivid sense of Jesus' presence in the early church. Acts, for example, makes the westward spread of Christianity contingent on the control of men by the Spirit. "The Acts of the Apostles" is really "The Acts of the Holy Spirit Through the Apostles"; human ingenuity fades from the picture; the actions of the apostles are directed by the Holy Spirit (8:29; 10:19-20; 13:4; 16:6; 20:22; 21:11; 28:25-28). The fourth evangelist inherited this belief (and, we may add, knew this experience). But the sense of personal intimacy is heightened in the Gospel, and the concept of the Spirit refined.

The function of Jesus as reminder grows out of the new perspective of the church on his words, his deeds, and his death in the light of the resurrection faith. The specific passages which reflect this are the following: 2:22; 12:16; 13:7; 14:26, 29; 16:4, 25-26.

The greatest problem in interpretation that confronted the primitive church was that of Jesus' death. Viewed in its bare historical aspect the cross was an instrument of execution for the lowest criminals; suffering, death, and shame were its accompaniments. Paul well knew this when he wrote that the message of Christ crucified was a stumbling-block to Jews and foolishness to Greeks (I Cor. 1:22). It is difficult to imagine the almost insuperable psychological and theological obstacles which had to be overcome before the Cross could be spoken of as "the power of God" (I Cor. 1:18) or as the only object in which men might glory (Gal. 6:14).

Now the fourth evangelist would meet in his sources, as a part of the Christian story, both the element of the human Jesus shrinking from the ordeal of the cross (Mark 14:32-42; Matt. 26:36-46; Luke 22:40-46) and Jesus' awareness of his own destiny thus to die (e.g., Mark 8:31; Matt. 16:21; Luke 9:22). He disposes of the first element by eliminating it, at the same time making the most of the second by stressing Jesus' complete self-determination. On the other hand, the protestations of the disciples (cf. Mark 8:32, the crucial passage in the Marcan outline) are due to their ignorance of what is taking place before their eyes. But their ignorance will be dispelled after Jesus dies. This enlightenment is synonymous with the reinterpreted cross, or, in other words, the cross vested with theological meaning. This meaning (for the church not dependent on a single interpretation) is viewed by John as the work of the Spirit within the fellowship, reminding its members of what Jesus had said in this regard.

In view of his imminent death, Jesus now bequeaths a legacy of peace to his disciples (14:27). This gift is dependent on the bestowal of the Spirit. The great Pauline trilogy—love, joy, and peace—comes into prominence in the Gospel at precisely the point where the future operation of the Spirit is under discussion: (a) the new commandment (13:34 with its sequel in 15:15-16); (b) the bestowal of the legacy of peace (14:27); (c) the abiding joy occasioned by the Spirit's presence (16:20-22). For Paul the accompaniments of the Spirit are characteristically these:

The mind of the flesh is death, but the mind of the Spirit is life and peace. (Rom. 8:6.)
For the kingdom of God does not mean food and drink but righteousness and peace and joy in the Holy Spirit. (Rom. 14:17.)
But the fruit of the Spirit is love, joy, peace, patience, kindness, goodness, faithfulness, gentleness, self-control. (Gal. 5:2?)

It is notable that our evangelist, while appropriately enough stressing love, joy, and peace, does not catalogue ethical virtues as accompaniments of the Spirit's presence as Paul does, unless we see in his stress on love the all-embracing virtue which subsumes all the rest. But of this there is no hint. But love, joy, and peace, characterized by Paul as the fruit of the Spirit, are in John also, and appear in the "Spirit" passages.

The peace which Jesus gives is of the same quality as that which he himself possesses: it is his peace (14:27). This means that the disciples will be steadfast and basically undisturbed in the time of persecution, for they will have at their command the same power which enabled Jesus to declare in the face of the cross, "Be of good cheer, I have conquered the world" (16:33).

The Allegory of the Vine
15:1-27

CH. 15 PRESENTS US WITH THE BEST EXAMPLE OF ALLEGORY found in the Gospel. Jesus is the true vine, God is the cultivator, the disciples are the branches. The allegory ideally serves John's purpose, which is to illustrate the intimate character of the relation between Jesus and the disciples. Just as the branches draw their life from the vine, so the disciples draw their life from Jesus. And since Jesus derives his life from God, so the life which the disciples draw from Jesus is the divine eternal life of which the Gospel everywhere speaks.

The test of discipleship is fruitfulness. Unfruitful branches are taken away by God, the caretaker of the vineyard, and even fruitful branches are "cleansed" that they may bear more plentifully. It is important to note that the word translated "cleansed" is καθαίρω; the same root is used in 13:10-11 to denote the cleansing of the disciples. The connection between the two chapters is made explicit by the cross reference in vs. 3.[76]

Operating within the orbit of the love of Jesus, the disciples are

---

[76] Supra, p. 188.

to love one another. To love one another just as Jesus has loved them turns out to be the new commandment (15:12). And the quality of Jesus' love is demonstrated by his willingness to lay down his life (τίθημι), indicating the kind and quality of love incumbent on the disciples.

Along with the test of fruitfulness and the active demonstration of a loving relationship within the fellowship, the evangelist affirms the necessity of "abidingness' as a mark of discipleship (15:4-7, 9-10). The reiteration of this idea brings into perspective the pervasive emphasis on belief that is not true belief because it will not continue. Left now with his disciples (the fringe-group that belongs more to the world than to Jesus having returned to its natural habitat), Jesus turns to his true disciples with instructions regarding the dangers which they themselves will encounter (15:18–16:33).

This theme of identification and isolation of true, as contrasted with false, disciples is a continuation of the symbolical cleansing of ch. 13. In that case, inability to learn the lesson of servanthood was the refining agent. Interestingly enough, this idea is now repeated (15:15) and a new element added; namely, the designation of the disciples as "friends" as contrasted with "slaves." It is true that the servanthood of ch. 13, when seen in relation to the cross as glorification, is a far cry from a menial function; but now the meaning is made explicit. For the disciples to lay down their lives as Jesus is to do elevates them to a new dignity; the designation "slave" no longer appropriately applies; they are, rather, "friends" of Jesus.

This constitutes one of the important insights of the Fourth Gospel. The evangelist would not have agreed with Paul that the way of the cross was a *kenosis*, a way of humility, in the sense that it emptied Jesus of his divine life. The cross was effective only because Jesus died vested with all the attributes of divinity. Similarly, followers of Jesus who give themselves in love for one another participate in the divine life while in the act of self-giving, and, while to the outsider it might appear that nothing more is involved than an act of humiliation, the

198

Christian knows that in the act he has been raised to a new status: he has become the friend of God, and works in harmony with him. This involves, of course, a drastic shift in the usual scale of values. Viewed externally the cross was a thing of shame, but from the perspective of the Fourth Gospel it was the glorification of the Son of Man. The Fourth Gospel lifts apparently shameful things to the level of the divine; and the men who participate in them, for the love of God and for one another, are elevated to the status of friends of God. This is the level of eternal life.

The Farewell Discourses as a whole are concerned with the future when the pressure from the world will be on the disciples. This feature is introduced in ch. 15 and is continued in an even more striking form in ch. 16. In the present chapter it takes the form of a warning that the world will hate the disciples. The hatred grows from the basic dualism on which the Gospel is structured: the realm above and the world below. Hatred for the disciples on the part of the world is inevitable since the two levels stand in a state of tension. But the disciples are to take courage from the fact that Jesus was the object of the world's hatred before it was turned on the disciples (15:18-20). Reverting to the analogy of the master and his slave, the evangelist makes it plain that persecution of the disciples is to be expected since they can scarcely escape the hatred to which their master had been subjected (15:20); master and slave belong together, share the same fate, and the same glory.

Reference to the Helper as the Spirit of Truth in 15:26 ought not to be construed as limiting the function of the Spirit. "Truth" (ἀλήθεια) does not signify merely the truth of particular ideas and experiences, but stands for the whole order of spiritual reality from which the Spirit operates. Speaking from this order of reality, the Spirit may testify to the oneness of Jesus with that order. To hate Jesus is to hate God (15:23), since Jesus is the embodiment of the spiritual order.

The "witness" idea, so prominent in the earlier pages of the Gospel, is thus continued in the Discourses. Not only is the

199

Spirit a witness, but this function is now ascribed to the disciples also (15:17). The ground of their ability to testify to Jesus is that they have been with him from the beginning (15:27). But along with this continuing experience of the disciples with Jesus must be placed a second factor, namely, the disciples' connection with the higher world to which Jesus belongs. Jesus has chosen them out of the lower world (15:16-19) so that their testimony, like that of the Spirit, is the testimony of spirit, not flesh, persons.[77]

Future Events Disclosed

16:1-33

IT SHOULD BE UNDERSTOOD THAT CH. 16 CONTINUES THE THEME of ch. 15 in which Jesus had made clear the future events of persecution and of the Spirit's coming. Ch. 16 now makes it clear that Jesus had so spoken in order that forthcoming persecution might occasion no surprise, and that the disciples will know they have not been forsaken (16:1-15; note especially vss. 1-4). The kind of persecution to which they will be subjected will have religious sanction: "They will excommunicate you from the synagogues; indeed the hour is coming when any one who kills you will think he is performing an act of worship" (16:2). This is reminiscent of Paul's experience prior to his revolutionary experience:

For you have heard of my former conduct in Judaism, how I persecuted the church of God and brought destruction to it; and I advanced in Judaism beyond many of my own age among my people. I did this out of extreme zeal for the traditions of my fathers. (Gal. 1:13-14; cf. Acts 22:1-5.)

It is well known that the pressure which Paul brought against

[77] It is interesting to note that the two ideas, witness based on continuous experience with Jesus, and the disciples as the chosen of Jesus, are clearly expressed in the Acts account of the choosing of Matthias as the replacement for Judas (Acts 1:15-26; note especially vss. 22, 24).

the Christians was not the action of an evil man, but rather of a man eager to protect the religious tradition to which he was committed. It is reasonable to suppose that the difficulties which Paul met from the Jews as a follower of Christ were motivated by the same fanatical zeal for the Torah that had characterized his own activity. In a very real sense Jews like Paul thought that by suppressing this messianic movement they were performing a religious service.

The fourth evangelist relieves Jesus of all emergency situations, to which either he or his followers might be victims, by giving Jesus foreknowledge of future events, and by having him instruct the disciples as to these events. He thereby makes the whole historical development subject at every step to divine control. In the context of ch. 16 this is true both for the coming period of persecution and for the scattering of the disciples at the time of the Crucifixion (16:32). This element of foreknowledge is akin to the device of apocalyptic where the writer takes his stand in the past and "predicts" the future. The Gospel literary form provides a natural medium for this device. To be sure, it had not been absent from the earlier Gospels, but in John it is more consistently and precisely articulated.

From this perspective, the cross is no arbitrary action in which a group of unsympathetic men connive to put Jesus of Nazareth to death. It is, rather, the act necessary for the redemption of the world, the voluntary self-giving of God, and the instrument which makes possible the abiding presence of the Spirit in the Christian community. That is why we are confronted with the radical interpretation of 16:7: "It is to your advantage that I go away."

The "going away" of Jesus means the coming of the Spirit, which, in turn, convicts the world (a) of sin, (b) of judgment, and (c) of righteousness (16:8-11). Hence, the judicial function of the Son of Man is extended into the future. The Helper convicts the world of sin "because they do not believe" in Jesus (16:9); that is, sin and unbelief, being the same thing, are revealed for what they are by the Spirit of Truth, which is the

201

revealer of Reality. As the disciples are led "into all truth," the world emerges for what it is—a force in active opposition to the truth, and it will be convicted of the crime of rejecting it.

As the Spirit enlightens men's mind the world which now condemns the Christian, and takes credit to itself for so doing (16:2), will itself be on trial with the Spirit as accuser; the result will be "conviction"—that is, the demonstration of the truth is so clear a light that it must be acknowledged as the truth, and the consequent condemnation of those who in spite of light reject that truth.[78]

Similarly, the Helper convicts the world of righteousness. This term, "righteousness," seems out of place in our Gospel; yet it constitutes, in its broadest sense, a fitting answer to the righteousness of Torah. Paul had spoken of the righteousness of God (Rom. 1:17), and the first evangelist had spoken of the higher righteousness which Jesus demanded (Matt. 5:20). What seems to be meant here is that righteousness is summed up in the person of Christ, his death and resurrection being the actual verification of the fact: he is exalted to the Father, and carries on his work invisibly through the agency of the Spirit. Hence, the return of Jesus to the Father and his unseen presence are themselves evidence of his victory over the forces of unrighteousness. This tendency to focus attention on the Person, not on ethical precepts, as gathering to himself all the richness of the Gospel is part of the development of the Christian movement as expressed in the New Testament as a whole. Where the Jews would have said, "Righteousness is revealed in Torah," the Christian would have said, "Righteousness is revealed in Christ." Death, resurrection, and abiding Presence were evidential as to the correctness of the assertion. Righteousness, in this sense, refers to the whole content of the revelation, and is akin to the thought of Paul (cf. Rom. 1:17; 3:5, etc.).

Again, the Helper is said to convict the world of judgment (16:11). The contrast is between the judgment of the Jews

[78] Macgregor, op. cit., p. 297.

which is external, κατ' ὄψιν, and that of Jesus which is with true discernment: τὴν δικαίαν κρίσιν (7:24). Two kinds of judgment are thus involved. On the part of the Jews there is the accusation that Jesus is a sinner (9:16), an evildoer (18:29-30), and so deserves to die. This is the judgment "of this world," a kind which operates on the basis of "factual" evidence. But in Jesus a different kind of judgment is evident; his judicial function stems from his quality of life. In the very act of pronouncing judgment upon Jesus, his judges place themselves under sentence of death. Pilate, the judge, becomes the accused, and Jesus, the accused, becomes the judge (18:33-38). The cross, which implements judgment of "this world," becomes a cosmic judgment seat: "The judgment of this world is now. The ruler of this world shall be cast out now" (12:31). So Jesus can declare (as though it were an accomplished fact) "the ruler of this world has been judged" (16:11). But the perfect tense of the verb (κέκριται) suggests that the judgment of the world which the cross entailed is a completed action with permanent results. The Spirit's presence in the church serves as a continuous reminder that what happened in the cross constitutes God's judgment upon the world.

This means that the function of the Spirit is in a real sense different from that of Jesus during his earthly career. The career left a permanent deposit, not only in the fact that it gave the Spirit to the world, but also in the fact that the cross laid bare the true nature of sin, revealed what constitutes righteousness, and reversed the ordinary claim as to where judgment belongs. For the church this is an event of history, something demonstrated in the past. The function of the Spirit, on the other hand, relates to the future—a future, to be sure, in which the implications of the past events are assumed as a living reality, but is in its own turn novel and creative: "When the Spirit of Truth comes, he will guide you into all the truth, for he will not speak of his own accord, but he will tell you what he hears, and will declare to you the things that are to come" (16:13).

This does not mean that there is a break in the continuity of

203

the "career of Jesus—Spirit-in-the-church" continuum. Jesus can say, "When the Spirit comes he will take what is mine and declare it to you" (16:14); that is, fresh revelations of the truth which come to the church are of the same quality revealed in the historical career, so that the possessive pronoun "mine" may be applied to them.

It is obvious that the double reference to "a little while" of 16:16 refers (a) to the period before Jesus' death; and (b) to the period between death and resurrection. The ignorance of the disciples as to the meaning of the words (16:17-18) is an appearance in the Discourses of the device employed in the dialogues with Nicodemus and with the Samaritan woman. It occasions an explanatory comment on the part of Jesus as in the two earlier cases. The Synoptics had pictured the emotional upheaval of the disciples at the time of the arrest and death: fear as represented by Mark (Mark 14:50; 16:8) and Matthew (Matt. 26:56), and disillusionment as represented by Luke (Luke 24: 21). The author of the Fourth Gospel shows that he is aware of the problem, though he removes fear and disillusionment from the picture and speaks only of sorrow (16:20-22). This agrees with his story of the betrayal in which Jesus dismisses his disciples, allowing for no accusation of cowardice to attach to them (18:8). By using the analogy of a woman in labor, soon to be delivered of her child, he graphically suggests pain followed by joy which the death and resurrection will bring (16:21-22). Yet 16:32 predicts the scattering of the disciples, and is strongly reminiscent of Mark 14:50.

The section on prayer in the name of Jesus (16:23-28) is of special interest. It suggests the importance of the sacred name in the early church. The words ἕως ἄρτι, translated "until now," "hitherto," indicate that the evangelist is aware that the practice began in the church after Jesus' death. The expression is common in Acts (e.g., 3:6; 4:10, 18, 30; 9:21; 16:18; 22:16). But we must not conclude that the allusion to petition in the name of Jesus means the same thing in the Fourth Gospel that it does in Acts. The Fourth Gospel conceives of a direct, personal relationship as existing between the believer and God. That is why its author hastens to add, "I do not tell you that I will ask the Father for you, for the Father himself loves you" (16:26-27). This corrects a wrong impression implicit in the phrase, "in my name." The unity of the believer with Christ and Christ with God (17:10, 21, 23) rules out the function of Christ as a mere intercessor in the sense advanced, for instance, by the writer of Hebrews (e.g., Heb. 7:25). Prayer in the name of Christ places the believer in close, personal relationship with Christ; this makes prayer effective. But it is in no sense a magical device.

A second idea which calls for consideration here is contained in the reference to Jesus' origin and destiny (16:27-28). Vs. 28, the main passage, seems to have been prompted by the final clause of vs. 27 where Jesus makes the basis of God's love for the disciples the fact that they believe he has come from the Father. His divine origin is confirmed in vs. 28 and combined with the additional reference to his return to the Father. This verse puts succinctly the theological scheme in terms of which the whole Gospel is constructed: Jesus comes into history from the Father, he leaves the historical scene and returns to the Father. There is no suggestion of a loss of his former glory; instead, there is a dipping into history with a redemptive purpose to fulfill, and a return to the glory which he had with God before the world was made (17:5). With his return to the Father the circuit is complete. But it is not a casual incursion of divine life into history; the world is different from what it was because of the deposit left behind. It has been made aware of God's love, a love focused in the cross, and made permanent by the Spirit's presence within the fellowship of believers.

Prayer for Christian Unity

17:1-26

CH. 17 ASSUMES THE FORM OF A PRAYER. THE DIFFERENCE IN literary style between John and the Synoptics is clearly seen by a comparison of this prayer with the Lord's Prayer (Matt. 6: 9-13; Luke 11:2-4). The former is long, repetitious, and quasi-philosophical, while the latter is brief and simple. The prayer in John is often referred to as the high-priestly prayer, a characterization which could scarcely be made of the Lord's Prayer. Whether there is any connection between the two prayers is not clear. E. F. Scott holds that "the great 17th chapter of John is inspired by the Lord's prayer, and is meant, in some measure, to interpret it." [79] But the Lord's Prayer (even if construed as a model prayer for the disciples) is too human a prayer for the fourth evangelist to place on the lips of Jesus. The prayer of his gospel is the communication of one divine being with another, not the prayer of a human being engaged in the human struggle. The only petition of Jesus for himself here is for his own glorification, that he might receive the same exalted place which he had with God before the world came into being (17:5).

At no point in the Fourth Gospel is the ecclesiastical interest more evident than here. Jesus' prayer is for his disciples (17:9) and for future believers (17:20), that is, for the church. The dominant interest in the church is at the point of its unity. Couched in the form of a prayer, the chapter is in reality a discourse on Christian unity. Perspective is gained if we remember that this "prayer" is actually second-century Christianity's understanding of the intention of Jesus on the problem of Christian unity.

The prayer form is used for a variety of reasons. For one thing, the evangelist found references to Jesus praying in his sources. But it is interesting to note that the kind of prayer employed

[79] *The Lord's Prayer* (New York: Charles Scribner's Sons, 1951), p. 33. Used by permission.

makes it clear that Jesus himself stood in no need of prayer, a fact which the choice of the verb ἐρωτάω (17:9, 20), "to ask," underscores in contrast to the employment of προσεύχομαι, "to pray" (Matt. 6:9; Luke 11:2; Mark 14:35, etc.) by the Synoptists. The latter is distinctly a term related to worship while the former has no necessary relation to it. Jesus may ask the Father for something, as one divine being to another, but he is not a suppliant praying in the sense that προσεύχομαι would suggest. Thus the prayer has the advantage of "correcting" the impression left by the Synoptists that Jesus needed the strengthening afforded by prayer. This interpretation is reinforced by the passage which reflects the Gethscmane scene (12:27), and in which the Synoptic plea, "If it be possible let this cup pass from me" (equals "Father, save me from this hour"), is repudiated.

The prayer form also adds an element of variety in terms of a new literary device, and so breaks the monotony of the long discourse section. The genius of a gospel demands sustained action. Consequently, the writer repeatedly introduces into the discourse section statements which give the impression of movement. This may be the reason for the inclusion of the much-debated words, "Rise, let us go hence," at the close of ch. 14.

Our next inquiry has to do with the nature of the Christian unity advanced here. It is clear that the evangelist's interest is not in organizational unity. Coming from the general period when an Ignatius could claim the paramount importance of the bishop for the catholic church, our writer emphasizes a kind of spiritual unity which transcends organization. This is consistent with his negative reaction to sacramental religion with its emphasis on rites, and is solidly based on his concept of God as spirit and of true worship as being "in spirit and truth."

This spiritual unity is treated in terms which convey a warmth of feeling lacking in argumentative treatments of the subject. This feeling is due partly to the fact that Jesus himself is represented as sharing in the concern for unity; and partly to the prayer form which lends itself naturally to warm religious concern; Jesus himself calls on God the Father for the welfare of his own beloved community. This strengthens the plea for unity.

What is frequently designated "Johannine mysticism" is most plainly evident here. The Gospel as a whole affirms the oneness of Jesus with God. But now this concept is developed so as to include the disciples, i.e., the church. It is helpful to view the relevant verses together:

I am asking for them; I am not asking for the world, but for those whom you gave me, for they are yours, and all mine are yours, and yours are mine. . . . I do not ask for them alone, but also for those who are to believe in me through their message, that they may all be one, just as you, Father, are in me and I in you, that they also may be in us. . . . I have given them the glory which you have given me, that they may be one as we are, I in them and you in me, that they may be completely one. . . . And I have made your name known to them, and continue to make it known, that the love with which you have loved me may be in them, and that I may be in them also.

This is a remarkable interlacing of the concepts of God, Jesus, and the disciples. The union of the three is possible because of the action of the Spirit within the fellowship. Just as Jesus became God's Son by the Spirit's descent, so the disciples become divine beings by the indwelling Spirit; they are no longer "of this world" (17:9, 14, 16). There is, therefore, a strong parallel between Jesus as sent by God and the disciples as sent by Jesus. It is probable that the parallel is specifically between the descent of the Spirit on Jesus and the breathing of the Spirit on the disciples (20:22-23): "Just as you sent me into the world, so I send them into the world" (17:18).

In view of the nature of the relationship of the disciples with God and with Jesus ("that they may be one as we are, I in them and you in me, that they may be completely one"), the possibility is ruled out that this is mere identity of will; it is rather identity of nature, resulting in a concept of the church as a holy fellowship caught up in the higher order of being. In view

208

of this fact, it is easy to understand the Gospel's emphasis on *life*. Life is the normal consequence of participation in the life of God. Death is as foreign to the participant as it is to Jesus or to God. It is likewise easy to understand the evangelist's position on the sacraments as of (at least) secondary importance, for without this sharing of divine life they "profit nothing."

By way of summary, we may say that the seventeenth chapter reflects a strong ecclesiastical interest on the part of the evangelist. But this ecclesiastical concern prompts him to say not a word about church organization: on the contrary, his whole emphasis is on the life in the Spirit which unites the believer with Jesus. It represents part of the evangelist's protest against the deadening effect of an overemphasis on ritualistic practices in the church; at the same time it bears witness to the impact of the divine Spirit upon the spirit of man, so well illustrated in the life of Jesus himself, and carried forward by the young, spiritually powerful, first- and early second-century church.

The Betrayal
18: 1-11

THE SYNOPTIC ACCOUNTS OF THE BETRAYAL ARE FOUND IN MARK 14:43-50, Matt. 26:47-56, and Luke 22:47-53. In each case the story is preceded by the agony in Gethsemane. Characteristically, John omits this. However, reflections of it are present in 12: 27 and in the present account at vs. 11: "Shall I not drink the cup which the Father has given me?" But they must not be considered mere reflections of a neutral sort; they amount to a refutation of the impression left by the earlier tradition that Jesus was subject to temptation.

Changes in the story, as it occurs in the Fourth Gospel, make it a new one. Judas betrays Jesus with a kiss in all three Synoptic accounts (Mark 14:44-45; Matt. 26:48-49; Luke 22:47-48), but not in John; instead, Jesus invites identification with the words, "Whom do you seek?" (18:4). In Mark and in Matthew, Jesus is seized immediately following identification (Mark 14:46;

Matt. 26:50), but in John this is delayed until Jesus has dismissed his disciples (18:12). In this regard John is closer to Luke than to Matthew or Mark (Luke 22:54). Perhaps the most radical change has taken place in connection with the reference to the sword. In Mark, a bystander cuts off the ear of the high priest's slave (Mark 14:47). There is no protest to this action on Jesus' part. In Matthew, the amputation of the ear is accomplished by "one of those who were with Jesus," and Jesus rebukes him thus:

Put your sword back into its place; for all who take the sword will be destroyed by the sword. Do you suppose that I cannot appeal to my Father, and he will send me now more than twelve legions of angels? But how then would the scriptures be fulfilled that it must be so? (Matt. 26:52-54.)

In Luke, the incident of the sword is introduced by the question put to Jesus by "those who were about him": "Lord, shall we strike with the sword?" Then follows the incident proper in which one of them cuts off the *right* ear of the slave. A heightening of the miraculous occurs when Jesus rebukes his impetuous defender and heals the slave's ear (Luke 22:49-51). In John, Simon Peter is identified as the man who used the sword. As in the Lucan account, the amputation of the *right* ear takes place. In John, the slave is identified as a man by the name of Malchus. And Peter is rebuked with the words, in the first part reminiscent of Matt. 26:52a but accommodated to the Johannine view of the Crucifixion as the divinely appointed hour: "Put your sword into its sheath. *Shall I not drink the cup which the Father has given me?*" (18:10-11).

One of the most striking departures of the fourth evangelist from his Synoptic predecessors comes at the point of the conduct of the disciples. Mark has it that "they all forsook him and fled" (Mark 14:50), followed by Matthew (26:56). Luke, however, is more cautious at this point and omits any reference to the flight of the disciples. Similarly, the fourth evangelist makes no

210

mention of the flight of the disciples. But he goes beyond Luke in that he is content with no mere omission; he has Jesus dismiss the disciples, a dismissal which fulfills his words spoken in 17:12 to the effect that no disciple of his should be lost (18:8-9).

Additional changes may be noted. For one thing, the setting of the betrayal is described as a garden. This is uniquely Johannine. The observation that Judas knew the place, because Jesus met there frequently with his disciples, may be a shrewd historical observation on the evangelist's part (18:1-2). A further point to observe is that Mark, followed by Matthew and Luke, has Jesus refer to his public teaching activity in the temple (Mark 14:49; Matt. 26:55; Luke 22:53). This reference is omitted by the fourth evangelist at this point. However, when Jesus is questioned by the high priest about his teaching, he replies in words highly reminiscent of the Synoptic material: "I have spoken openly to the world; I have always taught in a synagogue or in the temple where all Jews assemble, and I have said nothing in secret" (18:20). Finally, it is noteworthy that the event in John has more the character of well-ordered procedure than in the Synoptics. Mark has it that the arresting party consisted of a crowd armed with swords and clubs (Mark 14:43). This mob action elicits from Jesus the words: "Have you come out as against a robber, with swords and clubs to capture me?" (Mark 14:48). But in John the arresting party consists of Roman soldiers and officers from the chief priests and Pharisees (18:3). This helps to explain the apparent discrepancy in the Fourth Gospel where the Romans generally are placed in a good light. The introduction of the Roman soldiers into the arresting party guarantees order, and guards against the impression of mob action. Consequently, Jesus does not need to protest against the manner of the arrest. It possesses a dignity which the earlier accounts lack.

The effect of these changes is to transform the betrayal and arrest into a divinely planned event. All elements of an "emergency" nature have been removed. This fact, together with the additions, shapes the account in terms of the Crucifixion conceived as the consummation of the divine purpose. "Betrayal" is hardly the word for this event in John!

Jesus Before the High Priest and the Denial by Peter

18:12-27

TWO MAIN PROBLEMS EMERGE HERE: (a) THE INTENTION OF the evangelist in introducing both Annas and Caiaphas in relation to the office of high priest; and (b) the identity or function of the "other disciple" in the account of Peter's denial.

Looking first at the problem of the high priesthood, it is to be noted that Mark in his account of the trial before the Jewish authorities makes no mention of the high priest's name; he is simply referred to as "the high priest" (Mark 14:53, 54, 60, 61, 63). The same is true for Luke (Luke 22:54). In Matthew, however, he is identified as Caiaphas (Matt. 26:57; cf. 26:3). But there is a Lucan passage which deserves more attention than it has received. Luke 3:2 holds that John the Baptist began his preaching in the "high priesthood of Annas and Caiaphas." Bultmann believes that the fourth evangelist used a source other than the Synoptics at the point and that in this source Annas was said to be high priest.[80] This represents a possibility, but it is wise to look for other motivating forces in this kind of material. As we have noted, Luke refers to a joint high priesthood of Annas and Caiaphas. Furthermore, in the Acts section of his work, the third evangelist speaks of Annas as still high priest: "The next day, the leaders, elders, and scribes, were gathered together in Jerusalem with Annas the high priest and Caiaphas and John and Alexander, and all who were relatives of the high priest" (Acts 4:5-6).

But is this Lucan basis sufficient to account for the Johannine reconstruction of the trial account? It is, in part at least, if we

[80] *Op. cit.*, p. 497.

212

view the development in the light of the evangelist's method. For one thing he has already used Caiaphas at an earlier point in the story to prophesy ex cathedra that Jesus should die for the nation (11:49-52). There is therefore no reason, in terms of the story's development, for Jesus to appear before him. The verdict is already in so far as Caiaphas is concerned. And yet the story demands a trial before the high priest, both because the tradition carried it, and because a situation must be created for the Jews to carry the full weight of responsibility for Jesus' death. Joint high priesthood stood our author in good stead. Needless to say, perhaps, the question of the historical reliability of the assumption is irrelevant.

With the projection into the account of Annas as high priest, as is certainly assumed in vss. 19-24, the hostile attitude of official Judaism can be given full expression. Here we find Jesus' "disrespectful" words to the high priest together with the response when Jesus is slapped by one of the officers. Caiaphas fades from the picture. It is simply said that Annas sent him bound to Caiaphas, but there is no sequel in which Jesus stands before him. Caiaphas has played his role in the drama, a role which places him outside the camp of Jesus' real enemies, for his words were fully in line with the divine plan.

A second point which has relevance here concerns the twice-repeated phrase regarding Caiaphas: he was "high priest that year" (11:51; 18:13). It is frequently stated that this reveals the evangelist's ignorance of the facts relating to the office of the high priest and that he assumed an annual appointment. Again, historical accuracy seems to be beside the point. The emphasis to be placed on the phrase has no implication of annual appointment; instead, it relates to that particular year, that fateful year, when Jesus was to die.

Part of the solution turns on the peculiar Greek phrase translated "that year": τοῦ ἐνιαυτοῦ ἐκείνου (18:13). It is instructive to note that Luke has Jesus quote the Septuagint text of Isa. 58:6 in the account of the Nazareth rejection (Luke 4:18-19), closing the quotation with the words, "to proclaim the year of the Lord's

213

favor." The Greek word used here for "year" is ἐνιαυτός (4:19). As Gilmour has pointed out, the phrase in the Lucan context refers to the messianic age.[81] The same idea is conveyed in John except that the latter uses it in connection with the great event of the new age when the Spirit is released into the world. This gives it a more precise time-reference than the Lucan context permits.

Coming now to the second problem of the section; namely, that of the function and identity of the "other disciple," we find it related to the incident of Peter's denial. This incident is interwoven with the account of Jesus before the high priest (18:15-18, 25-27). This interweaving serves to heighten the dramatic element: Peter is more concerned about his own comfort and safety than about the fate of his Lord. So he is pictured as warming himself by the fire which Jesus' captors had kindled for themselves (18:18), and as denying any connection with Jesus or his disciples (18:16-17, 25-27). The interruption of this incident by the scene of the trial before Annas (18:19-24), a scene which even has Jesus slapped by an officer of the high priest, gives the whole the character of high drama. The arrangement of material heightens the contrast between the weakness of Peter and the strength of Jesus.

The story of Peter's denial was firmly fixed in the earlier tradition (Mark 14:66-72; Matt. 26:69-75; Luke 22:56-62). While it varies in details, the story in John is essentially the same. The most important Johannine addition is that of the "other disciple" (18:15-16). He is described as one "known to the high priest," a phrase which is twice repeated (18:15, 16). It may be that it is superfluous to inquire further as to his identity. The evangelist probably thought it inappropriate that Peter should enter the high priest's court without a proper point of contact. Moreover, he serves the function of subordinating Peter, a tendency which is apparent elsewhere: Peter is introduced to

---

[81] S. M. Gilmour, *The Interpreter's Bible* (New York and Nashville: Abingdon Press, 1952), VIII, 92.

Jesus by Andrew (1:40-42); the identity of the traitor is requested by Peter through the mediation of the beloved disciple (13:23-26); and this same disciple outdistances Peter in their race to the tomb (20:2-9).

The identification of the "other disciple" with "the disciple whom Jesus loved" is entirely gratuitous. When in 20:2 the phrase "the other disciple" is used it is qualified by another, "the one whom Jesus loved," as if to make a clear distinction between him and the man previously mentioned.

The problem of the "other disciple" and of the "beloved disciple" brings to the forefront the whole question of the disciples of Jesus in the Fourth Gospel. Only as that problem is solved can the questions relating to a particular disciple be satisfactorily answered. This, then, may be a good point at which to assess the larger problem.

The Fourth Gospel assumes twelve disciples (6:67, 70, 71; 20:24). There is no attempt, however, to give a complete list of their names. The nearest approach to this is in 1:35-51 where Andrew, Peter, Philip, and Nathanael are named in that order. Another disciple is left unidentified (1:35-40). Contrary to the Synoptic lists, where Peter always stands at the head, the fourth evangelist mentions Andrew first, and through him Peter is brought to Jesus (1:40-42). Nathanael has no place in the Synoptic lists.

Three other disciples appear in the Gospel who had a place in the earlier lists. These are Judas Iscariot, who appears in his familiar role as betrayer (6:71; 13:26-30; 18:2-3), Judas ("not Iscariot," 14:22), probably to be equated with Judas the son of James mentioned in the Lucan list (Luke 6:16), and Thomas (14:5; 20:24, 26).

This means that of the disciples mentioned in the Synoptic lists, six are mentioned by name: Andrew, Peter, Philip, Judas ("not Iscariot"), Thomas, and Judas Iscariot. The names which appear in the Synoptic lists but which John omits are James and John (the sons of Zebedee), Bartholomew, Matthew,

215

Thaddaeus, Simon (the Cananaean), Levi, and James the son of Alphaeus.[82]

Of the six Synoptic disciples whom John mentions, Peter assumes the most dominant, if not the most important, role. He figures in the account at five points in the narrative: at the time of his call (1:40-42); at the end of the discourse on the Bread of Life, where he utters the Johannine equivalent of the Synoptic confession (6:68-69); at three places in the Supper scene (13:6-9, 24, 36-38); at the time of the arrest (18:10, 11); and in the denial scene (18:15-18, 25-27).

Philip runs a close second to Peter in the number of times mentioned: at the time of his call (1:43-44); in connection with the call of Nathanael (1:45-48); in the scene of the Feeding of the Five Thousand (6:5-7); in connection with the coming of the Greeks (12:21-22); and in the Farewell Discourses (14: 8-9). This gives us a total of five times. However, Philip's call and the call of Nathanael are closely related to the call of Peter; perhaps the two should be considered as a unit.

Judas is referred to specifically at three points in the Gospel (6:71; 13:26-30; 18:2-3). But he appears by implication at several other points (13:11, 18; 17:12).

Thomas appears only in the later pages of the Gospel: in the Lazarus story (11:16); in the Discourses (14:5); and twice during the resurrection appearances (20:24-25, 26-69).

Judas ("not Iscariot") is mentioned but once: in the Discourses (14:22).

The problem of the disciples is complicated by the fact that there appears a group of disciples, some of whom have no connection with the traditional "twelve," others whose connection with the twelve is uncertain.

Joseph of Arimathea is mentioned plainly as a disciple (19: 38). The explanation is made that his discipleship was secret

[82] The membership of the original twelve (if such there were) constitutes a separate problem. Our lists, taken together, add up to a total of fourteen, not counting Nathanael, the three unnamed disciples of John, or Joseph of Arimathea and Nicodemus.

216

because he feared the Jews. He is described in Mark as a respected member of the Sanhedrin and as one who was looking for the kingdom of God (Mark 15:42-43). In Matthew, he is characterized as a rich man and as a disciple of Jesus (Matt. 27:57). Luke is close to Mark, but adds that Joseph was a good and righteous man, and that he had not consented to the purpose and deed of the Jews (Luke 23:50-51).

The fourth evangelist adds an element to the story of Joseph of Arimathea by introducing Nicodemus into the story (19:39). This is the third time Nicodemus has been mentioned. His first appearance was in 3:1 ff., and his second in 7:50-51. In the passage under discussion (19:38-42), he comes to the tomb to anoint Jesus' body. This act undoubtedly classifies him as a disciple also.

Joseph and Nicodemus must be considered disciples in a wider sense than is true of the twelve. That this wider meaning of the term "disciple" is Johannine is demonstrated by such passages as 6:66 and 7:3.

The idea of "secret disciples," such as Joseph of Arimathea is said to have been, is at home in the Gospel. That Nicodemus came to Jesus by night (3:2), a phrase repeated in 19:39, and is placed in relation to Joseph of Arimathea whose discipleship was secret because of his fear of the Jews, might lend some credence to the notion that Nicodemus' initial visit was surreptitious. It is probable that ambiguity is intended. In any case, it is evident that the evangelist intended to indicate a group of secret disciples. This is plainly stated in 12:42 where it is asserted that many even of the authorities believed in Jesus, but did not make it known because they were afraid of the Pharisees. Joseph would belong to this class.

So far we have seen that the Fourth Gospel envisages three groups of disciples; namely, the twelve, a group larger than the twelve, and a group of secret disciples. The first group is but representative of the persons named in the Synoptic lists, only six out of fourteen appearing. The second group is, of course, largely anonymous, except for Nathanael and, possibly, Nicodemus. The third list is also anonymous except for Joseph of Arimathea. It is possible that Nicodemus should be included in this category.

It is now our problem to consider still another group made up of the beloved disciple (13:23-25; 19:26-27; 20:2-8) and the "other disciple" (18:15-16); these may be classified as anonymous disciples.

The first question to be raised is whether or not the two are to be identified as one and the same. The question cannot be answered with assurance, but it is notable that when the phrase "other disciple" is used in 20:2, it is qualified by another, namely, "the one whom Jesus loved." On the other hand, the beloved disciple is placed in close relation to Peter both in the Supper scene and in the race to the tomb. This is also true of the "other disciple" in the trial scene. Bultmann thinks that the two are not to be identified.[83] He feels that the unnamed disciple of ch. 18 is introduced only to provide a motive for the entrance of Peter into the court of the high priest. It is probable that the disciple's anonymity is intentional, and that it is quite beside the point to ask, "Who is he?"

But can the same thing be said of the beloved disciple? His threefold appearance certainly suggests that he was more for the evangelist than a mere literary convenience. But, even so, his character does not emerge; we do not see him as a person.

As far back as Irenaeus, tradition has made him the author of the Gospel, identified as John, the son of Zebedee. Modern scholarship, in the main, has rejected this identification but has been unable to give a satisfactory solution to the problem. Various names have been suggested: Paul, the Rich Young Ruler, Lazarus, Matthias. Perhaps more plausible is the suggestion that he is a representative type, and stands for the ideal disciple. But Macgregor feels that the evangelist's allusions to the disciple are not numerous or pointed enough "to create any

[83] Op. cit., p. 499, n. 6.

well-defined impression of the ideal which he means to portray." [84]

Certain pertinent observations can be made in relation to our problem: (a) The beloved disciple appears at the point at which Jesus turns to his own, the point at which the story stands in immediate relation to the cross; (b) in two out of the three instances of his appearance he is placed in relationship to Peter; (c) in all three instances he is given some kind of superior recognition. In the first appearance he, of all the disciples present, has the courage (and, apparently, the recognized right) to question Jesus as to the identity of the betrayer. He is also here described as reclining on the bosom of Jesus (13:23; cf. 1:18). In the second instance, he is given sonship with respect to Jesus' mother, and Jesus' mother is entrusted to his care. The third scene pictures him as outrunning Peter in the race to the tomb. This suggests that he is to be thought of as a superior disciple, superior, that is, to the twelve.

Having surveyed the question of the Johannine disciples in general, and having classified them (the twelve, a group beyond the twelve, secret disciples, anonymous disciples), the question arises as to their function, and, in some cases, as to their identity.

Dealing first with the twelve, it is obvious that the evangelist had no need to add a new and complete list. He found it sufficient to preserve the tradition of the twelve, and, in addition, to make use of certain established names in the lists. Since John is writing for the church, the designation "the twelve" would be sufficient to provide Jesus with a Christian community. In this Gospel Jesus speaks to the church.

The disciples, of course, represent believers as distinct from the Jews. The author's method is largely that of dialogue, so that when the Jews are absent or when a particular end is more aptly served the disciples are used as foils to assist the development of a given idea; that is, they serve a purely literary purpose; An-

[84] Op. cit., pp. xlv f.

drew, Philip, Thomas, and one Judas ("not Iscariot") are employed to fulfill this function.

But a second function must be added; namely, the use of *particular* disciples as more suitable than others with reference to given situations. Thus Andrew and Philip are placed in relationship to the coming of the Greeks; Andrew, perhaps, because of his Greek name, and Philip because he has been identified with Philip the evangelist of Acts.

The dominant role of Peter in the earlier tradition could hardly be denied. But the role of Peter in the Fourth Gospel is not highly creditable. It is dominated by his rashness, if not supidity, and by his threefold denial of Jesus. Of the six of the twelve disciples mentioned by John, Peter most closely follows the Synoptic pattern. But even in the Synoptics the disciples are little more than names apart from Peter, the sons of Zebedee, and Judas Iscariot. It is interesting, and perhaps significant, that apart from Peter and Judas Iscariot, the disciples about whom some note is attached in the Synoptic records (as, for example, Matthew the publican, Simon the Zealot, and the sons of Zebedee) play no part in the Johannine Gospel. Andrew comes to us in the Synoptics only as the brother of Peter and as a fisherman, while Philip, Thomas, and the other Judas are given no real character. The dominant roles of Peter and Judas Iscariot, however, could hardly be denied by the fourth evangelist.

It is probable that the partial listing of the twelve and the tendency to use the more obscure persons from the twelve are but part of the trend which finds its ultimate expression in anonymous disciples. The less personality attaching to a name the more flexibility it could have as a symbol. Seen in this light, the role of the beloved disciple becomes understandable. He is the true disciple, whose faith, unlike Peter's, is unwavering. He is in the bosom of Jesus as Jesus is in the bosom of the Father. He is the one who alone can be entrusted with the care of Jesus' mother. His faith brings him first to the empty tomb. No member of the twelve could quite properly fill that role. But the ideal disciple who met the standard of Jesus' prayer,

"that they may be one as we are, I in them and you in me"—
that disciple met the requirements.[85]

It is therefore probable that his anonymity is intended, and
that an attempt at identification in terms of a particular individual runs counter to the evangelist's interest. If he had wanted
him identified he would have given his name. Unless the Gospel is a book of riddles we must accept his anonymity as intentional, and find meaning in terms of the role played in the
various scenes. It is entirely beside the point to say that John
Mark, Lazarus, etc., had a home in or near Jerusalem and thus
meet the requirements, for that is to treat this symbolic Gospel
as history. The point is not that someone had a home in Jerusalem, but that here is a disciple enough like Jesus himself that
Mary becomes his mother, and he her son. By implication he
is the brother of Jesus, not in the biological sense, of course,
but in the spiritual. One is reminded of Jesus' words recorded by
Mark: "Whoever does the will of God is my brother, and sister,
and mother" (Mark 3:35).

Jesus Before Pilate
18:28-40

THERE IS NO ACCOUNT IN THE FOURTH GOSPEL OF A TRIAL BE-
fore Caiaphas. This omission is due to the fact that Caiaphas
has already uttered his ex cathedra prophecy of the necessity
of Jesus' death (11:49-52). Annas has been introduced on the
basis of Luke-Acts to fulfill the requirement of a hearing before
the Jewish authorities. The account therefore moves rapidly to
the trial before Pilate.

The story is given in three scenes: (a) Pilate and the Jews:
the question of a charge (18:28-32); (b) Pilate and Jesus: the

---

[85] A reasonable suggestion as to the Beloved Disciple's identity is given by
Bultmann. He holds that this disciple is representative of Gentile Christianity
(see infra, pp. 237-38). This conjecture is given support by the fact that that
disciple's first appearance (13:23) follows the coming of the Greeks (12:20). This
position does not run counter to the suggestion given in these pages; the evangelist
undoubtedly felt that the true example of discipleship lay with Gentile Christianity.

question of Jesus' kingship (18:33-38a); (c) Pilate and the Jews: the verdict of "not guilty" (18:38b-40).

The question which Pilate puts to the Jewish captors of Jesus ("What charge do you bring against this man?") is answered only with evasion: "If this man were not a criminal, we would not have turned him over to you." This is really no answer at all. Pilate, who has found Jesus innocent, attempts to place responsibility on the Jews: "Judge him according to your own law." But the Jews insist that they have no right to do this. This point of law is still questioned by scholars, but the comment of the evangelist to the effect that this was to fulfill the word of Jesus about the manner of his death, i.e., by crucifixion (18:32), suggests that he considered the Jewish argument mere subterfuge, though, at the same time, in harmony with the divine purpose.

The scene now shifts inside the governor's house (18:33). There follows a most dramatic scene: the representative of imperial Rome questioning one who, presumably, is a Galilean peasant, but who, in fact, is the Son of God. The questioning begins with the crucial query: "Are you the king of the Jews?" Following the pattern characteristic of the Gospel, the answer is delayed and indirect. The Jews, not Pilate, are responsible for the charge (18:34). With great scorn Pilate asks, "Am I a Jew?" His real concern is expressed in the words, "What have you done?" Then follows Jesus' reply in which the claim to kingship is implicit. It is like saying, "I have control over a kingdom, but it is not one such as you or the Jews have in mind. It has nothing to do with Roman control or popular Jewish aspirations for national independence; this is evidenced by the fact that my followers made no effort to preserve my freedom. My kingdom is not a kingdom of this world." The implications of this statement are at least twofold: Jesus is a king, and his kingdom is not a political one. Pilate is quick to seize upon the first implication: "So you are a king?" But he is not able to grasp the second. That remains as the point of further dialogue.

This scene moves to its climax when Pilate exclaims, "So you are a king?" Jesus responds with the much-debated words σὺ λέγεις ὅτι βασιλεύς εἰμι. Commentators are divided on the meaning of σὺ λέγεις. Bultmann holds that it is equivalent to "Yes." [86] Dodd, on the other hand, thinks of it as constituting an ambiguous answer.[87] The form is found in Mark 15:2, Matt. 27:11, and Luke 23:3. It is probable that in John, at least, the ambiguity is intended. Direct answers are usually, if not always, avoided. In this case Pilate, not Jesus, registers the truth about Jesus. The same motive is at work which has Pilate write above the cross, "Jesus of Nazareth, the King of the Jews" (19:19), and then speak with finality against the protesting Jews, "What I have written, I have written" (19:22).

But the ambiguity constitutes only part of Jesus' reply. He affirms that the purpose of his coming into the world was to testify to the truth. All men who belong to that kingdom "hear his voice," i.e., obey him (18:37). There is no doubt about his kingship. The only question is as to the kind of realm over which he is king. This realm is that of ἀλήθεια, "truth." Pilate is mystified. He has not heard of this kingdom. "What is ἀλήθεια?" he asks (18:38). The question is left unanswered with powerful dramatic effect. Pilate, the Roman governor, while asking the question stands in the presence of the king of that realm; his answer is before him.

For the third of our present series of scenes the setting reverts to a place outside the governor's house (18:38b). Pilate now announces his verdict to the Jews: "I find no grounds for a charge in him" (18:38). Apparently Jesus' claims to sovereignty over the strange realm of truth have not convinced Pilate that he is guilty of seditious action. Consequently, Pilate makes a suggestion in obvious hope that Jesus will be liberated; he points to a custom which would release one prisoner at the Passover. How about releasing "the king of the Jews?" "No," they cry, "not this man, but Barabbas!" Then, with great simplicity and effective-

[86] Op. cit., p. 506, especially n. 7.
[87] Op. cit., p. 427.

ness, the evangelist explains, "Now Barabbas was a robber" (18: 40).

Pilate Presents Jesus
19:1-11

THIS IS A MOST DRAMATIC SCENE! THE ESSENTIAL THING ABOUT it is Pilate's presentation of Jesus who is clad in royal attire. The scourging lends further drama to the scene (19:1). It is useless to argue that Pilate must have passed sentence already, since, according to Roman custom, scourging followed sentence of death. Nowhere in this Gospel does Pilate sentence Jesus; quite the contrary, he states repeatedly that Jesus is innocent of any crime (18:38; 19:4, 6). The evangelist found references to the scourging in his sources; he includes it, since it enhances the dramatic element. Here we find the beaten man, the soldiers mockingly arraying him in royal garments, the brutal cry of demand for crucifixion, and Pilate's memorable words, "Here is the man!" But the reader knows what the Jews do not know (it is the thing that haunts Pilate)—he knows that this man *is* a king. He knows further that Pilate's fear induced by the claim of the Jews, "he made himself out to be the Son of God," is in a real sense justified, for he is indeed the Son of God. The tension between the apparent and the real finds its most graphic expression at this point.

The words of Pilate, "Here is the man!" must be understood in relation to this high drama. Pilate repeatedly makes assertions which go far beyond the literal meaning of the words, far beyond his own discernment. Dodd thinks that "the man" here has reference to the Son of Man:

> May not the famous ecce *homo*, ἰδοὺ ὁ ἄνθρωπος (xix. 5), contain a disguised confession of Christ? Ostensibly, the words are contemptuous: "Look! the fellow!" But the evangelist was hardly unaware that "Son of Man" means "Man," and it would be entirely consistent with the Johannine irony that ἰδοὺ ὁ ἄνθρωπος should have the veiled

meaning: Behold the heavenly Man, now about to be exalted to reign over mankind! [88]

In vs. 9 the scene shifts from outside to inside the governor's house. This shift of scene makes it possible for Pilate to question Jesus privately. Both in the earlier private scene (18:33-38) and here one gains the impression of a certain congeniality toward Jesus on the part of Pilate, as if he were half convinced of the rightness of Jesus' claims. Pilate's words about his power to release Jesus or to crucify him (19:10) are unconvincing. Even if his claim were true it is only because he is promoting the divine purpose. His authority is really delegated authority, for it is given by God (19:11).

Pilate's question, "Where are you from?" reintroduces the whole question of Jesus' origin. The response on the part of Jesus is silence (19:9). Mark has it that the silence of Jesus made Pilate wonder (Mark 15:5). But the reader of the Fourth Gospel fills in the silence with his knowledge of what has been made evident in the earlier pages of the story. Jesus' silence is more eloquent than many words!

Jesus upon the Judgment Seat
19:12-16

THE HIGH DRAMA OF THE PRECEDING SECTION IS CONTINUED through these verses. Now it is expressed in a judgment scene. It is probable that the verb ἐκάθισεν (19:13) should be construed as causal, i.e., Pilate made Jesus sit upon the judgment seat. This is likely because (a) the verb itself is frequently used transitively; (b) the evangelist's method, generally, reinforces this interpretation; (c) the Gospel's frequent emphasis on judgment supports the assumption that the evangelist makes Jesus judge here; (d) the mockery of Jesus as king is probably extended to the mockery of Jesus as judge; and (e) the words of Pilate to the

[88] Ibid., p. 437.

Jews, "Here is your king," are better understood if Jesus has been placed upon the judgment seat.[89]

The role of Pilate in all this is amazing and demands separate consideration.[90] For the present it is sufficient to point out that his words, "Here is your king," while perhaps spoken in mockery, convey much more meaning than that. The reader is already aware from 18:33-38 that Jesus is king of the realm of truth. Pilate speaks better than he knows. But one has the impression that Pilate is himself more a champion of Jesus than an enemy. Again, when the Jews shout, "Crucify him, crucify him," Pilate asks, "Shall I crucify your king?" And when the chief priests profess complete loyalty to the emperor (19:15), Pilate hands Jesus over to *them* to be crucified (19:16). It is plain that the author intended that the blame for Jesus' death should fall on the Jews.

The Crucifixion

19:17-22

THE CRUCIFIXION NOW TAKES PLACE. TO FEEL ITS PECULIAR FORCE one has to keep in mind that this is the *hour* toward which the story has been moving. Behind the simple line, "There they crucified him" (19:18), lies the whole Johannine position on the glorification of the Son of Man and the redemption of the world. In view of this, it is remarkable that the evangelist shows such restraint at this point. In Mark, when Jesus dies, the temple curtain is torn in two; in Matthew there is an earthquake, the rocks are split, and the tombs opened; in both Mark and Matthew occurs the allusion to darkness; in Luke there is an eclipse (?) of the sun. But in John no such phenomena occur. In a Gospel which gives such glory to the cross we should expect

[89] Macgregor, following Moffatt's translation, takes this position. He points out that the passage is so understood by Justin Martyr (*Apology* I, 35), and by the author of the Gospel of Peter (Macgregor, *op. cit.*, p. 342). Goodspeed interprets the verb transitively also. Bultmann, on the other hand, holds to the intransitive meaning (Bultmann, *op. cit.*, p. 514, n. 2).

[90] *Infra*, pp. 227-28.

the event of the Crucifixion to be described in extravagant supernatural terms. Instead, we find the title hailing in universal language the kingship of Jesus, the soldiers casting lots for the garments of Jesus, the scene at the foot of the cross in which Jesus' mother and the beloved disciple figure, the cry, "I thirst," and the words of complete fulfillment, "It is finished."

Since this section contains the last major appearance of Pilate, it might be a strategic point to assess the problem of his role in the passion narrative.

In the first place, Pilate is in no sense a co-conspirator of the Jews. It might be said that there is a greater degree of antagonism between him and the Jews than between him and Jesus. The narrative in general supports this view, but the words, "What I have written, I have written," make clear his attitude (19:22). In one of its aspects this is a rebuke to the Jews for the persistent pressure which they have applied.

Secondly, it is evident that Pilate finds Jesus innocent of any crime. Three times he gives his verdict: ἐγὼ οὐδεμίαν εὑρίσκω ἐν αὐτῷ αἰτίαν ("I find no grounds for a charge in him": 18:38; 19:4, 6). Under pressure from the Jews, he attempts to free Jesus by giving them an opportunity to choose between Jesus and Barabbas as to who should be given freedom according to custom (18:39-40). Obviously, his hope is that Jesus will be chosen for freedom. Twice Pilate suggests that the Jews themselves should crucify Jesus (18:31; 19:6). Once it is stated explicitly that Pilate sought to release Jesus (19:12). Finally, Pilate turns Jesus over to them (the Jews) for crucifixion (19:16).

In the third place, there is reason to think that, in this Gospel, Pilate is well on his way toward being a Christian. His attitude toward the Jews and his affirmation of Jesus' innocence represent one aspect of this position. In addition, his questions and answers in Jesus' presence, and his attitude throughout these scenes, suggest a strong resemblance to the role of Nicodemus. We may note, for example, the character of certain of Pilate's questions: "Are you the king of the Jews?" (18:33), "What is truth?" (18:38), "Where are you from?" (19:9). At least it can be said that

227

Pilate's role as Roman inquisitor is mixed with that of a religious seeker.

This element of congeniality on Pilate's part is reinforced by two additional passages. After Pilate has persistently tried to free Jesus, and has then been forced to turn him over to the Jews for crucifixion, an amazing development takes place at the cross. One would expect that with the crucifixion Pilate's part would have been completed. But this is not the case; instead, he appears as the composer of a title to be placed on the cross (19:19). Forthrightly, this title proclaims Jesus as the King of the Jews. When the Jews protest that the title makes a fact of what is really a false pretension, Pilate says with the utmost finality, "What I have written, I have written" (19:22). In other words, the literal meaning stands: Jesus is the King of the Jews; this is Pilate's decision, and it must remain. Pilate stands at the end as the champion of Jesus' cause. The question which he had formerly raised, "Are you the king of the Jews?" is now answered by his own hand with a finality which cannot be challenged.

The second passage has to do with the burial of Jesus (19:38). This, of course, has a Synoptic counterpart (Mark 15:43; Matt. 27:57-58; Luke 23:50-52). But it is significant that the fourth evangelist does not reject it. The request of Joseph of Arimathea for the body of Jesus is granted by Pilate, thus placing the latter in a favorable light. Nicodemus appears in this story also (19:39). So appear in friendly association, Pilate, Joseph of Arimathea (a secret disciple), and Nicodemus. Pilate is already firmly established in the process which was to culminate in the laudatory characterization of the Acts of Pilate and sainthood in the Coptic church.

The Soldiers Cast Lots for Jesus' Clothing

19:23-24

IT IS NOTABLE THAT THIS IS THE FIRST OF THREE INSTANCES IN ch. 19 which resort to scripture (cf. 19:28, 36-37). This suggests that the prime motivation for the latter's inclusion was to demonstrate that the Crucifixion was the working out of the divine plan. The meticulous way in which the evangelist attempts to meet the demands (as he interprets them) of Ps. 22:18 reinforces this suggestion. In the same manner that Matthew misconstrues Hebrew parallelism and has Jesus ride into Jerusalem on two animals to fulfill the prophecy of Zechariah (Matt. 21:2, 5), our author must meet the precise conditions of a literal reading of Ps. 22:18. The Roman soldiers are, of course, ignorant of the fact that they are fulfilling scripture, so an excuse must be given for their action in casting lots. This excuse is provided by the device of the seamless tunic. It seems improbable that symbolism is to be read into this feature. Suggestions to the effect that the seamless tunic makes Jesus the world's high priest or that it is a symbol of the Logos or of the church seem too far-fetched in this context. The point is that the evangelist feels the need of a proof text, so he constructs the incident to conform to his interpretation of the passage most appropriate to the division of the clothing. He had found reference to the division of the clothing and the casting of lots in his Synoptic sources (Mark 15:24; Matt. 27:35; Luke 23:34).

Jesus Speaks to His Mother and the Beloved Disciple

19:25-27

THIS LITTLE UNIT OF THE STORY CONTAINS ONE OF THE THORNIEST problems facing the interpreter: What is the meaning of the

229

words of Jesus to his mother and to the beloved disciple? It is obvious that Jesus, his mother, and the beloved disciple constitute the main characters in the scene. The women are there only because of the tradition that there were women present (Mark 15:40; Matt. 27-56), though, with the exception of Mary of Magdala, they can be identified with the characters of John only by resort to the harmonistic method. Their presence also gives an appropriate setting for the appearance of Jesus' mother. The real point of the story has to do with the three characters; and, of the women, only with the mother of Jesus.

The significance of this scene is derived from a combination of factors. In the first place, it must be recalled that the only other place in the Gospel where Jesus is associated with his mother occurs in the wedding scene at Cana (2:1-5). On that occasion he had rejected her assumption of parental authority since his status as son of a human parent has been changed to a new one as Son of God. Furthermore, in the Cana story the suggestion of Jesus' mother that he give the Spirit (implicit in the phrase "They have no wine") was rejected by him, for his hour (that is to say, the crucifixion hour) had not yet come.

But now his hour has come! He is exalted, lifted up on the cross, and so the earlier suggestion that the Spirit be given is ready to find fulfillment. So also is there a correction of the earlier impression of the abandonment of his mother. Now, as the last act before the giving up of his Spirit, Jesus establishes a filial relationship between his mother and the special disciple —a disciple who was in his bosom as Jesus was in the bosom of the Father, and was closely enough identified with Jesus as to be, in effect, his alter ego.

This suggestion reinforces our interpretation of the beloved disciple as a type of the true believer;[91] in other words, he is a symbol of the true church. Jesus' mother is taken into the church by a special act of Jesus himself.[92]

[91] Supra, pp. 218-19.
[92] Goguel thinks of the passage under discussion as antidynastic in character (Maurice Goguel, The Birth of Christianity, New York: The Macmillan Company, 1954, p. 114; English translation by H. C. Snape).

Jesus Gives Up His Spirit

19:28-30

WHEN JESUS DELIVERS HIS MOTHER INTO THE KEEPING OF THE beloved disciple his earthly career has been completed (19:28). But in fulfillment of scripture he yet must say, "I am thirsty" (19:28). The scripture referred to must be Ps. 69:21. This "sour wine" should not be confused with the wine refused by Jesus in Matthew (Matt. 27:34, 48). However, there could be dependence on Mark 15:23 and Luke 23:36 for the idea. The idea of a drugged wine offered out of compassion is not present in John, but the offering of wine *in fulfillment of scripture* is certainly there. There is no warrant to see in this an antidocetic reference. The note, "to fulfill the scripture," signifies its function, and constitutes the second item in a series of such appeals to scripture in the immediate context of the Crucifixion (cf. 19:24, 36-37).

In terms of the total dramatic structure of the Gospel vs. 30 is of great importance. In truly Johannine style the words "It is finished" are ambiguous. They mean, on the one hand, his career has now ended, he is about to die (this is what the onlooker would grasp). On the other hand, the words signify the completion of the work of redemption which is accomplished in the cross. And since this redemption is due to the giving of the Spirit, the bowing of the head in death is paralleled by the giving up of the Spirit.

It is important to dwell for a moment on this point. Mark has it that Jesus "breathed his last" (ἐξέπνευσεν, Mark 15:37); Matthew puts it that he "gave up the spirit" (ἀφῆκεν τὸ πνεῦμα, Matt. 27:50); Luke states that Jesus "breathed his last" (ἐξέπνευσεν, Luke 23:46). It is to be noted that in none of these cases does the verb ἀποθνῄσκω, "to die," appear; instead, we find in each case some connection with πνεῦμα, "spirit." This may be significant. While in the earlier Gospels it may be merely idiomatic for "Jesus died," it would be easy for the fourth

231

evangelist to read more into it. But one is not sure that a deeper meaning is not intended even in the Synoptics. The question is most acute in relation to the Lucan account. Luke 23:46 reads, "And uttering a great cry, Jesus said, 'Father, I place my spirit into your hands.' And when he had said this he breathed his last" (ἐξέπνευσεν). In the act of "breathing out his Spirit," he commits it to the Father. It would be an easy step from this idea to that of John where death by crucifixion means the return of the Spirit to the Father.

One might well expect the phrase "he gave up the Spirit" to be the final, climactic act of Jesus and the terminal point of the book. Instead, we find the narrative extended to resurrection stories plus a structured account of the giving of the Spirit to the disciples by Jesus in terms of an insufflation (20:22-23). Why does the narrative continue beyond the point where the Spirit has been released at the time of Jesus' death?

The answer seems to lie in the area of the Gospel's stress on the personal relation between Jesus and the believer. Not even in the momentous event of Pentecost in Acts is the Spirit bestowed personally by Jesus; yet John has his own story of the bequeathing of the Spirit—a Johannine "Pentecost," which relates the Spirit and its accompanying power directly to Jesus himself (20:22-23). Dodd has pointed out that

although it is declared that at the moment of the death of Jesus on the cross all is accomplished, and that the life-giving stream, which is the Spirit (vii. 38), is now released (xix. 34) for the salvation of man, it is yet necessary that the Spirit should be given by the risen Lord to His disciples (xx. 22). *Sub specie aeternitatis*, all is fulfilled in Christ's one complete self-oblation. Yet there was a moment in history when men received the Spirit as they had not received it before, and this moment is represented by the incident of the "insufflation," which is securely anchored to the empirical history of the Church by the commission to forgive sins—a commission strictly relative to the existence of the Church in time.[93]

Op. cit., p. 442.

232

Descent from the Cross

19:31-37

THE REFERENCE TO THE DAY OF PREPARATION IN VS. 31 IS ONE of a series of chronological notes (13:1; 18:28) which indicate that John placed the death of Jesus on the fourteenth of Nisan, coincident with the death of the Passover lamb. It will be recalled that John the Baptist had hailed Jesus as the Lamb of God.[94] It is probable that the evangelist intended his story of the passion to continue the Lamb symbolism of the earlier chapter. Paul had written, "Christ, our paschal lamb, has been sacrificed" (I Cor. 5:7). In all probability this symbolism prompted our evangelist to deviate from the date for Jesus' death indicated by the Synoptists; namely, the fifteenth of Nisan. This interest in Jesus as the Passover lamb is established by the reference to Exod. 12:46 (cf. Num. 9:12) in that failure to break the legs of Jesus identifies him with the Passover lamb of the scripture passage quoted (19:36). It is true, of course, that the evangelist does not develop a theory of the death of Jesus in terms of sacrifice. But that fact does not prevent him from suggesting symbolically that in the death of Jesus, God gave his Son. It is this "givingness" of God that he finds of value in the lamb symbolism.

From the use made of Old Testament passages in ch. 18, we may infer that the evangelist found appeal to its authority of special value in relation to the Crucifixion. Colwell has observed that

almost every event of the Passion happens to fulfill Scripture; while there are not more than six or seven allusions to the Old Testament elsewhere in John. Moses and the serpent set the type for the death of Jesus (3:14); the Messiah enters on an ass's colt (12: 14-16); the disbelief of the Jews was predicted by Isaiah (12:37-41; 15:25); the betrayal by a disciple was foretold (13:18; 17:12); the

[94] *Supra*, pp. 73-74.

escape of the disciples and the execution by the Romans were predicted by Jesus himself (18:9, 32); the division of Jesus' clothes
was controlled by Scripture (19:23-24); so also what he said from
the cross (19:28), and the fact his legs were not broken and his
side was pierced (19:31-37). If John's quotations of Scripture are
numerous only in the Passion story, it is because that part of the
career of Jesus was hardest to deify. The Jesus of John needed no
divine prediction to support the account of the public ministry,
but the crucifixion story could be transformed into the triumph of
a god only with the greatest difficulty. To support this transformation the author of the Fourth Gospel turned to the Scriptures.[95]

This tendency to appeal to the scriptures for support finds
its final expression in the references to the breaking of the legs
and the piercing of the side with the lance (19:36-37). Aside
from the symbolic reference to Jesus as the Passover lamb, the
main problem centers in the phenomenon which accompanied
the piercing of the side, namely, the flow of blood and water.
What is the meaning of this peculiar phenomenon?

In the first place, we do well to observe that it is tied to the
reference to the reliable witness. Goguel identifies the witness
as the beloved disciple, and asserts that the fragment belongs
to the earliest parts of the Gospel.[96] Macgregor, who holds to
the theory of a redactor, thinks that the reference to the witness
belongs to him. He points out that the witness passage breaks
the continuity between vss. 33 f., and 36; also that it seems to
be a "throw-back" of the point of view of the Appendix into the
body of the Gospel (cf. 21:24).

If Macgregor is right about the witness passage (and it is a
strong possibility), then it is also possible that the reference
to blood and water is an addition by the same hand, and that
it was added to enhance the wondrous and mystical character
of the event. It is this phenomenon of the flow of blood and
water to which the witness testifies, not the breaking of the

[95] John Defends the Gospel, pp. 86-87. Used by permission of Harper &
Brothers.
[96] Op. cit., p. 545, n. 1.

234

legs and the piercing of the side as such. The reference to blood and water is therefore closely connected with the witness passage. If the addition is inclusive of both the witness passage and the reference to blood and water, i.e., of 19:34b, 35, then the original would have read as follows:

32 So the soldiers came and broke the legs of the first man and of the other who had been crucified with him. 33 But when they came to Jesus and saw that he was already dead, they did not break his legs. 34 But one of the soldiers pierced his side with a lance. 36 For these things took place that the scripture might be fulfilled, "Not one of his bones shall be broken"; 37 and again, another scripture says, "They will look at him whom they pierced." [97]

This would result in a balanced parallel structure, allowing the two Old Testament passages to refer to the breaking of the legs and the piercing of the side, respectively, without the complicating additions of the blood and water and the witness reference.

We must hasten to add, however, that this can be no more than a suggestion. In a book like the Fourth Gospel one cannot place a great deal of trust in literary reconstruction apart from textual evidence to support it. And for this there is none. On the other hand, there is strong internal probability that the witness passage, at least, is an interpolation into the text. Our suggestion merely extends this to include vs. 34b.

If we proceed now on the assumption that the reference to blood and water should stand in the text, the question remains as to its meaning for the evangelist. The usual procedure is to equate the blood with the eucharist and the water with baptism. But if it is the case, as we have suggested, that the Fourth Gospel is nonsacramental and relegates water baptism to an in-

[97] This suggestion was originally made in a seminar on the Fourth Gospel by Richard Olds, a graduate student in the School of Religion, University of Southern California. One suspects that there is some connection between the reference to the blood and water in the Gospel and a similar reference in I John 5:6-8, and that there is a literary relationship between the Gospel proper, the Appendix, and I John at this point.

ferior position,[98] the explanation of the symbolism is likely to be found elsewhere. Dodd has pointed out (and probably rightly so) that association of the passage with 6:55 and 7:38 is inevitable. While the meaning of 6:55 is not immediately clear, that of 7:38 is explained: the water which issues from the body of Jesus is the Spirit to be given when Jesus is glorified.

From the crucified body of Christ flows the life-giving stream: the water which is the Spirit given to believers in Him (vii. 38-39), the water which if a man drink he will never thirst again (iv. 14), and the blood which is ἀληθὴς πόσις ["true drink"] (vi. 55).[99]

The allusion to blood and water would be another (symbolic) way of saying that the life to which the first twelve chapters attest, and to which the signs point, now finds its fulfillment in the Crucifixion. "Blood" and "water" are therefore not symbolic of the eucharist and of baptism, but are meaningful symbols already built into the Gospel's structure intending to say, "Now the richness of divine life is poured out."

The Burial
19:38-42

THE MAIN IMPRESSIONS LEFT BY THE READING OF THIS PASSAGE are those of dignity and munificence. Joseph of Arimathea, characterized by Mark as a respected member of the council (Mark 15:43), and Nicodemus, mentioned formerly as "a ruler of the Jews" (3:1) and "Israel's teacher" (3:10), men of high repute, come together in this scene of the anointing. The former requests permission from Pilate to remove the body of Jesus, while the latter brings a lavish amount of expensive ointments; these are their respective roles. "Judas had been scandalized at the use of one pound of perfume for the living Jesus (12:3-5), and here are one hundred pounds brought to his corpse!" [100] The

[98] Supra, pp. 123-24.
[99] Op. cit., p. 428; cf. p. 438.
[100] Loisy, quoted by Macgregor, op. cit., p. 353.

Synoptics leave the impression that the body of Jesus had not been anointed for burial, but that impression is corrected by John. Not only was his body lavishly anointed, but the anointing was done by devoted disciples of high social standing. The burial is carried out with all the dignity appropriate to the occasion.

Two other items reinforce the dignity of the event: Jesus is buried in a *new tomb* located in a *garden* (19:41). The "garden" is a feature peculiar to the Fourth Gospel. John seems to think of the garden location as a fitting place, both for the arrest of Jesus (18:1) and for his burial (cf. II Kings 21:18, 26). Mark speaks of a tomb hewn out of rock (Mark 15:46); Matthew has the tomb the property of Joseph, and describes it as "new," and as hewn in the rock (Matt. 27:60); Luke has it that the tomb was rock-hewn, and adds that no one had yet been placed in it (Luke 23:53). John's account seems to be in part a reconstruction from Matthew and Luke, deriving the "newness" of the tomb from Matthew, and the phrase, "in which no one had yet been put," from Luke. In John, these two items become complementary, and must be construed as a mark of honor.

The Race to the Tomb
20:1-10

THE IMPORTANCE OF THIS SECTION SEEMS TO LIE IN THE ASSOCIATION of two disciples, Peter and the beloved disciple, in connection with belief engendered by the empty tomb. The introduction of Mary Magdalene in 20:1-2 stems from her part in the Synoptic account (Mark 16:1; Matt. 28:1; Luke 24:1, 10); obviously, she has no part to play in the story of the race to the tomb. Her appearance in 20:1-2 serves to lead to the scene in which Jesus appears to her, although there is no record of her advance to the tomb from the position in vss. 1 and 2.

What is the meaning of this story of the race to the tomb? Bultmann thinks that Peter and the beloved disciple have symbolic meaning: Peter is a representative of Jewish Christianity while the beloved disciple represents Gentile Christianity. The

237

first community of the faithful is established out of Jewish Christians; then, after them, the Gentiles come to believe. But the fact that Jewish Christians come first gives them no superiority over Gentile Christians; indeed, readiness to believe on the part of the Gentiles is often greater than that of the Jews: the beloved disciple runs more rapidly to the tomb than Peter.[101]

There is a second aspect of this, the first of the postcrucifixion scenes, which needs to be considered. It stems mainly from the reference to the linen cloths which remained inside the tomb (20:6-7): καὶ θεωρεῖ τὰ ὀθόνια κείμενα καὶ τὸ σουδάριον ὃ ἦν ἐπὶ τῆς κεφαλῆς αὐτοῦ οὐ μετὰ τῶν ὀθονίων κείμενον ἀλλὰ χωρὶς ἐντετυλιγμένον εἰς ἕνα τόπον ("And [Peter] saw the linen cloths lying there, and the handkerchief which had been on Jesus' head, not lying with the linen cloths, but rolled up separately in one place"). This careful description suggests that a peculiar meaning attaches to the position of the grave cloths. As Howard puts it:

The meaning of the Greek word applied to the napkin (ἐντετυλιγμένον) seems here to be "wound around." As the evangelist regards the sight as a faith-creating phenomenon for **the other disciple** . . . , the interpretation that thinks of the linen clothes as merely having been "rolled up" is too jejune for the context. The explanation that best fits the Johannine view of the mode of the Resurrection is that the body had been swifty dematerialized, leaving the swathing clothes as they were, with the cloth that had been wrapped around the head still lying on the slightly raised ledge where the head had been laid, and keeping its annular shape. . . . In other words, if the body of Jesus had been carried away from the tomb, either the grave clothes would have been taken away with the body, or else they would have been scattered on the floor of the sepulcher. It was their position that made the disciples leap to the conclusion that the material body had been transformed into

[101] *Op. cit.*, p. 531. It should be noted that Bultmann is consistent in this interpretation of the beloved disciple, relating it to 13:23-25 and 19:26-27, as well as to the passage under discussion here. See Bultmann, *op. cit.*, pp. 369-70.

a spiritual body. This seems to correspond with the Pauline doctrine (cf. I Cor. 15:20, 44, 50).[102]

This concept of the Risen Jesus is supported by his ability to go through closed doors (20:19, 26). Once again the evangelist reveals his dependence on the thought of Paul.

The reader of the Fourth Gospel confronts the story of the empty tomb with the background of the Lazarus story in mind. Here we find the same phenomenon of resurrection, but with important differences. Lazarus had been raised from the dead by Jesus. The lesson to be drawn was that Jesus is the source of life—life giving spirit (cf. I Cor. 15:45); Lazarus is not raised on his own accord. But in the case of the resurrection of Jesus it is different. No one is present when the resurrection takes place; no one needs to be, for the life which is in him is intrinsically superior to the powers of death. In the case of Lazarus the dead man emerges from the tomb still bound with the bandages, and they are removed only at the command of Jesus. In the case of Jesus the bandages are left undisturbed, for Life rises unfettered from the bonds of death. Lazarus has life mediated to him; but life is original with Jesus.

But vestiges of the unbelief of the earlier, sign-type, story still remain attached to the resurrection of Jesus. Mary Magdalene infers from the fact that the tomb is empty that Jesus' body has been removed surreptitiously (20:2, 13). And the disciples run to the tomb with Mary's fears fresh in their minds. It is only when they see the empty tomb for themselves, and especially the position of the linen cloths and the handkerchief, that they believe (20:8). Then the note is added, "For they did not yet know the scripture, that he must rise from the dead." The point seems to be that through the experience of viewing the empty tomb they came to believe in Jesus' resurrection apart from a knowledge of the scripture's teaching. What passage is intended it is impossible to tell; possibly Ps. 16:10 (cf. Acts 13:35).

[102] Wilbert F. Howard, in The Interpreter's Bible, VIII, 790. Copyright 1952 by Abingdon Press and used by their permission.

Jesus Appears to Mary Magdalene

20:11-18

THIS IS THE SECOND OF THE POSTCRUCIFIXION SCENES. THERE seems to be movement toward a climax from the idea of the empty tomb, to an appearance of Jesus to Mary, to the bestowal of the Spirit, to the belief of Thomas, and to the climactic words of Jesus in 20:29. In the present scene Mary appears, weeping because Jesus' body has apparently been removed from its burial place. But, looking into the tomb, she is confronted by an angelic scene (20:11-12). The angels' question, "Woman, why are you weeping?" prompts her to express her fears: her Lord's body has been lost to her.

The next step is the appearance of Jesus himself (20:14). As in the case of the two disciples on the Emmaus road (Luke 24:13-35), she fails to recognize him. Jesus then asks the same question the angels had asked, "Woman, why are you weeping?" with an additional one, "Whom do you seek?" (20:15). This second question betrays his knowledge of her reason for being there. Still unaware of his identity, Mary supposes that he is the gardener, and suggests that she be told of the resting place of Jesus' body (20:15). Then with one word Jesus makes himself known; in the speaking of her name, "Mary" (20:16).

This mode of revelation is in striking contrast to that in the Lucan Emmaus-road story. In the latter, Jesus makes himself known to the two disciples in the breaking of bread (Luke 24:30-31, 35). It is difficult to escape the impression that the fourth evangelist wrote this scene with the Emmaus-road story in mind. Luke's story of the empty tomb refers to "two men in dazzling apparel" (Luke 24:4), and in the Emmaus-road passage itself they are described as angels whom the women had seen at the tomb during their early morning visit (Luke 24:22-23). This feature, together with the elements of lack of

240

recognition and disclosure through a precise event, suggests literary dependence.

If this is so, then the fact that Jesus discloses himself through the utterance of Mary's name and not in the eucharist (for a eucharist it appears to be in Luke) has special significance. *The risen Jesus is known by his intimate, personal relationship to his people.* The attentive reader of the Gospel will associate this scene with words which Jesus had already spoken: "The sheep hear his voice, and he calls his own sheep by name and leads them out" (10:3). There is something startling (and appealing) in hearing one's given name spoken by another who appears to be a total stranger. It makes one ask, "Do I know him?"

A further important aspect of this section occurs in vs. 17. With Mary's recognition of Jesus, Jesus admonishes her with the words, "Do not touch me, for I have not yet ascended to my Father and your Father, to my God and your God" (20:17). Dodd seems to have found the key to this enigmatic statement when he says:

The reappearance of οὔπω ["not yet"], which is so natural and so significant . . . in the Book of Signs, is surprising here, after the hour has been declared come, and all things accomplished. While Christ's ascent, or exaltation, is fully accomplished on the cross, *sub specie aeternitatis,* it cannot be fully accomplished in relation to men and to human history until the resurrection, as return to His disciples, in this world, and at a particular time, is an established fact. Thus the process by which Jesus is establishing renewed contact with His disciples after His resurrection is accompanied by a process of ascent, which can be (temporally speaking) complete only when this renewed contact is consolidated; that is, in the sense of xiv. 15-18, xvi. 13-16, when they possess the Spirit. When therefore the disciples have received the Spirit through His "insufflation" (xx. 22), we may know that Christ has finally ascended. And this seems to be implied when Thomas is invited to touch His hands and side, in contrast to Mary Magdalene, who was not permitted to touch Him, because He was not yet ascended.[103]

[103] *Op. cit.,* pp. 442-43.

241

The Giving of the Spirit

20:19-23

THE GREAT CLIMAX OF THE GOSPEL COMES AT THE POINT OF THE giving of the Spirit to the disciples (20:22-23). Care is taken to show the difference in the resurrection body of Jesus as compared with the Jesus of the precrucifixion period. It is twice mentioned that the doors of the room were shut (20:19, 26); yet Jesus entered their midst. It is as the Spirit that he gives the Spirit. Nevertheless, his spiritual body still bears the identifying marks: he shows them his hands and his side (20:20). John differs from the Synoptists in that he speaks of the marks of the nails (20:25), and substitutes "his side" for "his feet" (cf. Luke 24:39), the substitution being the natural sequel to 19:34.

Jesus greets the disciples with the beautiful salutation, "Peace be with you"—twice repeated (20:19, 21). This fulfills his words spoken in the valedictory address (14:27).

Three elements are combined in vss. 21-23: (a) the disciples are "sent" by Jesus just as Jesus was "sent" by the Father; (b) Jesus breathes the Spirit on the disciples; and (c) the disciples are given authority to forgive or to retain sins. But these three are not to be thought of as in any sense independent; the first and last elements are rooted in the second. The disciples are sent just as Jesus was sent. That is to say, just as the Spirit was sent into the world to remain in Jesus of Nazareth, so the Spirit is now sent into the world to remain in the disciples. In each case the Spirit is the important factor; it was the essential element in Jesus, and it will be the essential element in the disciples.

Similarly, the authority given the disciples to forgive or retain sins cannot be understood apart from its relation to the giving of the Spirit. In form the statement resembles that of Matt. 16:19 and 18:18, but is less technical.

The words "binding" and "loosing" are used there (Matt. 18:

242

18) in their technical meaning of a rabbi's responsibility for declaring in the light of tradition and experience that an action was forbidden (i.e., "bound"), or permitted (i.e., "loosed").[104]

The Johannine passage must be understood in terms of the Gospel's own teaching. As Macgregor puts it:

By the inbreathing of the Spirit Christ himself becomes incarnate in the community of the disciples, i.e. the Church. Accordingly there is a sense in which the world (separate from that Church, 17:6, 14) will be judged by its attitude towards the Christian community and its message. Just as to accept Jesus as Son of God means forgiveness of sin and to reject him means the "retaining" of sin (8:24, 9:41), and in this sense Christ is said to "judge" men (3:17 f.), so may the Church be said to "judge" men—to forgive or retain their sin—when, as a result of either accepting or spurning the Church's message, men deliberately choose either life or death (2 Cor. 2:16, Is. 6:9 f.). . . . Just as in Matthew the life and authority of the Church are to be founded on faith exemplified in Peter, so here are they derived from the gift of the Spirit bestowed on the gathered disciples.[105]

Belief in the Seen and the Unseen
20: 24-29

THE AFFINITY OF CH. 20 WITH LUKE 24 (ESPECIALLY WITH 24:36-43) is again evident here. Luke relates that Jesus appeared to the disciples, that they supposed that he was a spirit, that as evidence of the corporeal nature of the Resurrection, Jesus draws attention to his body as consisting of flesh and bone, and that he ate fish before the disciples. The antidocetic character of the Lucan narrative is obvious. But the Johannine account is geared to another interest. Thomas, absent at the first appearance of Jesus, doubts the simple statement of the disciples, "We have seen the Lord." He wants tangible proof of its truth; the body

---

[104] Howard, op. cit., p. 798.
[105] Op. cit., pp. 365 f.

of Jesus will furnish the evidence (20:25). When Jesus appears a second time the evidence is before him and (though there is no word to the effect that he touched Jesus) he makes his great confession: "My Lord and my God!" But it must not be thought that this is the climax of the scene; that follows, in truly Johannine fashion, in the climactic words, "Have you believed because you have seen me? Blessed are they who have not seen, yet believe." This is the main point of the Thomas story. Belief based on seeing Jesus externally is inferior to belief which is independent of it. This, of course, is the only kind of belief which the church of John's time could possess. But the superiority of this belief is not affirmed merely because of the chronological accident that John's own generation failed to coincide with the historical career of Jesus. Its superior quality is due, rather, to the divine economy in which the unseen world is the real world to which the Son of God truly belongs. His Presence becomes a living reality if seen by the eyes of faith. This passage, then, is not antidocetic. If anything it is more congenial to docetism than hostile to it, though it is probably more correct to say that it is neutral with respect to the problem. Its interest is in belief that goes beyond tangible evidence.

Vs. 29 may well have a bearing on the problem of authorship. From the time of Irenaeus the author of the Gospel has been identified with John the disciple. Modern scholarship, in the main, has repudiated this identification, maintaining that the Gospel was written either by an anonymous Christian or by the elusive John the Elder. For the latter assertion there is no precedent in antiquity. External evidence helps us not at all since it is relatively late, and is biased in favor of apostolic authorship. Even the tendentious Appendix must be ruled out. Any light as to the author's identity must come from the Gospel itself, and even this can be of value only in the most general terms.

It is possibly more fruitful to approach the problem from the standpoint of the evangelist's concept of the ideal disciple. Assuming that he, like Paul before him, considered his gospel to be *the* gospel, we may conclude that he was one who had not known Jesus, and who indeed considered historical knowledge of Jesus to be an inferior basis of faith. The words of Jesus to Thomas, "Have you believed because you have seen me? Blessed are they who have not seen, yet believe," represent the evangelist's personal testimony; he is one so blessed! On the other hand, had he been a disciple of Jesus he might well have argued for the priority of the faith of disciples like Peter or John. But the burden of the Gospel's thought is in the opposite direction. There is no discernible tendency toward a looking to the past for the norm of the church's authority. The idea of apostolic authority as constituting a rule of faith is foreign to the Gospel's outlook; authority is rooted in the believer's contemporary experience of the living Spirit in the community. It is to this group that the author belongs, and it is of this experience that he speaks with authority. He therefore invites his public to share with him the same richness of life which he himself enjoys, confident that it is independent of a historical relationship to Jesus: "Blessed are they who have not seen, yet believe."

Postscript
20: 30-31

THIS PASSAGE CONSTITUTES THE STATED PURPOSE OF THE GOSPEL. It says, in effect, that out of a multiplicity of signs which Jesus performed, a certain number have been selected to create belief in Jesus as the Son of God, in the knowledge that such belief leads to life. This means that, for the evangelist, it is unnecessary to gather together all existing records of Jesus' activity; the signs which he selects are sufficient in themselves (rightly understood) to convey knowledge of Jesus.

It should be observed, however, that this *stated* purpose does not exhaust the purpose of the evangelist. It may be said that it constitutes his main purpose from the point of view of religious experience, but a survey of changes made in material borrowed from the Synoptics indicates many other purposes.

Ernest Cadman Colwell's book *John Defends the Gospel* was written to show that many interests were "fused together" in his purpose; that John wrote to show that Jesus was not a magician, he was not a follower of John the Baptist, he was not a Jew, he was not a human being, that he did not associate with sinners, he was not a criminal, that Christianity was not a superstition, and not a revolutionary movement. He points out that these purposes are to be understood in relation to the cultural level of John's audience, a culture superior to that which lies back of Paul and the earlier gospels.[106]

But when all is said and done it is the religious interest that dominates the Gospel writer's thought. While it is true, as Colwell points out, that all four Gospels were written for the purpose stated in 20:31, and that the purpose as stated does not make the Fourth Gospel distinctive,[107] it is also true that the whole theme, "that you may believe that Jesus is the Christ, the Son of God, and that by believing you may have life in his name," has a meaning for our evangelist which is different from that of any other Gospel extant. In this sense it is peculiarly *his* theme. He could say, like Paul before him, "This is *my* gospel!"

The Appendix

21:1-25

SCHOLARS ARE ALMOST UNANIMOUSLY AGREED THAT CH. 21 was not a part of the original Gospel, but that it was added later. This agreement is remarkable in view of the fact that there is no manuscript evidence to support the view. But the internal evidence against its being an authentic ending of the Gospel is extremely strong. The main points may be summarized as follows:

1. The Appendix, as now placed, constitutes a second conclusion to the Gospel. The first, and most natural, conclusion comes at 20:30-31.

[106] Pp. 1-109.
[107] *Ibid.*, p. 10.

2. The inclusion of the Appendix results in a conflation of the two traditions of the resurrection appearances of Jesus: the Judean and the Galilean. The likelihood that any Gospel writer would do this is, in itself, remote. It is even less likely that the fourth evangelist with his stress on Jerusalem would include a Galilean appearance.

3. The role of Peter in the Appendix suggests that one of its major functions was to reinstate him to a place of primacy. This is shown by his eagerness to go to Jesus (21:7), and by a three-fold confession of his love for Jesus, paralleling his threefold denial (21:15-17; cf. 18:15-18, 25-27).

4. It is obvious that vs. 24 is an attempt to identify the author of the Gospel with the Beloved Disciple, and possibly (though this is not certain) with John the son of Zebedee. Yet vss. 24 and 25 are undoubtedly an addition to the Gospel and there is no good reason to think that they are by a different hand than the Appendix itself. As Macgregor remarks, "These verses seem closely connected with the rest of the chapter, and if we amputate 24 f. not only do we leave the chapter without any suitable ending, but we deprive it of its whole *raison d'être*." [108]

5. Commentators vary in their judgments as to the value of evidence in terms of language and style. Macgregor thinks it argues strongly against the authenticity of the Appendix.[109] Bultmann, on the other hand, does not think that language and style present conclusive evidence.[110] But he points out certain peculiar features of ch. 21: ἀδελφοί as a designation for Christians (21:23); ἐξετάζειν in place of ἐρωτᾶν (21:12); ἐπιστραφῆναι in place of στραφῆναι (21:20; cf. 1:38; 20:14, 16; ἰσχύειν in place of δύνασθαι (21:6); τολμᾶν followed by an infinitive (21:12); the disciples are called παιδία (21:5); causal ἀπό (21:6; partitive ἀπό in place of ἐκ (21:10); ἕως in place of ἕως ὅτου (21:22; cf. 9:18),

[108] Op. cit., p. 367.
[109] Ibid.
[110] Op. cit., p. 542.

or ἕως οὗ (cf. 13:38); πλέον in place of μᾶλλον (21:15; cf. 3:19; 12:43); οὐ μακράν in place of ἐγγύς (21:8; cf., e.g., 11:18); ὑπάγειν with infinitive (21:3; cf. 4:16; 9:7; 15:16); peculiar also is τι πρὸς σέ (21:22; cf. 2:4).[111]

Bultmann also notes certain words which occur in ch. 21 but nowhere else in the Gospel: αἰγιαλός (vs. 4), ἁλιεύειν (vs. 3), ἀποβαίνειν (vs. 9), ἀριστῆσαι (vs. 12), ἀρνίον (vs. 15), βόσκειν (vs. 15), γηράσκειν (vs. 18), γυμνός (vs. 7), δίκτυον (vss. 6, 8), ἐκτείνειν (vs. 18), ἐπενδύτης (vs. 7), ζωννύναι (vs. 18), οἶμαι (vs. 25), πῆχυς (vs. 8), πιάζειν (vss. 3, 10), ποιμαίνειν (vs. 16), προβάτιον (vs. 16), προσφάγιον (vs. 5), πρωΐα (vs. 4), σύρειν (vs. 8).[112]

It may safely be assumed, on the basis of these factors, that ch. 21 constituted no part of the original Gospel. But in view of the lack of manuscript evidence to the contrary, it must be granted that the Appendix became affixed to the Gospel at an extremely early date, probably for purposes indicated in points 3 and 4 above.

The Appendix is divided into two episodes: the first dealing with an appearance of the Risen Lord to seven disciples by the Sea of Galilee (Tiberias) (21:1-14); the second with Peter and the Beloved Disciple (21:15-23).

Several sources seem to lie behind the first episode. Certain disciples named are drawn, apparently, from the Fourth Gospel itself, giving the impression of continuity. These are Peter, Thomas ("The Twin"), Nathanael, who is said to belong to Cana of Galilee, although the Gospel does not specify Cana (1:43-51), and two anonymous disciples. The sons of Zebedee are mentioned but not by name. This item must be drawn from the Synoptic tradition. Mention is also made of the disciple whom Jesus loved. Since the disciples present are listed, he must be identified with one of the seven.

The episode of the appearance of Jesus by the sea (21:1-14) seems to be dependent in part on Luke 5:1-11. The account of

[111] Ibid., pp. 542-43.
[112] Ibid., p. 542, n. 5.

248

the miraculous catch of fish parallels the Lucan story. The latter account itself may have been originally a resurrection tradition. If so, the Johannine Appendix has restored its original function.

But the Appendix introduces several significant changes in the Lucan source: In Luke, only three disciples are present—Peter, and the two sons of Zebedee—while in the Appendix there are seven, one of whom, significantly, is the Beloved Disciple. In Luke, Jesus teaches "the people" from the boat, but in the Appendix only the disciples are present, and Jesus is on the shore. In the earlier Gospel, Jesus initiates the action by commanding Peter to push off from shore and let down the net. But in the Appendix it is Peter who begins the action by his words, "I am going fishing." Luke speaks of a great shoal of fish, while in the Appendix the number is specified as 153. In Luke, there is no failure to recognize Jesus, but in the Appendix recognition comes through the Beloved Disciple, expressed by the words, "It is the Lord." Peter confesses his sinfulness in Luke; this is absent from the Appendix. Luke has Jesus announce to Peter that henceforth he will be catching men. While this is absent from the Appendix, perhaps its equivalent is to be found in the reference to the threefold commission, "Feed my lambs," "Tend my sheep," "Feed my sheep." This commission, however, involves a threefold confession of love for Jesus on Peter's part, so more properly balances the threefold denial of Jesus by Peter.

A second source lying behind the Appendix appears to be Luke 24:13-35. The meal is the counterpart of the one described in that section of Luke. In Luke, the two disciples recognize Jesus in the breaking of bread. This is reflected in the Appendix by vss. 4 and 12. It is probable that here the eucharist is intended as in Luke. The art of the Christian catacombs in Rome depicts the eucharist as consisting of bread and fish.

The sources for the second episode are (a) the tradition of Peter's threefold denial (indicated in the Synoptics and the Fourth Gospel); (b) the tradition of Peter's martyrdom; (c) the Fourth Gospel proper; and (d) the tradition that a certain disciple would be alive at Jesus' coming.

249

Vss. 1-14 present two main elements: the miraculous catch of fish, and the meal of bread and fish. It seems likely that the number of fish caught (153) has a symbolic meaning, and probably refers to the great number to be added to the Church by the apostolic preaching,[113] perhaps to the nations of the earth.

The second element, the meal of bread and fish, probably signifies the recognition of Christ through the eucharist. Luke has it that the two disciples recognized Jesus in the breaking of bread (Luke 24:35). The writer of the Appendix is somewhat limited with respect to the idea of recognition through the meal, since he has already indicated recognition through the medium of the Beloved Disciple (vs. 7). Yet he betrays his interest in the concept in vs. 12: "None of the disciples had the courage to ask him, 'Who are you?' They already knew it was the Lord." Why introduce the question, "Who are you?" at all if they already possessed knowledge as to Jesus' identity? The reason is that the writer is caught between the thought of his source (probably Luke 24), and the element of vs. 7. But his present concern is to suggest recognition through the eucharist on the basis of his source.

The second episode (21:15-23), contains three main ideas: (a) the threefold commission to Peter (vss. 15-17); (b) the prediction of Peter's martyrdom (vss. 18-19); and (c) the tradition regarding the Beloved Disciple (vss. 20-23).

Ch. 13 lies in the background of this scene. In the earlier chapter there appear the elements of the meal, the dominant role of Peter (though in an unfavorable light), and the appearance of the Beloved Disciple, placed in close relationship to Jesus. That the author of the Appendix wrote with ch. 13 in mind is proved by the cross reference in 21:20. In both chapters the dialogue takes place after the meal (13:3; 21:15).

[113] The precise meaning of the number cannot be determined with assurance. Since it is not a round number, it is likely that its meaning is more than "a large quantity." Jerome points out that ancient naturalists specified 153 kinds of fish. For a good statement on the various theories advanced see Bultmann, op. cit., p. 549, n. 1.

There is no doubt that the threefold commission to Peter ("feed," "shepherd," "tend") is intended to reinstate Peter to a place of dominant leadership among the disciples. As such it parallels his threefold denial. The main problem relates to the meaning of the two words for love (φιλέω and ἀγαπάω) in vss. 15-17. Are they to be regarded as interchangeable and present simply for the sake of euphony or is a distinction in thought intended? Commentators are divided on the matter. Macgregor takes the position that

the words are interchanged simply for euphony, just as "feed" is changed to "shepherd" below (16) and "lambs" to "sheep." It is not concern about the quality of his love that is apparent in Peter's answer, but surprise that the question should be asked at all.[114]

Bultmann sees in the use of φιλέω by Jesus in the third instance evidence simply that the two words are used interchangeably.[115] Goodspeed, on the other hand, argues strongly for a clear distinction between the two words:

Not only does translating these two Greek words alike reduce the conversation to mere iteration but the phrase, "the third time" seems to lose all its force. For the Greek does not mean that what hurt Peter was Jesus' repetition of his question; the Greek means that what hurt him was that the third time Jesus had changed his question to the word Peter himself had chosen . . . . In short, using the same Greek word in all seven places in verses 15-17 loses the point of the story, which seems to be that the third time Jesus gave up his word ἀγαπᾷς and used Peter's word, φιλῶ.[116]

In attempting to reach a decision on the problem several facts must be kept in mind. For one thing, if the Appendix is not by the author of the Gospel, it is faulty method to assume that the method of the author of the Appendix is the same as that

[114] Op. cit., p. 373.
[115] Op. cit., p. 551, n. 2.
[116] E. J. Goodspeed, *Problems of New Testament Translation*, p. 118. Copyright 1945 by the University of Chicago. Used by permission of the University of Chicago Press.

of the evangelist. The latter delights in play on words, but with the scanty materials which we have from the author of the Appendix it is precarious to assume that he has adopted the same technique. And, in any case, the evangelist uses these two words (φιλέω and ἀγαπάω) interchangeably (13:23; cf. 20:2; cf. also 11:3, 5, 36). Moreover, the interchange of the words "lambs" and "sheep" with no apparent difference in meaning indicates the author's interest in euphony. Finally, it is doubtful if precise distinctions between the two words were maintained in Hellenistic Greek. The Gospel proper is itself evidence to that effect. The confusion on this point emerges in discussions on this passage, some interpreters holding that φιλέω is the nobler word, others the reverse. In view of these facts we must conclude that an intended distinction between the words is highly improbable.

The prediction of Peter's martyrdom (vss. 18-19) is conveyed by the words, "You will stretch out your hands," signifying crucifixion, as vs. 19 makes clear. Ch. 13 had not made it plain that Peter would die a martyr's death. When Peter exclaimed, "I will lay down my life for you," Jesus had answered with a prediction of his denial (13:37-38). However, a cryptic allusion to Peter's martyrdom is certainly contained in 13:36. But in ch. 21 the element of doubt is removed, and Peter, it is indicated, is to follow his Lord in crucifixion. What higher tribute could be paid Peter than that? The command, "Follow me" (21:19), must be construed in these terms. In 13:36 Jesus had said that Peter would follow him later on; now the meaning is made clear: Peter will follow Jesus in crucifixion and is commanded to do so.

Vss. 20-23 contain the tradition regarding the Beloved Disciple. They make it clear that the person whom the author of the Appendix has identified as the Beloved Disciple was already dead at the time the Appendix was written. That is, the Beloved Disciple, a representative type in the Gospel proper, has been identified with a particular individual in the Appendix. The tradition apparently developed that Jesus had predicted the Beloved Disciple's long life not to be terminated before the Parousia. But now he is dead; so the problem of reconciling his death with the tradition has arisen. The Appendix solves the problem by making the prediction of Jesus conditional; Jesus had not said that disciple was not to die, but, "If I wish him to remain until I come, what is it to you?"

Vs. 24 makes the Beloved Disciple both witness and author. The words, "We know that his witness is true," betray the fact that the author of the Appendix wrote as a representative of the community.